Caring for Children with Chronic Illness:
Issues and Strategies

Ruth E. K. Stein, M.D., is Professor of Pediatrics at the Albert Einstein College of Medicine where she is Director of the Pediatric Ambulatory Care Division. Dr. Stein works as a clinician, administrator, teacher, and researcher in the area of health care delivery for children with ongoing health conditions. In 1970 she organized a multidisciplinary comprehensive care outreach program, Pediatric Home Care, and she works with children with serious ongoing health conditions in that setting. She was the Principal Investigator of the Pediatric Ambulatory Care Treatment Study (PACTS), a randomized controlled evaluation of the home care program sponsored by the Health Services Administration, Bureau of Community Health Service. She is also the Principal Investigator of the Preventive Intervention Research Center for Child Health at the Albert Einstein College of Medicine/Montefiore Medical Center, the only such center for the prevention of mental health problems that result from serious illness in childhood. The Center is funded by the National Institute of Mental Health. Dr. Stein is a member of the Research Consortium on Chronic Illness in Childhood and has served on numerous regional and national advisory committees for the improvement of pediatric health care, teaching, and research. She is a member of several national associations and has just completed a term as President of the Ambulatory Pediatric Association.

Caring for Children with Chronic Illness: Issues and Strategies

Ruth E. K. Stein, M.D.
Editor

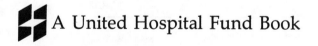 A United Hospital Fund Book

SP SPRINGER PUBLISHING COMPANY
New York

Springer Publishing Company, Inc.
536 Broadway
New York, NY 10012

89 90 91 92 93 / 5 4 3 2 1

LIBRARY OF CONGRESS
Library of Congress Cataloging-in-Publication Data

Caring for children with chronic illness: issues and strategies
   Ruth E. K. Stein, editor.
      p.   cm.
   "A United Hospital Fund book."
   Includes bibliographies and index.
   ISBN 0-8261-5900-1
   1. Chronically ill children—Medical care.   2. Child health services—United States.   I. Stein, Ruth E. K.
   [DNLM: 1. Child Health Services—United States.   2. Chronic Disease—in adolescence.   3. Chronic Disease—in infancy & childhood.   4. Health Policy—United States.   WS 200 C277]
RJ380.C37 1989
362.1'6'088054—dc19
DNLM/DLC
for Library of Congress   89-20169
                                                                          CIP

Printed in the United States of America

Contents

Preface

This book is intended to provide a framework for considering the range of issues and dilemmas posed by serious ongoing physical illness in infants, children, and adolescents. It grew out of a conference entitled "New Directions in Care of Children with Chronic Illness" that was jointly sponsored by the United Hospital Fund of New York together with the Preventive Intervention Research Center for Child Health and the Department of Pediatrics of the Albert Einstein College of Medicine/Montefiore Medical Center. The chapters are written so that each can stand alone, but together they outline key concerns in the field of childhood chronic illness.

Part I discusses the major public policy issues in the field of chronic illness. The introduction defines the population of youngsters under consideration and the reasons the topic has gained national attention. In Chapter 1, Vince Hutchins and Merle McPherson provide an overview of the history of national initiatives and review a number of political, social, and economic forces that have molded current policy. Further, the chapter provides the background for understanding both the origins and nature of pressures for further change in the way health care policy is shaped. In Chapter 2, Diane Rowland examines the specific role of public financing on the health care of these youngsters, outlining the range of economic programs that provide financing of services. The chapter also highlights some of the gaps that such diversified initiatives create.

The book then continues, in Chapter 3, with an examination by Henry Ireys of the oldest and most substantial public program for children with serious ongoing conditions. It describes the radical changes in this program in recent years, demonstrating not only how it has evolved over time from the Crippled Children's Service to the Program for Children with Special Health Needs, but also something about society's struggle with the changing nature of this population and its service needs.

In Chapter 4, Deborah Klein Walker moves from the oldest public program to one of the newest as she describes the increasing role of public education in providing services to children with special ongoing health needs. The involvement of the educational system represents important new recognition that the overwhelming majority of children with chronic conditions are going to survive. Thus, they not only must receive health care, but also should be prepared to participate to the maximum extent possible in the activities of our society. This chapter raises important questions about the adequacy of the newer initiatives for addressing the needs of this population. The discussion in this section of the book also suggests some polarities between health care oriented and educationally dominated models. These polarities reflect real, unresolved tensions in the field.

Part II covers a number of general themes, revealing the complexity of the concerns and critical perspectives that must be considered in dealing with these children. It begins with a chapter by Dorothy Jones Jessop and Ruth Stein on individuals and families, which discusses the diversity of family needs and structures, the impact of illness on the family, and the interaction between the family and the health care system. The chapter emphasizes some of the demands and burdens placed on the family by the health care system and by the long duration of chronic illness. Chapter 6 deals with the roles of institutions and professionals. Antoinette Eaton, Daniel Coury, and Richard Kern consider how these roles have been characterized in the past and at present, and project some future directions. They stress the importance of reorienting medical educational programs to educate and train physicians so that they are equipped with the knowledge and skills necessary to deal with this population, and so that they have an appreciation of how to deliver comprehensive family-oriented care.

The discussion on ethics by Alan Fleischman in Chapter 7 examines societal values toward children with chronic illness, posing concerns about how these children should be treated, how decisions should be made for them, and the role of their families in their care. It outlines the major ethical principles that need to be considered in making difficult decisions. Chapter 8, entitled "With a Parent's Eye," is a moving account by Julianne Beckett of her family's experience with a prolonged serious physical illness. It illustrates that such illnesses can strike anyone and also vividly portrays the complicated obstacles and systems with which a family must deal in obtaining needed services. It is a powerful example of how one family's struggle can alter the system of care for many others.

After these overviews, Part III of the book directs attention to new frontiers and challenges. Elaine Lugovoy's chapter on children without homes examines the important interaction between the burden of the child's care and the capacity of the family to mobilize to meet it. These interactions are shifting the boundaries between those families that can manage to care for their seriously ill children and those that cannot. In earlier times, when care needs at home were much less complicated, it was generally easier to determine whether or not families could manage successfully. This chapter also points out the irony of making services and supports available for alternate homes and care schemes, while natural families often find it difficult to obtain the same help, if they need it.

In considering community-based self-help efforts, in Chapter 10, Leslie Borck emphasizes an important and growing movement for lay support for families. However, she also stresses that, at the present time, this type of service is not readily available for all types of families.

In Chapter 11, on transition to adulthood, Stephen Richardson outlines a major new crisis that is occurring as large numbers of youngsters with chronic conditions reach adulthood. Their survival raises new dilemmas for our service systems and for our society—dilemmas that go far beyond the health care system to encompass all aspects of the transition into adult roles of social and employment competence. The final chapter in Part III by I. Barry Pless and Michael Wadsworth provides some new and compelling data from the British cohort studies which demonstrate that when children with chronic illness become adults their troubles are not over; they experience considerably more psychological and social consequences in adulthood than do their healthy peers. We have only begun to scratch the surface in dealing with these concerns.

Part IV examines model programs developed and staffed by pioneers who set out to create a system that would work. Each represents an exciting new approach to a complex set of problems and deals successfully with some universal concerns. While the models operate in diverse environments and attack different problems, all are very innovative projects that provide significant evidence of progress and that are having dramatic effects on the families they serve. They offer important lessons that could easily be adapted to address similar problems and needs in other sites. The programs range in scope from an institutional hospital-based outreach program to a major effort to reorganize services in a large region of the country. Throughout the descriptions, it is clear that individual efforts make a difference through caring and making the "non-system" work, as well as through innovation, restructuring, and advocacy efforts.

In Chapter 13, Henry Adam deals with one of the oldest programs for chronic illness management outside the hospital. It is an urban inner-city model and the only one for which efficacy has been demonstrated through a randomized controlled evaluation. In contrast, Chapter 14 by Steve Freedman and Patricia Pierce considers a rural case management project that employs virtually identical principles, but serves fairly isolated communities in northern Florida. The similarities between these programs are striking, but latter chapter also demonstrates the economic viability of a program for chronically ill children, something that had not previously been shown.

The Illinois model described by Gene Bilotti in Chapter 15 focuses on the highest technology-dependent children, for whom economic incentives originally drove the program development. The Illinois program is one of five high technology demonstration projects in the country. Over the years, these high technology programs have moved from a narrow definition of high technology children to much broader services for children who need varying degrees of technical assistance, but require many critically important elements of care in an ongoing way after hospital discharge. Thus, they are now closer to the first two models in Chapters 13 and 14.

Project SERVE, described in Chapter 16, is a statewide planning model that looks at the revamping of an entire state's systems and bureaucracies for the large number of children with diversified needs. This program is now being replicated throughout the New England region.

In Part V, several areas are targeted for future efforts. In Chapter 17, Morton Silverman and Doreen Spilton Koretz deal with the mental health consequences of chronic illness both for the child and for family members. This is an area where preventable morbidity threatens to increase as a result of advances in biomedical technology. The more highly specialized and demanding the care becomes, the more difficult the consequences may be for the family and the child. After stressing the importance of preventing these problems, the next chapter by Ronnie Halper and Henry Ireys considers a model program that addresses prevention issues in the mental health arena. It was selected because it illustrates an interdisciplinary approach to complex problems resulting from chronic conditions. Such approaches will be the cornerstone of much of the new research, services, and training in the area of chronic illness, where single disciplines can no longer adequately address the problems in isolation. While an integrated approach is a prerequisite to progress in a field as complex and multifaceted as chronic illness, a center of the sort described requires sustained economic stability in order to allow for initial investments in collaboration to bear fruit.

The book then examines some newer and more tangible research technologies. Chapters 19 and 20 describe applications of scientific discoveries to improve the lives of children with chronic illness, illustrating the opportunities to extend our frontiers of care through the use of new scientific information. In Chapter 19, Karen Hein considers the effects of new pharmacologic understanding about the way in which the adolescent's body metabolizes medications on the improvement of treatment of adolescents. In Chapter 20, David Rubin looks at applications of the computer for enhancing the care of chronically ill children. In some cases the computer assists in the actual monitoring of treatment of the diseases; in others it provides ways of compensating for deficits or serves as a tool for educating patients and their families about self-care.

In Chapter 21, Arthur Kohrman examines the financing of care, taking a futuristic approach and suggesting some radical alternatives and some new techniques. Although finances tend to dictate the way the care system is designed, the chapter stresses that, despite the ever increasing pressure to contain costs, economics must not be allowed to be the only consideration in assessing services for children. Finally, Bruce Vladeck's Epilogue deftly weaves the threads of all the discussions together and outlines some of the options for future directions.

The work in this book builds on an important earlier study of children with chronic illness and their families conducted by the Center for the Study of Families and Children of the Vanderbilt Institute for Public Policy Studies. That study defined many areas of concern and placed the needs of these families on the public agenda. In the intervening years, it has become even clearer that there is an urgent need for addressing the problem in a way that empowers families and insures opportunities to develop caring, flexible, and fluid systems for care of children with chronic conditions. Additionally, the urgency of the problem compels us to move ahead with policy changes, perhaps even before all the answers are in. It is our hope that the materials in this volume will provide a stepping-stone to help bring the concerns to public attention and hasten their resolution.

RUTH E. K. STEIN, M.D.

Acknowledgments

This book could not have been completed without the efforts of many people who generously contributed their time and energy. I am indebted to Bruce C. Vladeck and George Schneider, who encouraged us in the development of the original conference on "New Directions in Care of Children with Chronic Illness" and provided the support through the United Hospital Fund of New York to make it a reality. I am also grateful to my colleagues at Albert Einstein College of Medicine, Ronnie Halper, Henry T. Ireys, and Dorothy Jones Jessop, who shared in the planning process and worked to make the conference a success. Secondly, I want to thank all the speakers and their co-authors, who not only agreed to participate, but then extended their cooperation by authoring full-scale chapters when we belatedly decided to develop a volume based in part on the conference. Several other authors enthusiastically agreed to contribute material as well.

There are a number of key individuals at the United Hospital Fund of New York who have always been available and helpful in working with me during the editorial process, especially Sally J. Rogers and Bruce C. Vladeck. Above all I owe special thanks to Carol Ewig, Editorial Consultant to the United Hospital Fund, for her untiring efforts throughout the process. She has been a devoted and energetic colleague in overseeing this project and her contribution to it has been immeasurable. Additional thanks are due to Barbara Watkins of Springer Publishing Company.

I especially want to thank the many children and families with whom I have worked over the past two decades for the countless lessons they have taught me about their needs and strengths in facing the issues of living with serious ongoing illnesses. Last, but by no means least, I am most grateful to my colleagues, friends, and especially my own family for supporting me throughout my career and during the completion of this project.

RUTH E. K. STEIN, M.D.

Contributors

Henry M. Adam, M.D., is an Assistant Professor of Pediatrics at the Albert Einstein College of Medicine. Currently he is the Associate Director of Pediatric Ambulatory Care at the Bronx Municipal Hospital Center, and the Medical Director of a Day Care Center for children with AIDS, also at Bronx Municipal. A graduate of Hamilton College and Yale University, Dr. Adam also studied at the University of Paris, in France, and the University of Warwick, in England. He attended medical school at the State University of New York Upstate Medical Center, and was a resident in Pediatrics at Mount Sinai Hospital in New York. After completing a Fellowship in Ambulatory and Behavioral Pediatrics at Albert Einstein, he joined the staff of the Pediatric Home Care Program in 1983. From 1984 to 1986, he directed the Home Care Program and continues now to be involved in its clinical work.

Julianne E. Beckett, M.A., is Associate Director for Consumer Affairs for the National Maternal and Child Health Resource Center at the University of Iowa College of Law. She has served as Vice-Chairman for the Task Force on Technology-Dependent Children, a congressionally mandated Task Force within the Department of Health and Human Services. The Task Force concentrates on building family-centered, community based, coordinated systems of care. She spends most of her time travelling the country educating and training parents, educators, health care professionals, and community leaders focusing on the requirements of children with special health care needs and their families. She earned her Bachelor's degree from Clarke College in DuBuque, Iowa, and a Master's degree from the University of Dayton in Ohio.

Gene E. Bilotti, M.S.W., is Assistant Director of Special Projects and External Affairs at the University of Illinois Division of Services for Crippled Children. He is an ordained Presbyterian minister who earned his Master's of Divinity at the Eastern Seminary in Philadelphia. Mr. Bilotti earned a Master's degree at the State University of New York at Albany.

Leslie E. Borck, Ph.D., is Executive Director of the Westchester Self-Help Clearinghouse of Westchester Community College in Valhalla, NY. Dr. Borck earned a Ph.D. in Counseling Psychology, specializing in Community Psychology, at the University of Kansas. She received her Master's degree in Behavior Therapy at the University of Rochester.

Daniel Lee Coury, M.D., received his medical degree from the University of Tennessee Center for the Health Sciences. Following his pediatric residency, he pursued a Fellowship in Ambulatory Pediatrics at Brown University. He is currently an Assistant Professor of Clinical Pediatrics at The Ohio State University. His academic duties include serving as Director of the Continuity of Care Clinic and Co-director of a Behavioral Pediatrics Fellowship program. He has published several articles on behavioral pediatrics issues, including fellowship training, child abuse, and failure to thrive.

Antoinette P. Eaton, M.D., is Professor of Pediatrics and Preventive Medicine at Ohio State University and Associate Medical Director for Ambulatory Services for Children's Hospital, in Columbus, Ohio. She is also the Director of Governmental Affairs at Children's Hospital, Inc., and President of the Ohio Chapter of the American Academy of Pediatrics. She served Ohio for six years in public health as State Maternal and Child Health Director. After receiving her M.D. degree from the Medical College of Pennsylvania, Dr. Eaton completed post-doctoral pediatric specialty training at Ohio State University-Columbus Children's Hospital. She is a recipient of the Ambulatory Pediatric Association's National Teaching Award for her work in developing a written behavioral-developmental curriculum that prepares academic pediatricians to deal with children who have special health care needs.

Alan R. Fleischman, M.D., is the Director of the Division of Neonatology and Professor of Pediatrics at the Albert Einstein College of Medicine and Montefiore Medical Center. He is currently an Adjunct Associate at the Hastings Center and a member of the New York State Governor's Task Force on Life and the Law. He is also a member of the American Academy of Pediatrics Bioethics Committee. After receiving his M.D. degree at the Albert Einstein College of Medicine, Dr. Fleischman completed pediatric training at Johns Hopkins Hospital. He completed advanced studies in fetal physiology at the National Institutes of Health.

Steven A. Freedman, Ph.D., is currently the Director of the Institute for Child Health Policy of the State University System of Florida. He holds academic appointments as Associate Professor of Pediatrics at the College of Medicine and within the Department of Health Services Administration at the University of Florida. Dr. Freedman is the Principal Investigator of the Case Management Information Base for Chronically-Ill and Disabled Children, a Special Project of Regional or National Significance of the Division of Maternal and Child Health of the U.S. Public Health Service. He is also a member of the Task Force on Technology Dependent Children, a Task Force mandated by the U.S. Department of Health and Human Services. Dr. Freedman earned his Ph.D. degree at Florida State University.

Ronnie Halper, M.S.W., M.P.H., is the Associate Director of the Preventive Intervention Research Center for Child Health and the Administrator of Pediatric Ambulatory Care for the Albert Einstein College of Medicine. She received Masters' degrees in Social Work and Public Health from Columbia University. Ms. Halper combines a clinical background with extensive experience in program development and administration in the areas of pediatrics and mental health.

Karen Hein, M.D., is Associate Professor of Pediatrics and of Epidemiology and Social Medicine with the Albert Einstein College of Medicine. She serves as Director of the Adolescent AIDS Program at the Montefiore Medical Center. She was recently appointed to the National Advisory Panel on Adolescent Health for the Office of Technology Assessment (OTA). After receiving her M.D. degree at Columbia University's College of Physicians and Surgeons, Dr. Hein completed a 3-year residency in Pediatrics at the Albert Einstein College of Medicine. She performed her post-doctoral Fellowship in Adolescent Medicine at Montefiore Medical Center. Specializing in adolescent health for the past 15 years, Dr. Hein has published extensively on adolescent growth and reproductive health care, developmental pharmacology, and most recently on AIDS in adolescence.

Vince L. Hutchins, M.D., M.P.H., is currently Deputy Director of the Bureau of Maternal and Child Health and Resources Development of the United States Public Health Service. He received his medical degree from the University of Iowa in 1952, and a Master's of Public Health from the University of California School of Public Health in 1968. Dr. Hutchins is certified by the American Board of Pediatrics, has been in the private practice of pediatrics, and has held several academic appointments in pediatrics at the Medical College of Pennsylvania. He was appointed Regional Medical Director for Maternal and Child Health in Region III, in 1971, and in 1972, Dr. Hutchins accepted an appointment with the Central Office of the Department of Health, Education and Welfare. Since that time, he has held several positions in Maternal and Child Health at the national level and is the recipient of numerous honors and awards. These include the APHA Martha May Eliot Award in 1987 and the Presidential Meritorious Executive Rank Award in 1988.

Henry T. Ireys, Ph.D., is Co-director of the Preventive Intervention Research Center and an Associate Professor of Pediatrics at Albert Einstein College of Medicine. Graduated from Williams College, Dr. Ireys received his Doctorate in Clinical Psychology from Case Western Reserve University and completed a post-doctoral Fellowship in Public Policy at Vanderbilt University. Before moving to his current work on the prevention of mental health problems in children, he was involved in research on public policy issues for children with chronic illness and is a co-author of *Chronically Ill Children and their Families: Problems, Prospects and Proposals from the Vanderbilt Study.*

Dorothy Jones Jessop, Ph.D., a sociologist, is a Research Scientist with the Office of Policy and Program Development of the New York City Human Resources Administration (HRA). She has an academic appointment as a Visiting Associate Professor in the Department of Pediatrics at Albert Einstein College of Medicine. Prior to joining HRA, Dr. Jessop spent seven years at Einstein working on studies of children with chronic illness, first as Project Director of the Pediatric Ambulatory Care Treatment Study and later as Co-director for Research and Evaluation of the Preventive Intervention Research Center for Child Health.

Richard A. Kern, M.D., received his M.D. from Ohio State University College of Medicine in 1982, and completed his residency in Pediatrics at Columbus Children's Hospital in 1985. In 1987, he became the first graduate of the Hospital's fellowship program in Developmental-Behavioral-Pediatrics. He is currently Clinical Assistant Professor of Pediatrics at Ohio State University College of Medicine, and works with developmentally handicapped, learning-disabled, and sexually-abused children.

Doreen Spilton Koretz, Ph.D., is currently Assistant Chief of the Prevention Research Branch, Division of Clinical Research, National Institute of Mental Health. For the past ten years she has worked in a variety of applied research settings, performing program evaluations and policy analyses related to the physical and mental health of children and families. She has special interests in developmental psychopathology and preventive research methods. Dr. Koretz received her Ph.D. in Developmental Psychology from Cornell University in Ithaca, NY.

Arthur F. Korhman, M.D., is currently Professor and Associate Chairman, Department of Pediatrics, at Pritzker School of Medicine at The University of Chicago; and is also Director, LaRabida Children's Hospital and Research Center. He earned his medical degree from the Western Reserve University School of Medicine in Cleveland. He has published extensively on ethical and policy issues of chronic diseases of children.

Elaine Lugovoy, R.N., M.A., has received an M.A. from Columbia University, a B.S. from Hunter College, and a Nursing Diploma from Jewish Hospital of Brooklyn. She is currently Child Health Nursing Consultant, New Jersey Division of Youth and Family Services. She has previously been Associate Director of Nursing, Community Health Care of North Jersey, an Administrator of Pediatric Home Health Care Nursing Services for high-risk infants and chronically ill children, and Director of Health Services for the Children's Aid Society in New York. She has administered health care programs for children in foster care, children with chronic illness in a summer residential camp, homeless children in transient hotels, and adolescents at high risk of unintended pregnancies. She was adjunct lecturer at Columbia University School of Public Health from 1981 through 1987 and was recipient of the Greater New York March of Dimes Outstanding Maternal Child Health Nurse Award in 1985.

Merle McPherson, M.D., M.P.H., is currently Director of the Division of Services for Children with Special Health Needs of the Bureau of Maternal and Child Health and Resources Development. She received her medical degree from the University of Saskatchewan in Canada in 1959, and holds the Master's of Public Health degree from the Johns Hopkins School of Public Health. Dr. McPherson is certified by the American Board of Preventive Medicine and has worked in pediatric clinical settings at the local, state, and international levels. She has had adminstrative responsibilities for the Title V Crippled Children's program and for primary pediatric care in the District of Columbia, and for the Title V Maternal and Child Health Program and for Family Health Services in the state of Hawaii. Dr. McPherson has held various positions in Maternal and Child Health at the Federal level since 1976, and is the recipient of numerous honors and awards.

Patricia M. Pierce, R.N., Ph.D., is currently the President of Prescribed Pediatric Extended Care, Inc., and is also a member of the Consultant Statewide Nurse Specialist Program, Children's Medical Services, of the Florida Department of Health and Rehabilitative Services. Dr. Pierce is the Secretary/Treasurer of Family Health and Habilitative Services, Inc. She was the Principal Investigator of a Special Project of Regional or National Significance (SPRANS) supported by the Division of Maternal and Child Health, a division of the Public Health Service. Dr. Pierce has published numerous journal articles. She earned her Ph.D. at the University of Texas at Austin.

I. Barry Pless, M.D., F.R.C.P.(C), Professor of Pediatrics and Epidemiology at McGill University has held the position of Director of the Community Pediatric Research Program at the Montreal Children's Hospital since 1975. The most recent of his awards is the 1988 George Armstrong Award of the Ambulatory Pediatric Association. He is a National Health Scientist; Chairman of the Canadian Institute of Child Health; an associate member of The Canadian Institute for Advanced Research; and a member of the Scientific Advisory Council for the Alberta Heritage Foundation for Medical Research, as well as an active member of 12 Societies. After receiving his medical degree from the University of Western Ontario, he did graduate work at Harvard University and the London School of Hygiene. Dr. Pless has published extensively in peer-reviewed journals and books, and has given numerous scientific presentations, workshops, and seminars in Canada, the United States, and abroad. His major areas of interest are the care of children with chronic disorders, and childhood traffic accidents.

Project SERVE, which included **Susan Gilbert Epstein, M.S.W., Ann Boyd Taylor, Ed.D., Deborah Klein Walker, Ed.D., Allen C. Crocker, M.D., Jane Gardner, R.N., Sc.D., Alexa S. Halberg, B.A., Serena E. H. Mailloux, M.D., Ann Murphy, M.S.W.,** and **Gerald A. Tuttle, Ph.D.,** was a collaborative effort of the Massachusetts Department of Public Health's Division of Family Health Services, the Department of Maternal and Child Health at the Harvard School of Public Health, and the Developmental Evaluation Clinic at The Children's Hospital (Boston), managed by the Massachusetts Health Research Institute, Inc., and funded with a 3-year federal grant from the Bureau of Health Care Delivery and Assistance and the U.S. Department of Health and Human Services. This Policy Planning Project focused on developing recommendations for the Massachusetts Department of Public Health that define future directions in serving children with special health care needs.

Stephen A. Richardson, Ph.D., is Professor Emeritus at the Albert Einstein College of Medicine in the Departments of Pediatrics and Epidemiology and Social Medicine. He is a Senior Investigator at the Kennedy Center for Research in Child Development and Mental Retardation. He has been at Einstein for 20 years. Previously, he was with the Association for the Aid of Crippled Children. His interests have been in the causes and consequences of handicapping conditions in childhood. His research has dealt with physical disabilities, mental retardation, and the long-term consequences of severe malnutrition in infancy. His undergraduate training was at Harvard and he took his graduate training at Cornell.

Diane Rowland, M.P.A., Sc.D., is Assistant Professor in the Department of Health Policy and Management at the School of Hygiene and Public Health of the Johns Hopkins University. She has been at Johns Hopkins since 1981 and specializes in issues related to access to care and financing health for the poor, elderly, and disabled. She was recently awarded a Brookdale National Fellowship to enable her to pursue her research interests in aging. She is also Associate Director of the Commonwealth Fund Commission on Elderly People Living Alone. She also serves as a consultant on Medicaid and long-term care to the Subcommittee on Health and the Environment of the Committee on Energy and Commerce in the U.S. House of Representatives. Dr. Rowland is the author of numerous articles and the coauthor of the book *Medicare Policy*. She formerly served as the special assistant to the Administrator of the Health Care Financing Administration where her responsibilities included Medicaid and child health legislation.

David H. Rubin, M.D., is an Assistant Professor of Pediatrics in the Divisions of Pediatric and Perinatal Epidemiology and Ambulatory Care at the Albert Einstein College of Medicine-Montefiore Medical Center, Bronx, NY. After receiving his M.D. degree at Case Western Reserve University, Dr. Rubin completed his pediatric training at the University of California, San Francisco. He then spent two years as a Robert Wood Johnson General Academic Pediatric Fellow at Yale University, and one year as a Fulbright Fellow at the University of Copenhagen, Denmark.

Morton M. Silverman, M.D., is the Director of the Student Mental Health Service and Associate Professor of Psychiatry at the University of Chicago. He was previously Associate Administrator for Prevention in the Alcohol, Drug Abuse, and Mental Health Administration (U.S. Public Health Service). Dr. Silverman was also Chief, Center for Prevention Research, at the National Institute of Mental Health (NIMH) and has served as advisor to the Division of Mental Health of the World Health Organization.

He received his M.D. degree at Northwestern University and completed residency training in Psychiatry at the University of Chicago. Dr. Silverman has co-authored numerous monographs related to the prevention of mental disorders and also stress research.

Bruce C. Vladeck, Ph.D., is President of the United Hospital Fund of New York, the nation's oldest federated charity, which seeks to shape New York's health care through an integrated program of information, philanthropy, and policy development. Prior to joining the United Hospital Fund, Dr. Vladeck served as Assistant Vice President of The Robert Wood Johnson Foundation and as Assistant Commissioner for Health Planning and Resources Development of the New Jersey State Department of Health. Previously, he taught for more than four years at Columbia University. Dr. Vladeck is the author of *Unloving Care: The Nursing Home Tragedy,* and of numerous articles and book chapters on health policy, health care finance, and health politics. He is a member of the Prospective Payment Assessment Commission, the New York State Council of Health Care Financing, and the Institute of Medicine, National Academy of Sciences.

Michael E. J. Wadsworth, M.Phil., Ph.D., is Director of the Medical Research Council's National Survey of Health and Development in Great Britain, a longitudinal study from birth to age 43 years. His interests are in life course and intergenerational research in health and behavior, and in the childhood and early adult predictor of rates of midlife change and aging.

Deborah Klein Walker, Ed.D., is the Assistant Commissioner for the Bureau of Parent, Child and Adolescent Health in the Massachusetts Department of Health. Before assuming her current position, she was faculty member at the Harvard School of Public Health and the Harvard Graduate School of Education. In addition, she has served in a variety of roles related to the development and evaluation of educational and human service programs and policies. She is currently doing research on the social functioning of handicapped and chronically ill children in schools and evaluations of secondary prevention programs for adolescent pregnant and parenting teens. Her past work focused on the assessment of social and emotional factors in the development of young children, behavioral and learning problems in children and youth, and early intervention programs and policies, and community assessment of child health status and service access and utilization.

Introduction

Ruth E. K. Stein, M.D.

Modern science has opened new vistas in the care of the ill. Nowhere has this been more dramatic than in the treatment of infants and children. Although childhood is commonly thought to be a time of well-being, a large number of infants born prior to the last few decades died before reaching adulthood. In the past century, however, we have seen an almost miraculous reversal of this wasting of human potential through the prevention and cure of infectious diseases and the control of many serious medical conditions. However, one of the results of these changes has been the emergence of a new kind of morbidity—the creation of a population of youngsters with serious ongoing health conditions or chronic illnesses.

WHO ARE THESE CHILDREN?

The term chronic illness is an abbreviated designation that is most often used in connection with the elderly and not the young, whom we usually imagine to be vigorous and well. In fact, I, along with many others, prefer the term, "serious ongoing physical health conditions," but resort to the phrase chronic illness as a matter of convenience. The chronic illness rubric is not a list of specific illnesses. Rather, it is a framework for thinking about a whole range of conditions that threaten the health and developmental potential of youngsters and that often require special treatments and health care services. The definition used throughout this book is one drawn from the work of Pless and Douglas (1971) and Pless and Pinkerton (1975), who define a child's chronic illness as one that lasts three or more months or requires at least one month of hospitalization. The presumption is that either of these circumstances produces stress on the child and family unit and requires substantial time, energy, and personal resources in order to cope with the situation and these extra demands.

The youngsters whose conditions qualify as chronic under this definition are those with kidney, liver, or heart disease, with inborn errors of metabolism, and with a wide range of birth defects. They include those with cystic fibrosis, diabetes, hemophilia, and severe asthma, as well as the small number of low birthweight infants who have unresolved respiratory problems as a result of their prematurity. In addition, there are the victims of muscular dystrophies, malignancies, head trauma, seizures, and spinal cord injuries. Recently added to the list are those with pediatric AIDS. There are also quite a number of youngsters with a wide variety of very rare conditions or unusual combinations of more than one common condition. All are alive today because of the wonders of medical science. However, most now live their lives with some special threat to their continued well-being and have an ongoing need for special health care services.

LIMITATIONS OF TERMINOLOGY AND EPIDEMIOLOGY

There are several problems with the term chronic illness as a descriptor of these conditions. Some, such as spina bifida or cerebral palsy, are not illnesses in the usual sense. Many are long-term conditions that require special care, but do not render the child ill when the care is adequate. Diseases such as diabetes hemophilia or cystic fibrosis require special care in order to allow normal daily activities; but if that care is provided, most children function very well and often without much evidence of their physical vulnerability. Still other children have illnesses, such as juvenile arthritis or asthma, that are ongoing for long periods of time, but that may resolve over time and hence do not necessarily continue indefinitely. Nevertheless, because chronic illness is the usual term for these disorders, it is used throughout this text. In reading the book, however, the larger context of serious physical health conditions should be kept in mind.

There are no precise figures on exactly how many children in the United States have chronic physical conditions. Estimates range from a low of 5% to a high of almost 30%, depending on the definitions and methods used to collect the information. Most experts believe that the number is somewhere between 10 and 15% (Gortmaker & Sappenfeld, 1984). This translates into approximately 6 to 9 million children under the age of 18 years. While most, if not all, of these children need some increased health care services, the vast majority are able to carry out their daily activities with minimal, if any, obvious dysfunction. It is usually estimated that between 1 and 3% of children have functional limitations that affect their daily lives. Data from the National Center for Health Statistics Household Interview Surveys indicate that since 1967 there has been a significant increase in the number of American children who have a condition that limits their activities in some way (Newacheck, Budetti, & Halfon, 1986). On the most extreme end of this spectrum are medically fragile children, such as those who require ventilators to assist them to breathe. However, they represent a very small fraction of the larger group.

In general, the number of children with chronic conditions has increased as has the number of medically fragile children, although some authorities suggest that we may have reached a plateau. I would take issue with this on several grounds, including the continued development of life sustaining and saving technologies, the improvements in early detection and treatment of premorbid conditions, and the change in the gene pool. However, it is clear that even if the incidence of chronic illness does not increase further, we can still expect to see a growth in the child and adult populations because of their increased longevity. Consequently, the issues raised by living with chronic conditions of childhood are likely to become more important to individual families, health care professionals, and society at large.

WHY WE SHOULD BE CONCERNED

Beyond the specter of a growing population, there are several other critical reasons for us to be concerned about this group of children. First, the care of this population is extremely complex and fragmented. Second, these children are high-cost consumers of health care services (Butler et al., 1985). The total costs are magnified both because illnesses go on for a long time and because their cumulative toll on the children and their family members over time is high in social, psychological, and economic terms. Third, because of the developmental needs and tasks of childhood, the care needs of youngsters with chronic conditions differ in essential ways from those of adults with chronic illness, especially the elderly.

COMPLEXITY OF SERVICE NEEDS

Children with chronic physical health conditions receive their health care through a variety of different arrangements. Some are seen primarily in hospital-based clinics for both primary and tertiary care. Some attend public freestanding clinics or health maintenance organization facilities, and many are cared for in the office of private physicians. Surveys suggest that at least for those with serious physical health conditions, the private physicians tend to be pediatricians (Walker et al., 1981). Quite frequently, even those who receive their primary care in the private sector are seen for consultation and tertiary care services at major medical centers, whether in the private or public system. This produces many gaps in services (Kanthor, Pless, Satterwhite, & Myers, 1974; Palfrey, Levy, & Gilbert, 1980; Stein, Jessop, & Riessman, 1983).

Typically, in addition to the usual preventive and primary health care, such children need different types of services at different phases of their illnesses. At some time, virtually all come into contact with more than one health care provider, and often with a large number of different individuals and/or types of health care professionals. Moreover, the care is likely to be spread over many geographic sites, some of which may be local and others geographically distant from the child's home. In this fragmentation, it is often hard to know whether anyone has a complete picture of how things are going from the family's point of view. One result is that each provider may think that another is attending to the issues. In turn, the family may not form a strong attachment to anyone or know to whom to turn if they have a problem.

In addition, the passage of PL 94-142 extended some of the responsibility for the provision of services to the school system by putting it in charge of addressing and ameliorating those health conditions that interfere with school performance. This initiative will be extended further by PL 99-457, which is in the process of being implemented and which will increase the responsibilities of the education system to children with special needs from birth to 5 years.

It is important to realize that, in general, the care of a single child may involve one or more primary care physicians, subspecialists, nurses, social workers, and occupational, physical, speech, educational, or respiratory therapists, as well as nutritionists, developmentalists, pharmacists, teachers, and, most importantly, the family itself. In addition, each agency may have its own source of payment and eligibility requirements that necessitate the family's learning to negotiate with many levels and types of bureaucracies.

ECONOMIC PRESSURES

Aside from the complex systems that families must learn to negotiate, there is considerable economic cost associated with childhood illness. For some time now, children with serious long-term physical health conditions have been consumers of very intensive and expensive health care services. For example, according to Zook and Moore (1980), children with congenital anomalies rank among the top five high-cost consumers of general hospitals when all conditions and all age groups are included. Not only do they currently consume a large segment of the health dollar, but they are very likely to require more than average medical services throughout their lives. Additionally, the costs of maintaining large numbers of children in institutions is overwhelming. A single child who is ventilator-dependent has been estimated to generate a yearly hospital bill of over $300,000. What is becoming clear is that the majority of such children who now live in hospitals and other institutions for prolonged periods of time could be the beneficiaries of more normal experiences of childhood, if their lives could be spent outside the institutional walls.

It has been shown that the illness of a child impacts on families in many ways that include major physical, social, emotional, and financial strains. It also affects their participation in the work force (Breslau, 1983; Sabbeth, 1984). Some parents report that they are actively encouraged to go on public assistance programs in order to become eligible for third-party coverage for their children's health care expenses. Others are required to give up employment, and often its fringe benefits, because of the physical care demands of providing care. Aside from the fact that the parents have experienced the psychological devastation of having a very sick child, they may be subjected to a series of further emotional blows through loss of autonomy, job satisfaction, and financial independence. In the long run, such policies may also threaten mental health, individual pension and Social Security status, and insurance coverage for other members of the family unit.

DEVELOPMENTAL IMPACT

Finally, care needs of children differ quite dramatically from those of seriously ill adults. Generally, illness in adulthood occurs as a threat to the integrity of an already mature individual whose basic personal development has already passed many milestones. A major difference in considering chronic illnesses in children is that they occur at a time when they threaten the normal trajectory of the child's development. Unlike the adult, who may suffer major setbacks but has a significant personal history and developmental achievement to fall back on, the child is at an early stage of personal maturation.

There is a great deal of information documenting the fact that all aspects of normal child development are threatened by the presence of a chronic condition. While the majority of children overcome the obstacles, the fact that their development is threatened has led to the recognition of the need to do as much as possible to normalize the life experiences of children with ongoing medical conditions. Providing the opportunity for maximal psychological and social development involves minimizing hospitalizations and special institutional care and enabling youngsters with chronic conditions to have normal contact with the members of their family and community. In fact, many aspects of the therapeutic prescription for care of children with chronic conditions actually lie on fringe areas in which medicine and social policy overlap. At times this poses difficulties for a society that tends to compartmentalize responsibilities for different elements of service in separate agencies.

NEED FOR A NEW PARADIGM

In addition to these factors, it is also clear that family composition and economic, social, and personal resources greatly influence the ability of a family to meet the needs of an ill or medically fragile child. As a result of this, there is a need to change the paradigm used for the care of children with serious ongoing conditions from one that focuses exclusively on biomedical technology to one that addresses a more comprehensive need for services in biological, social, and psychological realms. This requires examination of the boundary zones between medicine and the social world of the child. The pressures to address this issue are increasing because of the mounting evidence that many, perhaps most, of these children will be physically well enough to become productive members of our society. However, if they are not provided the necessary life experiences to maximize their developmental potential to function in society, these youngsters will lack the educational, emotional, and social skills to succeed in the adult world. This will create a problem with very serious long-term implications for them personally and for our society as a whole. Without normalizing their experiences during their formative years, seriously ill children face considerable handicaps in terms of social and cognitive skills and will have limited opportunities for adult self-sufficiency, independence, and competence.

Additionally, the evidence is growing that children with serious ongoing health conditions and their families are at heightened risk for mental health problems. These are preventable dysfunctions. There is also some evidence that the effects of poor physical health may interact with other risk factors for mental health problems, such as family disruption and poverty, to place individuals at double jeopardy (Stein & Jessop, 1984, 1987; Gortmaker, Walker, & Weitzmann, 1987). Therefore, the social and economic consequences of illness may intensify the mental health risks.

CONCLUSION

All these factors suggest that chronic illness in childhood is an important topic that warrants our sustained attention. The purpose of this book is to provide a framework for considering the range of issues and dilemmas posed by this difficult topic. The issues outlined are designed to give the reader a sense not only of the complexity of the issues, but also of the potential for moving ahead.

It has been suggested that children are our most precious resources and that a society can be judged in part or in whole by how it treats its most vulnerable members. Children with chronic physical conditions represent a vulnerable population, and the time has come for us to go beyond the recognition of that fact to remedy the problems and address the needs. At present we lag behind many other nations in our willingness to assure a wide range of services to children and their families. The challenge for all of us is to continue to make our own individual and collective contributions to caring for children with chronic illness and to assume a leadership role in setting a high standard for the provision of comprehensive and humane services to these children and their families.

REFERENCES

Breslau, N. (1983). Care of disabled children and women's time use. *Medical Care, 21,* 620–629.

Butler, J. A., Budetti, P., McMannus, M. A., et al. (1985). Health care expenditures for child with chronic illness. In T. M. Hobbs, & J. M. Perrin (Eds.), *Issues in the care of children with chronic illness.* San Francisco: Jossey-Bass.

Gortmaker, S. L., & Sappenfield, W. (1984). Chronic childhood disorders: prevalence and impact. *Pediatric Clinics of North America, 31,* 3–18.

Gortmaker, S. L., Walker, D. K., & Weitzman, M. (1987). Chronic illness and psycholosocial problems in children: Results of a National Survey Program. Abstract American Public Health Association. New Orleans, LA.

Kanthor, H., Pless, I. B., Satterwhite, B., & Meyers, G. (1974). Areas of responsibility in the health care of multiply handicapped children. *Pediatrics, 54,* 779–785.

Newacheck, P. W., Budetti, P. P., & McManus, P. (1984). Trends in childhood disability. *American Journal of Public Health, 74,* 232–236.

Newacheck, P. W., Budetti, P. P., & Halfon, N. (1986). Trends in activity-limiting chronic conditions among children. *American Journal of Public Health, 76,* 178–184.

Palfrey, J., Levy, J. C., & Gilbert, K. L. (1980). Use of primary care facilities by patients attending specialty clinics. *Pediatrics, 65,* 567–572.

Pless, I. B., & Douglas, J. W. B. (1971). Chronic illness in childhood: Part I.

Epidemiological and clinical characteristics. *Pediatrics, 47,* 405–414.

Pless, I. B., & Pinkerton, P. (1975). Chronic childhood disorders: Promoting patterns of adjustment. Chicago: Year Book Medical Publishers.

Sabbeth, B. (1984). Understanding the impact of chronic childhood illness on families. *Pediatric Clinics of North America Symposium on Chronic Diseases in Childhood, 31,* 47–58.

Stein, R. E. K., Jessop, D. J., & Riessman, C. K. (1983). Health care services received by children with chronic illness. *American Journal of Diseases of Children, 137,* 225–230.

Stein, R. E. K., & Jessop, D. J. (1984). Relationship between health status and psychological adjustment among children with chronic conditions. *Pediatrics, 73,* 169–174.

Stein, R. E. K., & Jessop, D. J. (1987). Behavioral consequences to chronic childhood illness. Final Report to William T. Grant Foundation.

Walker, D. K., Gortmaker, S. L., & Weitzman, M. (1981). Chronic illness and child health studies. Harvard School of Public Health, August 1981.

Zook, C., & Moore, F. (1981). The high-cost users of medical care. *New England Journal of Medicine, 302,* 996–1002.

I

A Framework for Providing Care

1

Roots of Current Perspectives

Vince L. Hutchins, M.D., M.P.H.,
Merle McPherson, M.D., M.P.H.

National attention to the needs of children with chronic illness is a relatively recent phenomenon. Indeed, Nicholas Hobbs said in this regard less than a decade ago: "I continue to be surprised at the relative lack of attention that has been given these sorely burdened children and their families" (Hobbs, 1980).

What has happened to change this situation? And why are the needs of these children being increasingly recognized? The answer lies in the convergence of many recent developments—biomedical, political, social, and economic in origin—that have affected public policy regarding programs for the disabled and handicapped over the past quarter century. These social forces and the changes they have generated have completely altered our view of chronic illness so that it is no longer entirely negative. The result is an environment in which the health care community can—indeed, is encouraged to—promote the many services that families with children with chronic illness require as well as to reassess the policy implications of those needs and services.

---

*Opinions and beliefs expressed in this chapter are those of the authors and do not necessarily reflect the view of policies of the federal government.

FACTORS CONTRIBUTING TO INCREASED INTEREST IN CHRONIC ILLNESS IN CHILDREN

Political Factors

Legislative Forces

Major federal legislative action has significantly affected the approach to chronic illness in children over the past 20 years. Perhaps the most important was the passage of Section 504 of the Rehabilitation Act of 1973 (PL 94-271), which states that ''no otherwise qualified handicapped individual in the United States should solely by reason of his handicap be excluded from participation in, be denied the benefits of, or be subjected to discrimination under any program or activity receiving Federal financial assistance.'' This law requires, for example, that educational facilities and all new federal facilities be constructed to provide ready accessibility for the handicapped. The Civil Rights Act of 1964 indirectly laid the groundwork for Section 504. Other legislative forces that have had a more direct influence on Section 504, both before and after its passage, include amendments to the Community Services Act that added handicapped children to Head Start programs and amendments to the Social Security Act that mandated Supplemental Security Income (SSI) and disabled children's programs in Title XVI, Early and Periodic Screening, Diagnosis, and Treatment (EPSDT) in Title XIX, and Social Services for Handicapped Children and Their Families in Title XX. Additional support for Section 504 came from legislation to assure free and appropriate public education to all handicapped children (PL 94-142).

Other important legislation in recent years has included amendments to the Developmental Disabilities Act to prevent discrimination on the basis of handicapping conditions in federally funded programs (PL 94-013) and to establish a state-based protection and advocacy system for persons with developmental disabilities (PL 95-602), as well as amendments to Title V of the Social Security Act to establish a Maternal and Child Health (MCH) Services Block Grant (PL 97-35). Further, the federal Maternal and Child Health Program (Title V of the Social Security Act) has had a long and distinguished history of contribution to the area of chronic illness in children, having supported such activities as training programs at the interface between pediatrics and child psychiatry, child development and evaluation clinics, interdisciplinary training in university-affiliated facilities, pediatric pulmonary centers, adolescent health programs, and research leading to *Child Health and the Community* (Haggerty, Roghmann, & Pless, 1975), the Chronically Ill Children Project of the Vanderbilt Institute on Public Policy Studies (see ''Focus on the Family," below), Ruth Stein's evaluation of a home care unit, and, for the past 50 years, the individual states' Program for Children with Special Health Care Needs.* These activities have stressed early case identification, coordination of multidimensional approaches, quality assurance, community-based approaches, and primary, secondary, and tertiary prevention. Preventing the occurrence of disorders has also been a central concern of pediatricians and the Maternal and Child Health Program since its inception some 50 years ago.

Following many months of discourse and judicial action, the 1984 amendments to the Child Abuse Prevention and Treatment Act continued this positive lawmaking on behalf of children with chronic illness by requiring states to implement procedures or programs for responding to reports of medical neglect of disabled infants with life-threatening conditions. Indeed, a major consequence of this legislation was the establishment of Infant Review Committees by most hospitals serving disabled infants. The debate about the existence and composition of these local committees has played an instrumental role in resolving delicate issues surrounding the problem of caring for, or the desire to withdraw care from, chronically ill infants.

Taken together, these recent legislative mandates have recognized and bolstered the concept of civil rights for handicapped individuals and propelled it to the forefront of the agenda of both public and private agencies. In this regard, both Section 504 of the Rehabilitation Act of 1973 and the amendments to the Developmental Disabilities Act for the first time provided services to disabled children at the same time that they prohibited denial of services based on handicapping conditions. The language changes in these two pieces of legislation reflected a change in approach from providing medical care for children with designated disabling conditions to including all children in a comprehensive, systematic program of health care irrespective of handicapping conditions.

The potent political power of this legislation is especially clear when one considers that the legislation spawned the movement, instead of the other way around, as was the experience in the legislative system for women and blacks.

Judicial Forces

Landmark decisions in the 1970s that resulted in the deinstitutionalization of mentally retarded persons in Pennsylvania (*Halderman v. Pennhurst*) and in the mainstreaming of children in special education classes in Washington, D.C. (*Mills v. Board of Education*) are among many that have

---

*Name changed from Crippled Children's Services (CCS) by PL 99–272.

come out of the judicial branch, from the municipal courts through the state and federal appellate courts to the United States Supreme Court.

Executive Orders

Executive Orders are another important element of recent political change, reflecting a broadened scope of responsibilities for health agencies serving handicapped children. An Executive Order asserted that any hospital receiving federal funds would be in violation of Section 504 if it agreed to withhold life-sustaining efforts from infants born with Down syndrome. The controversy surrounding this interpretation of Section 504 ultimately led to the Child Abuse Amendments of 1984. The debate between the executive and other governmental branches and the public brought the issue of handicapped children to national attention.

Through Executive Orders, federal and state agencies are being moved and, it is expected, will continue to be moved in the direction of broadening the scope of their activities to maximize the health of children with handicapping conditions. Two prominent recent examples are the orders creating the President's Committee on Mental Retardation and the President's Committee on Employment of the Handicapped. The impact of these executive political forces on state agencies has been significant.

State Agencies

State agencies serving children with special health needs can have a key role in helping mentally retarded children and adolescents maintain healthy lifestyles and in determining what adaptations need to be made for disabled youngsters in programs designed to combat teenage pregnancy, alcoholism, and violence. In general, state agencies should provide leadership in coordinating and ensuring the multiplicity of services offered by medical and other health practitioners. This should be done in both the public and private sector and include services that are needed by all children with chronic illness and other disabilities.

Social Developments

The major social forces affecting the provision of care to chronically ill children, though less tangible, are nonetheless real, and they are entwined with many political forces in an alternating cause-and-effect relationship. The political force of the Section 504 legislation preceded the social movement of disabled individuals organizing and mounting an effective advocacy program. Since then, new coalitions of people with disabilities have become articulate advocates of their desire to lead productive lives. Moreover, advocacy efforts on behalf of these individuals have subsequently led to legislation that defines and protects the civil rights of disabled persons and have developed new and expanded health, education, and service programs.

Efforts to meet these increased demands have led to major changes and new concepts in the provision of service to disabled children. Health care professionals now recognize that disabled children have many developmental characteristics that are similar to those of so-called normal children. Thus it is neither necessary nor desirable to treat the disabled apart from the rest of society, and social attitudes have moved away from maintaining the handicapped child in an institutional setting and toward creating a less restrictive environment for the child within his or her own community. In addition, through federal legislation, the handicapped child has attained a right to a free, appropriate public education and to the related services required to assist him or her in benefiting from that education. To deny the disabled child access to the health and educational services he or she requires may be a violation not only of the law but of the child's civil rights. The relationship between these social and political forces can be felt in the system's approach to delivering services to these children. In this approach, the child is viewed as a member of a microsystem—the family—which is in turn part of a larger system—the community. A collection of communities can constitute a state-based system (Hutchins, 1984).

Economic Influences

The current economic force that has dictated change in the care of children with chronic illness is the increased demand for services in the face of decreased funds for human services. This factor, coupled with accelerated costs for public and private third-party payers, has shifted downward the level of state agencies' support for children with disabling conditions.

Cost effectiveness has become a criterion by which most programs are judged; too frequently, however, it has become the only criterion. Because such economic forces will continue to affect state agencies and the populations they serve, strategies for combating them must be developed. The basic problem to be addressed is how, at this time of public austerity, the health care system can modify and coordinate programs so as to provide comprehensive care to the greatest number of children with chronic illness and other disabilities. Medicare's Prospective Payment System, based on diagnosis-related groups (DRGs), is the latest arrival on the economic scene. This tool, based chiefly on data collected on the hospitalized elderly, will likely be extended to all payers and thus will have an effect on chronically ill and disabled children, both poor and nonpoor (NACHRI, 1984).

Other Influences

Increased Survival of Children with Chronic Illness

The recent biomedical advances that have improved outcomes for the disabled are central to the dramatic changes and increased interest in chronic illness in children. Surgical advances in congenital heart disease, improved prosthetic and orthotic technology for amputee children, blood concentrate therapy for hemophilia, protocols for treatment of leukemia, aggressive treatment for cystic fibrosis, and ventilation support for bronchopulmonary dysfunction are a few examples of our ongoing biomedical advances (McPherson, 1986).

Indeed, the increased survival of children with chronic illness over the last two decades has highlighted new problems concerning the pressing need for the provision and coordination of health, educational, vocational, and social services to these individuals as they prepare to enter adult life. At a conference in the spring of 1985 for these "youth in transition," Madeleine Will, the Assistant Secretary of Education, said, "The most crippling disability of all may not be found among disabled individuals but instead may be found in the very system Federal and state officials have created to help them. The system is uncoordinated, inconsistent, and often incomprehensible" (Will, 1985).

Changes in Physicians' Practice Patterns

Changes in practice patterns among pediatricians, owning in large measure to the virtual elimination of infectious disease and acute illness as threats to children's health, have led to a focus on psychosocial aspects of children's health. In 1975, Robert J. Haggerty and his associates noted that the social environment in which a child lives is a major determinant of his health and the care he will receive. This "new morbidity," exemplified by children's behavioral and psychosocial problems and family stress, was described as being beyond the boundaries of traditional medical care. Solutions to the "new morbidity" would require pediatricians to extend themselves into the community in collaboration with representatives from many other disciplines. These changes in practice patterns also raise the issue of the value of health care supervision, well-child visits, and management of long-term problems for the prevention of psychosocial problems of children. Haggerty warned, however, of two issues that may delay acceptance of the "new morbidity" by pediatricians. The first was an implicit loss of status and prestige by shifting from technical expertise to an interpersonal, managerial style. The second concerned the willingness of society to adequately compensate for the value of these services (Haggerty, Roghmann, & Pless, 1975).

Despite such reservations, in some instances where this approach has been tried, there have been positive results. The Hemophilia Program, for example, accomplished great feats between 1975 and 1985 when it began to emphasize outpatient and home care. This investment in comprehensive care programs that promote home infusion has paid off by reducing disability, unemployment, loss of school days, and the cost of medical care. Specifically, the number of patients seen at both primary treatment and affiliate centers increased more than 350%; the number of patients receiving comprehensive care and the number receiving home care more than quadrupled; the average number of hospital days per year per patient was reduced by 83%, from 9.4 hospital days to 1.6 hospital days per year and, moreover, there was a 73% reduction in the number of days lost from work or school each year; finally, the percentage of unemployed adults dropped from 36% to 9.4% overall and is as low as 4.5% in some regions (Smith & Levine, 1984/1986).

New Educational Options

In 1975, Congress passed PL 94–142, the Education for All Handicapped Children Act. Enactment of this law marked the culmination of a revolution in educational opportunities for handicapped children. The new provisions of this legislation included individualized education plans (IEPs) designed to meet a child's special needs by including parent participation—a concept that has become accepted in the provision of all human services, such as health education and social services. Early implementation focused on those children in need of special education and related services. More recently, attention has been given to those children with health impairments who do not need special education but who do require "related services" (see Walker, Chapter 4).

At the same time, however, the individualized plan can be detrimental to the family, which may have several conflicting plans developed by different agencies and real input into none of them. Although appropriate collaboration among agencies and providers of human services should avoid such complications for the family, this does not necessarily occur. Indeed, until a few years ago, it was possible for a child to have up to seven individual care plans. To solve this problem, providers must keep the focus on the child and the child's family. Their primary responsibility, then, is to plan a continuum of care utilizing the social, health, educational, and family resources that are available.

Another lesson from PL 94–142 is the concept of least restrictive environment for children consistent with their special needs, which has opened the normal classroom to children with disabilities and chronic illness. However, although revolutionary changes in attitude have occurred and are continuing to occur, "least restrictive environment" must not be interpreted to mean "normal." Universal mainstreaming is as inappropriate as blanket institutionalization for disabled children. The essential concerns should be whether the child is being given every opportunity to learn or to develop his or her inherent abilities and whether we, as a responsible society, have removed all barriers and have placed the child in the best available setting for development to occur.

Finally, a trend toward earlier intervention with disabled, developmentally delayed, and at-risk children is clearly evident. New amendments to the Education for all Handicapped Children Act, contained in PL 99–457, allowed states to address the needs of disabled and at-risk infants and toddlers and their families and strengthened the incentive for states to serve all handicapped children aged three to five.

FOCUS ON THE FAMILY

In recent years, American society has given almost unlimited support to technology, but support for the essential service systems outside the tertiary care environment has not kept pace with the increasing numbers of children and adolescents in need. During the 1982 Surgeon General's Workshop on Children with Handicaps and Their Families, the contributions as well as the complications and costs of high technology were discussed. Technology is expensive, essential support systems are also expensive, and funds are limited, but the one issue that must remain foremost is what is best for the child and the family (*Report of the Surgeon General's Workshop*, 1983).

The success of recent efforts to help children with chronic illness has resulted largely from an awareness of early intervention and, even more important, of the central role of families and the primacy of parents' roles in the lives of their children. Research by Ruth Stein and colleagues, for example, supported her hypothesis of commonalities across diagnostic categories in chronic illness of children (Stein & Jessop, 1982). Her study also began to provide detailed information about the impact of children's chronic illness on their families and the issues raised in the home care of these children (Stein & Jessop, 1984a; Stein, Jessop, & Riessman, 1983).

A report issued in 1980 by the Select Panel for the Promotion of Child Health agreed with this new emphasis on the crucial role of the family and concluded that, "Not only is the family the primary unit for the delivery of health services to infants and children, but the family environment is probably the greatest influence on a child's health" (Select Panel, 1981). Expanding on this theme, the panel further stated:

From conception on, a child is dependent upon his or her mother and other family members not only for the physical necessities of life—food, shelter, clothing and protection from harm—but also for the emotional support and intellectual stimulation needed for healthy growth and development. It requires no great expertise to recognize the importance to any child of a secure, loving, and stimulating familiy environment. . . . The family is not only the principal influence upon a child's development, it is also the inter-mediary between the child and the outside world, including the health care system. . . . Health providers can support, encourage, and enhance the com-petence of parents in their role as caregivers, or they can directly or indirectly undermine and denigrate it.

Four general themes emerged from the Select Panel's review of the health care needs of children with chronic illness. First, the panel found that coordination of care to eliminate duplication and unnecessary cate-gorical restrictions was urgently needed; that there were seven major ser-vice programs spanning the health, education, and welfare sectors; that no single agency or authority at any level of government was responsi-ble for identifying these children, diagnosing their needs, or ensuring that comprehensive health services were provided; and, finally, that the types of services received were, to a large extent, dependent on financial status. Second, the panel reported that professionals at all levels need additional training to deal more effectively with these children. Health providers' knowledge of child development, functional ability, and disa-bling conditions was noted to be particularly inadequate. Third, the panel stressed that prevention and early identification efforts need support and expansion. All three levels of prevention must be included. Primary prevention efforts must be taken to promote general health as well as to prevent diseases such as maternal rubella during the childbearing years. Genetic services and newborn screening are essential. Secondary preven-tion should be directed toward early diagnosis and correction of poten-tially disabling conditions, such as phenylketonuria (PKU) and hypothyroidism. Tertiary prevention should concentrate on the child with a disabling condition requiring medical, surgical, or other professional intervention in order to minimize the disability to the greatest degree pos-sible. Optimally, organized health care services for disabled children would provide an organized system of primary, secondary, and tertiary services linked together to ensure continuity and coordination. Finally, the Select Panel stated that families of children with chronic illness need significantly more financial and psychosocial support than presently exists.

In the late 1970s, not long before the panel's report was issued, the Vanderbilt Institute for Public Policy Studies created the Chronically Ill Children Project, under the assumption that children who suffer from severe, chronic illness are "a neglected group in our society who live out their lives in a twilight zone of public understanding."* This study, a review of existing public policies and their effects on children with chronic illness and their families, identified certain basic principles that should underlie all policy concerning chronically ill children.

> Children with chronic illnesses and their families have special needs that merit attention, beyond that provided to the health needs of able-bodied children. Families have the central role in caring for their own members and the goal of policy should be to enable families to carry out their responsibilities to nurture their children and encourage their most effective development. Policy should encourage professional services of a highly ethical nature. Key elements include truth telling, confidentiality, maintenance of dignity and respect for family preferences, professionals' recognition of limits of their own effectiveness, and emphasis on collaboration. (Hobbs, Perrin & Ireys, 1985)

As hoped, the Vanderbilt findings and recommendations have been distributed widely and are making a rich contribution to the national dialogue on improving services for children with chronic illness and their families.

Other important issues affecting the services available for children with chronic illness and their families include regionalization of care for these low prevalence conditions; the complications of high technology, including children dependent on gastrostomy tubes for feeding; the growing home care movement; the complex bioethical issues involved in high technology care; and, especially, the cost and financing of required services and the increasing problem of uncompensated care in hospitals. In addition, although hospitals have traditionally been the preferred treatment setting, leaders in children's services have begun to recognize that children have special needs requiring special hospice services. The growth of hospice-based care over the past few years suggests that feasible alternatives may be possible as well as preferable; indeed, the hospice philosophy and movement have had a strong influence on the care of chronically ill children and their families (Hutchins, 1986).

Perhaps most important, in recent years family resource programs, parent-to-parent networks, and other self-help groups across the country are supporting parents who are coping with the ordinary stresses

---

*In the development of the Vanderbilt project, an important step that strengthened the effort both substantively and symbolically was joint funding from both the Department of Education and the Department of Health and Human Services. The Robert Wood Johnson Foundation was also a key contributor to the support of the project. Moreover, from the beginning, the strengths of the Vanderbilt project were the concept of building public awareness of the problem of chronic illness in children and a deliberate plan for the dissemination of the findings.

of contemporary child rearing as well as families whose children face special challenges (see Beckett, Chapter 8; Borck, Chapter 10; Bilotti, Chapter 15). To this latter end, the Office of Maternal and Child Health of the Public Health Service is supporting four major national efforts at building an ongoing system of family-centered, community-based care for these children and their families. These initiatives are designed to develop systems and strategies at local and state levels that will allow for parent involvement in the health care and education of their children, encouraging families and health professionals to work together as partners. The individualized family services plans and case-management services specified in PL 99–457 are among the tools that can be utilized to achieve these ends.

FUTURE DIRECTIONS

Future Directions of Services for Children with Specialized Health Needs, a report currently being prepared by a team of national experts headed by John MacQueen, M.D., will identify and examine the major issues and problems confronting government-supported programs for children with special health care needs. The report will enunciate goals and objectives for state Programs for Children with Special Health Care Needs (see Ireys, Chapter 3); furnish guidance to state and local policymakers charged with allocating public resources to services for these children; and provide guidance to other organizations, groups, and individuals with an interest in the delivery of services to these children (MacQueen, 1984).

THE GOAL OF CARE

Ultimately, the challenge in caring for children is to maintain a sensitive awareness of the individual child while being cognizant of the influences of the child's environment—the family and the community. This is especially true when dealing with the promotion of a child's health and the prevention of further disease. Today, many of the health problems of children and youth have multiple causes and thus require multiple interventions. The pediatrician, to be effective, needs to possess, in addition to specific knowledge of the disease process, knowledge of growth and development, family development, function and culture, and reactions to stress, loss, and separation. We have now accepted the child as a citizen with the right to live, play, and grow in his or her own community. This requires changes in service delivery, with local pediatricians, school staff, community and mental health workers, and social service providers working effectively together in community-based networks. The pediatrician must have knowledge of community institutions, their resources, and their functions as well as the skills necessary to work with other professionals and other agencies in order to understand and treat the whole child in the context of the family (Hutchins, 1985).

Drs. Stein and Jessop have written: "The goal of care is to confine the consequences of the biologic disorder to its minimum manifestation, to encourage normal growth and development, to assist the child in maximizing potential in all possible areas, and to prevent or diminish the behavioral and social consequences" (Stein & Jessop, 1984b). Accepting this goal, we can move into the next century confident of providing the necessary resources for children with chronic illness and their families. These children will then be able to live, play, learn, and thrive in their own communities.

Acknowledgment: The authors gratefully acknowledge the critical reading and editing contributions of John E. Hutchins.

REFERENCES

Gortmaker, S. L., & Sappenfield, W. (1984). Chronic childhood disorders: Prevalence and impact. *Pediatric Clinics of North America, 31* (1), 3–18.

Haggerty, R. J., Roghmann, K. J., & Pless, I. B. (1975). *Child health and the community.* New York: Wiley.

Healy, A. (1983). Children with disabilities: Implications for care. In *Report of the surgeon general's workshop on children with handicaps and their families.* (DHHS Publication No. PHS-83-50194). Washington, DC: U.S. Government Printing Office.

Hobbs, N. (1980, February). Letter to Surgeon General Julius B. Richmond.

Hobbs, N., Perrin, J. M., & Ireys, H. T. (1985). *Chronically ill children and their families.* San Francisco: Jossey-Bass.

Hutchins, V. L. (1984, September). *Community-based services for children with disabilities and their families.* Dale Richmond Memorial Lecture presented to the American Academy of Pediatrics.

Hutchins, V. L. (1985). The goal of care. *Journal of Developmental and Behavioral Pediatrics, 6,* 179.

Hutchins, V. L. (1986). Pediatric hospice in the '80s—Enriching the circle of care. In M. Hunter (Ed.), *1985 Pediatric Hospice Conference Report* (pp. 2–4). Alexandria, VA: Children's Hospice International.

MacQueen, J. C. (1984, March). *Future directions of services for children with specialized health needs.* Paper presented at the annual meeting of the Association for MCH/CC Programs. March, 1984.

McPherson, M. G. (1983). Improving services to infants and young children with handicapping conditions and their families: The division of maternal and child health and collaborator. *Zero to Three* (Bulletin of the National Center for Clinical Infant Programs), *4*, (1) 1–4.

McPherson, M. G. (1986). Community-based services for disabled/chronically ill children and their families. In E. Eklund (Ed.), *Developmental handicaps: Prevention and treatment, III* (pp. 15–35). Silver Spring, MD: American Association for University-Affiliated Programs.

National Association of Children's Hospitals and Related Institutions, Inc. (NACHRI). (1984). *The use of case mix based prospective payment for inpatient hospital care.* Merrifield, VA: Cardinal.

Pless, I. B., & Douglas, J. W. B. (1971) Chronic illness in childhood I. Epidemiological and clinical characteristics. *Pediatrics, 47,* 405–414.

Report of the surgeon general's workshop on children with handicaps and their families. (DHHS Publication No. PHS-83-50194). Washington, DC: U.S. Government Printing Office.

Select Panel for the Promotion of Child Health. (1981). *Better health for our children: A national strategy* (Vol. 1). (DHHS Publication No. PHS-79-55071). Washington, DC: U.S. Government Printing Office.

Smith, P. S., & Levine, P. H. (1984, data updated 1986). The benefits of comprehensive care of hemophilia: A five-year study of outcomes. *American Journal of Public Health, 74,* 616.

Stein, R. E. K., & Jessop, D. J. (1982). A noncategorical approach to chronic childhood illness. *Public Health Reports, 87* (4) 354–362.

Stein, R. E. K., & Jessop, D. J. (1984a). Does pediatric home care make a difference? Findings from the pediatric ambulatory care treatment study. *Pediatrics, 73,* 845–853.

Stein, R. E. K., & Jessop, D. J. (1984b). General issues in the care of children with chronic physical conditions, *Pediatric Clinics of North America, 31* (1) 189–198.

Stein, R. E. K., Jessop, D. J., & Riessman, C. K. (1983). Health care services of chronically ill children. *American Journal of Diseases of Children, 137,* 225–240.

Will, M. C. (1985). Opening remarks. *Journal of Adolescent Health Care, 6* (2), 105–106.

2

Financing of Care:
A Critical Component

Diane Rowland, M.P.A., Sc.D.

In an era of wide-ranging constraints on federal domestic spending, the problem of inadequate financing for the care of chronically ill children will not be easily ameliorated. Children with chronic illness require comprehensive services, and the cost of that care is neither inconsequential nor short term. A chronically ill child can devastate the family's resources as episodes of illness and medical bills mount. The financial devastation complicates the already difficult emotional burden these families face as they struggle to provide for the health and well-being of the frail child.

This financial burden arises because most chronically ill children lack sufficient health insurance coverage for the medical care their conditions require. Lack of comprehensive Medicaid coverage and gaps in private insurance coverage leave many vulnerable children unprotected in the health care marketplace.

This chapter examines the extent of health insurance coverage for chronically ill children and the inadequacies in that coverage. The first section reviews the financial burden of caring for chronically ill children; the second describes current public and private financing for medical services; the third summarizes recent legislative developments; and the last discusses directions for improving coverage in the future.

THE FINANCIAL BURDEN OF DISABILITY

Recurring medical expenses are a major burden for seriously impaired children and their families, compounding the strain and stress of coping with the disabling condition itself. Children with chronic disabilities often need intense medical, physical, and social services; hospital and ambulatory care as part of special therapies; family support services; physical, speech, and occupational therapy; and psychiatric counseling.

Children with chronic illness use more physician services and are hospitalized more often than other children. Severely impaired children have, on average, 21.8 physician visits per year, compared to 9.5 visits per year for less severely impaired children with functional limitations and 4 visits per year for children without chronic health problems (Fox, 1984). Hospital discharge rates for severely impaired children are 1,677 per 1,000, compared to 256 per 1,000 for children with functional limitations and 58 per 1,000 for nondisabled children. When hospitalized, functionally limited children have an average length of stay that is twice that of other children.

The cost for this care is significant and the expenses are not one-time expenditures; they recur year after year and frequently increase as the condition becomes more disabling. In 1982, average annual hospital expenditures for a severely impaired child ranged from $5,000 to $10,000, compared to annual expenditures of $75 to $150 per nondisabled child (Fox, 1984). Similarly, the average physician bill for a severely impaired child was $600 per year, almost six times that for other children. It is not unusual for the most severely impaired children to incur annual health care expenses far in excess of $10,000.

Children with serious chronic illnesses or other disabilities are thus prominent among those with large health care expenditures. Children born with a congenital anomaly can incur enormous costs for corrective surgery, medical care, and attendant services before they ever leave the maternity ward (Butler, Budetti, McManus, Stenmark, & Newacheck, 1985). Children with prolonged and degenerative diseases often have frequent high-cost episodes of illness over their lifetime. In some instances costs can be very unpredictable and can fluctuate greatly. But even when the nature and level of expenditures are relatively predictable, families are often unprepared for the financial consequences. As a result, the child's illness often becomes a catastrophic burden for the family.

Children with chronic conditions, as measured by functional limitations, are more likely than children with acute illness episodes to incur catastrophic debts because the services they need are often not covered by private insurance and are unavailable or difficult to obtain from public programs. Many private insurance plans have limits on covered services and require substantial copayments for physician and nonphysician visits, medical supplies and equipment, and medications. Families with private coverage often exhaust their benefits and are left to finance needed care from their own resources or turn for help to charity and public assistance.

THE CURRENT FINANCING PATCHWORK

The sickest children with the greatest need for health care services are, unfortunately, also the children whose health care needs are most often inadequately financed. Parents are left to worry not only about the health and well-being of their sick child, but also about the economic consequences of the child's illness for the whole family.

Many chronically ill children have major insurance coverage, but others have no coverage at all. Fully 10% of children with functional limitations have no insurance coverage whatsoever (Butler et al., 1985). The interaction of family income, disability status, and insurance coverage is depicted in Table 2.1.

Lack of insurance is a financial burden for any family with a child with large medical expenses, but a true financial catastrophe for low-income families—almost 20% of disabled children from families with incomes below the poverty level are uninsured. Although a small percentage may receive some Social Security income supplementation, and there have been some initiatives involving more comprehensive services through the educational system (see Walker, Chapter 4), for the most part their impoverished families cannot afford the needed care and must try to finance it through charity or public programs. Such patchwork financing translates into uneven and episodic patterns of care that undermine comprehensive and effective treatment of a chronic illness.

TABLE 2.1 Insurance Coverage for Children Under Age 18, 1979

	Number of children (in millions)	Type of insurance		
		Private	Public (% distribution)	Uninsured
All children	62.6	75	17	8
Disabled children	3.7	62	28	10
Above poverty	2.7	78	15	7
Below poverty	1.0	18	63	19

SOURCE: Butler, et al., 1985. Reproduced by permission.

Poor disabled children are far more likely to rely on public programs for insurance than children from more affluent families. Among the 1 million disabled children from families with incomes below the poverty level, 63% are covered by public programs and 18% have private insurance (Butler et al., 1985). In contrast, among disabled children from more affluent families, 78% are privately insured and only 15% are covered by public programs.

Private Insurance Coverage

Most families of chronically ill children obtain private health insurance for their families from an employer, but chronic illness of a child may interfere with a parent's ability to work outside the home and therefore with eligibility for private insurance. This presents a problem, especially for the single parent with a child who has extensive need for special care. But even for those who are able to work and obtain insurance through an employer, being insured still does not mean that all necessary care is covered; private health insurance invariably falls short for families with a chronically ill child.

Private insurance is most beneficial for high-cost acute episodes of illness, but its coverage for routine and ongoing care tends to be less comprehensive. Benefits are limited and can often be exhausted. For some children with illness costs may even exceed the most liberal lifetime benefits. Moreover, most policies have poor coverage for such necessary health and social support services as physical and speech therapy, dental care, outpatient mental health services, and prescription drugs. Gaps in physician and hospital coverage also occur for some specialized services.

Among severely impaired schoolchildren with private health insurance coverage, only 22% had all of their physician visits paid by insurance. This was less than the 23% whose parents paid out of pocket for all physician visits despite having private insurance. Parents and insurance combined to pay for physician visits for nearly 49% of children with private coverage (Butler, Singer, Palfrey, & Walher, 1987).

Even for covered services, cost sharing can result in substantial out-of-pocket costs. Cost sharing combined with payments for uncovered services can prove catastrophic for many families. Data from 1980 show that approximately 421,000 noninstitutionalized children incurred out-of-pocket expenses greater than 10% of family income, and approximately 157,000 children had out-of-pocket expenses in excess of 30% of family income (McManus, Newacheck, & Matlin, 1986).

For some families, obtaining coverage for their chronically ill child under the family's health insurance policy may be impossible. Some private policies specifically exclude it. Riders that exclude treatment for certain conditions or for preexisting conditions can be especially problematic for families with disabled children. Moreover, even when policies cover the child, families face serious problems obtaining continuation of coverage after the child reaches age 21. In addition, many families are limited in terms of job mobility because they know that a change in insurance may result in loss of or lapses in insurance coverage.

Chronically ill children are therefore less likely to be covered by group policies than other children. Only 55% of all chronically ill children are covered by group insurance, compared to 76% of all children (Fox, 1984). If the child is not covered under the family's group insurance policy, the family may attempt to purchase an individually written one. Individual policies are often unaffordable, and in many cases insurers will not write policies for certain conditions that are considered "medically uninsurable." Thus, although private insurance coverage is important protection for most families with chronically ill children, it is neither complete nor comprehensive. Large numbers of chronically ill children are not covered, and for those with coverage, benefits are often inadequate.

Medicaid Coverage for Poor Children

Medicaid is the single largest health care program financing services to poor children and their families. It is a joint federal–state program, operated under federal guidelines, giving substantial discretion to states in terms of eligibility policy and program design. Unlike the federal Medicare program, Medicaid has a means test and is neither comprehensive nor universal. Variations among states mean that chronically ill children and their families receive different coverage from Medicaid depending on their state of residence. For example, it is estimated that 20% of low-income disabled children are covered in Nevada, compared to 86% in New York (Butler et al., 1985).

In all states, in order to be eligible for Medicaid, the family of a chronically ill child must be poor. How poor one must be before becoming eligible varies tremendously because the income level for program benefits is set by each state. In 1984, Medicaid income eligibility standards averaged about 44% of the poverty level across the states. Standards ranged from less than $2,000 per year for a family of four in Alabama and Tennessee to more than $7,000 per year for a similar family in Alaska, California, Connecticut, New York, and Wisconsin (HCFA, 1985).

In some states, families that are not poor enough for Medicaid coverage can qualify for assistance if their medical expenses reduce their available income to below the income standard for Medicaid eligibility. This process is known as *spending down,* and the states that offer this option for

Medicaid coverage are referred to as states covering the "medically needy." Thirty-four states provide coverage to the medically needy.

Moderate- and low-income families with a child with very high medical costs can thus sometimes receive assistance from Medicaid if they reside in a state offering coverage to the medically needy. But the income levels for eligibility under this option require virtual impoverishment, because the family must spend enough on medical care to reduce its income to well below the poverty level. In addition, there are severe limitations on the amount of assets that a family can have to qualify, which further restrict eligibility.

The medically needy spend-down option is useful mainly during periods of high medical expenses when income is substantially reduced by the cumulative effect of multiple medical bills. Medicaid eligibility often does not extend beyond the high-expense period because routine care expenses may not reduce the family income to Medicaid eligibility levels. The on-and-off nature of eligibility for the medically needy makes Medicaid coverage an ineffective means of providing routine and preventive care to chronically ill children.

Even if a family with a chronically ill child meets the Medicaid income and assets tests, the child still might not qualify for Medicaid coverage. Although Medicaid eligibility can be more liberal, it generally follows eligibility for welfare assistance and usually provides coverage to single-parent families with dependent children. However, a new federal Medicaid law requires states to cover pregnant women and young children in two-parent families under state welfare standards and gives states the option of offering broader coverage up to 185% of the poverty line.

In addition to variations in eligibility policy, states also vary widely in terms of the benefits offered under Medicaid. All states are required to offer basic medical coverage in terms of inpatient hospital care, physician services, laboratory and x-ray services, and screening and diagnostic services for children. Most states impose restrictions on utilization of services by requiring prior authorization for service or by limiting the number of covered physician visits or hospital days. Low provider reimbursement rates discourage provider participation and may promote unnecessary institutionalization. Such limitations could be especially problematic for chronically ill children who need extensive health care services and multiple physician visits.

Thus, although Medicaid is an important financing source for poor children with chronic and disabling conditions, it falls short in terms of both the number of poor children covered and the level of comprehensiveness for many of those who are covered. Medicaid covers only about 60% of disabled children from families with incomes below the federal poverty level (Butler et al., 1985). However, because Medicaid is a means-tested program for the poor, it offers no relief to moderate-income families struggling to provide for their chronically ill children. Medicaid is not an alternative to private insurance for most families.

Maternal and Child Health Services

The Maternal and Child Health (MCH) Program, Title V of the Social Security Act, is the most direct and sustained federal effort to serve chronically ill children (see Ireys, Chapter 3). First enacted in 1935, the MCH program provides states with federal funds to develop and provide services for high-risk pregnant women and children as well as crippled children. In 1979, the Crippled Children's Program spent $275 million in federal funds on services to one million handicapped children (Butler et al., 1985). However, large variations existed among the states in terms of the number of chronically ill children served, the eligibility rules for assistance, the types of conditions covered, and the generosity of benefits.

In 1981, the Title V programs for mothers and children were consolidated into a block grant to the states. Under the block grant, states have even broader discretion in designing and providing services than under the formula and grant programs. Many states still concentrate on covering orthopedic problems, but funds are no longer earmarked for crippled children. The block grant nature of the program also means that no longer is there federal control over the expenditure of funds and little state accounting of how the funds are actually used or how effective they have been in meeting health care needs. Over time, this lack of documentation could lead to an erosion of federal support to maintain or increase funding, which, in turn, would have serious implications for services.

However, the main drawback of the MCH program is that while it provides targeted assistance to chronically ill children, it does not entitle them to health insurance coverage or assure access to needed health care services. The total amount of services provided is limited to care that can be provided under the existing appropriation. Service needs that exceed appropriated levels are not covered. This results in the rationing of crippled children's services in virtually all states.

RECENT LEGISLATIVE DEVELOPMENTS

The plight of chronically ill children and their families has not gone unnoticed. The case of Katie Beckett, a ventilator-dependent child, dramatized the obstacles confronting families trying to care for their disabled child at home and led to amendments in the Medicaid statute to try to ease their burdens and facilitate home care for disabled children (see Beckett,

Chapter 8). Incremental improvements have been achieved, but broad-scale reform of financing still remains an elusive goal as Congress struggles to restrain federal domestic spending.

"Katie Becketts" and Model Waivers

The case of Katie Beckett of Cedar Rapids, Iowa, helped bring the plight of ventilator-dependent chronically ill children to the nation's attention when President Reagan intervened to help Katie be cared for at home by her parents instead of in a hospital. As long as Katie had been in the hospital for more than 30 days, she was eligible for Medicaid because her parents' income was not considered available to her for purposes of calculating income to determine Medicaid eligibility. However, if Katie were to have gone home, she would have been considered ineligible for Medicaid, even though care at home would have cost substantially less.

The Health Care Financing Administration (HCFA) set up a special review program to help keep the "Katie Becketts" at home with their families whenever possible. Initially, the "Katie Beckett waivers" were handled on an individual review basis. A special review board determined on a case-by-case basis whether the quality of care would be better and the cost cheaper to keep the chronically ill child in the community rather than in the hospital.

HCFA replaced the individual review system with a process through which the states could obtain "model waivers" to provide Medicaid assistance to "Katie Beckett-type" cases. Model waiver coverage is available only for chronically ill children and adults. A model waiver expedites approval from HCFA, and each waiver provides Medicaid coverage for up to 50 chronically ill individuals. Although each model waiver covers only 50 children, states are permitted to apply for more than one. It permits states to cover home modifications, case management, homemaker services, respite care, and transportation.

Most important, under the model waivers the states do not deem the parents' income to be that of the chronically ill child. This means that the child can qualify for Medicaid coverage at home even if the parents have income and assets in excess of Medicaid eligibility standards.

As of April 1986, fourteen states have actively pursued the use of model waivers to provide services to chronically ill children who would otherwise require hospitalization (Office of Technology Assessment, 1987). Such waivers are obviously state-initiated, and access to care under them depends on the state's policy with regard to coverage of this population. As with all other aspects of Medicaid coverage, individuals will receive differing levels of assistance depending on the state in which they reside. No matter how important these options are, some states will be reluctant to commit the funds to implement them without a specific mandate from Congress.

Home- and Community-Based Services Waivers Under Medicaid

As part of the 1981 Omnibus Budget Reconciliation Act, Congress set up a home- and community-based services waiver program. Under the waivers, also known as 2176 waivers, states are permitted to provide a comprehensive package of in-home and community-based services as alternatives to institutional care. Services offered can include personal care, case management, respite care, and homemaker services. States are permitted to use more generous income levels (up to approximately $12,000 per year) in determining eligibility for home- and community-based services.

The catch in the program is that in order to obtain approval for the waiver, the state has to demonstrate to HCFA that expenditures under the waiver will not exceed what would otherwise have been spent on institutional care. Documenting the budget neutrality of the proposed waivers has been a major problem for the states because HCFA has applied a very stringent formula.

In the 1985 Consolidated Omnibus Budget Reconciliation Act (COBRA), Congress clarified the formula to facilitate approvals for states. COBRA also contained provisions permitting ventilator-dependent children in hospitals to be eligible for home- and community-based services and including rehabilitation services in the benefits that could be covered as waivered services.

In the 1986 Omnibus Budget Reconciliation Act, Congress again broadened the application of the home- and community-based waiver provision to permit states to cover any individual who, but for the provision of home- and community-based services, would require the level of care provided in a hospital. This expansion is especially important for chronically ill children, who are more likely to be users of long-term hospital care than nursing home care. Medicaid coverage of respiratory services for ventilator-dependent individuals was also added as an optional benefit.

This 1986 provision provides an important expansion of Medicaid coverage, since any disabled child at risk of hospitalization, not just ventilator-dependent children, could conceivably qualify for waivered services. It helps to keep children out of institutions and at home with their families, as long as budget neutrality or savings can be demonstrated.

In addition to the expansion of the waiver authority in 1986, Congress also amended Medicaid to allow states, for the first time, to include case management as a Medicaid benefit and to target services to specific groups of Medicaid beneficiaries, such as children with special health needs, without obtaining home- and community-based waivers. This amendment opens up the possibility of Medicaid reimbursement to Title V agencies for the provision of case-management services to children with special health care needs.

Expansion of Medicaid for Pregnant Women and Children

The scope of Medicaid coverage for pregnant women and children, another area that affects the level of public support for chronically ill children, has been extended in recent legislation. Improved coverage of prenatal care for low-income women will, it is hoped, serve as a preventive strategy that helps improve birth outcomes.

In the Deficit Reduction Act of 1984, Congress required states to cover all children up to age five who meet state welfare standards, with coverage phased in beginning with infants born after October 1, 1983. States were also required to cover all pregnant women in families with an unemployed parent who meet state welfare standards.

In the 1985 Consolidated Omnibus Budget Reconciliation Act, Congress required states to extend Medicaid coverage to all pregnant women whose incomes are below state income standards, whether in single- or two-parent families. It also permitted states to accelerate coverage of children up to age five. In the 1987 Omnibus Reconciliation Act, Congress gave states the option to extend coverage to all pregnant women and young children with incomes up to 185% of the federal poverty level.

However, despite these important improvements in coverage for pregnant women and young children, the Medicaid program itself has been severely constrained in recent years. Since 1980, budget pressures have resulted in reductions in eligibility levels and scope of benefits in many states. This has meant a loss of Medicaid as an insurance option for many of the poor who would otherwise have been covered.

Task Force on Technology-Dependent Children

Concern for further documentation of the problems faced by technology-dependent children led to the establishment of a Task Force on Technology-Dependent Children in the 1985 Consolidated Omnibus Budget Reconciliation Act. The task force was charged with identifying alternatives to institutionalization for technology-dependent children.

In 1987 the Task Force submitted a report to Congress and the Secretary of the Department of Health and Human Services on barriers that prevent the provision of appropriate care in a home or community setting to technology-dependent children. The task force report includes recommendations on changes in the provision and financing of health care in private and public health programs to provide home- and community-based alternatives for these children.

Relevant congressional committees also requested a report on this subject from the Office of Technology Assessment of the U.S. Congress, which was published in May 1987.

Maternal and Child Health Block Grant

The 1981 Omnibus Budget Reconciliation Act created the Maternal and Child Health (MCH) Block Grant by consolidating the categorical and formula grant programs for financing the delivery of services to mothers and children under Title V of the Social Security Act. The Crippled Children's Services Program was folded into the block grant, which gives the states flexibility over program spending priorities and services.

Recent congressional activity has mainly focused on appropriations and authorization levels for the block grant. In 1984, the Deficit Reduction Act established a permanent authorization of $478 million for the MCH block. The 1985 Consolidated Omnibus Budget Reconciliation Act changed the words "crippled children" to "children with special health needs" in the MCH block grant to remove the stigma associated with the phrase "crippled children" and reflect a broader definition of its mission (see Ireys, Chp. 3).

The 1986 Omnibus Budget Reconciliation Act increased the authorization level for the next three years and provided that funds be set aside for the screening of newborns for sickle cell anemia and other genetic disorders. The states are also required to use additional funds to develop demonstrations that provide primary health care services and community-based service networks for children with special health care needs.

Vaccine Compensation

In the National Childhood Vaccine Injury Act of 1986, Title XXI of the Public Health Service Act, Congress created a no-fault compensation program for children who have been seriously injured by one of the seven vaccines required by state law prior to school entry. Although such injuries are rare, they may produce chronic disabilities and be expensive to treat. Public health experts estimate that there are about 80 serious vaccine-related injuries per year.

Under the new compensation program, victims of vaccine-related injuries receive expenses, rehabilitation services, and special education. The program requires victims to go through the federal compensation program first. If they do not accept the federal compensation award, the victims and their parents are free to sue under a modified tort system.

FUTURE DIRECTIONS

Clearly the serious gaps in insurance coverage for chronically ill children need to be filled. Families should not be impoverished by the medical expenses of a sick child. Furthermore, families should not receive differential assistance depending on the type of medical condition of the child, their employer, or the state in which they live. Concern for those with catastrophic health burdens is currently receiving increased public attention.

The HHS Task Force on Catastrophic Illness Expenses has stimulated discussion in both the public and private sectors. The President promised legislation on catastrophic coverage for elderly Americans in his 1987 State of the Union address. The Congress has begun to respond with hearings and legislative proposals of its own.

Yet most of the momentum to ease catastrophic burdens seems aimed at the elderly and disabled through improvements in Medicare. Such approaches are clearly essential improvements in health insurance protection for the elderly and disabled, but will not address the problems faced by most chronically ill children and their families. Separate and focused efforts to address their plight should accompany new protection for the elderly and disabled.

Caution should also be exercised in this competitive era to ensure that, in the quest for more cost-effective insurance coverage, we do not end up leaving those with the most serious or expensive health needs without assistance. Coverage of a child with chronic illness in a small group plan can result in very uncompetitive insurance premiums.

Action to expand health insurance protection for chronically ill children and their families needs to come from several directions. Private health insurance coverage could be improved through state risk pools for medically uninsurable children and mandated coverage for chronically ill children under family group policies. PL 100-360 mandates Medicaid coverage by 1990 for all infants up to one year of age in families with income at or below the poverty level and the option now exists to offer Medicaid to children up to age 5 in families with incomes up to 185% of the poverty level. States could be required to expand such coverage initiatives further. The MCH block grant needs to have services more targeted and reporting requirements improved to document program effectiveness. Finally, a strong preventive program, including better access to prenatal and well-baby/child care, could be developed as part of Medicaid and the Maternal and Child Health programs to help avoid chronic illness in the future.

One of the stumbling blocks for this reform agenda is the lack of dollars to finance the improvements. The private insurance reforms will be difficult to implement because they impose additional costs on private employers. The public-sector reforms will also face serious opposition because of federal budget constraints.

Today's environment involves, unfortunately, a fight to preserve existing programs that leaves little maneuvering room for necessary, but generally costly, program improvements. There is intense competition for limited federal funds. Programs such as the MCH block grant will not continue to grow if the evidence necessary to document effectiveness is not collected. Immediate action may come more in the form of studies and some incremental improvements than from broad initiatives, although the push for catastrophic insurance may help to broaden the debate.

The problems of chronically ill children and the financial burdens their families face must be documented so that the dollars to address these burdens at the federal level will be incorporated into the budget. Advocates of chronically ill children need to build their case for program improvements with good statistics and human stories to ensure that legislators and the public understand what is at stake in delaying necessary improvements.

REFERENCES

Butler, J. A., Budetti, P., McManus, M. A., Stenmark, S., & Newacheck, P. (1985). Health care expenditures for children with chronic illness. In N. Hobbs & J. H. Perrin, *Issues in the care of children with chronic illness* (pp. 827–861). San Francisco: Jossey-Bass.

Butler, J. A., Singer, J. D., Palfrey, J. S., & Walker, D. K. (1987). Health insurance coverage and physician use among children with disabilities: Findings from probability samples in five metropolitan areas. *Pediatrics, 79,* 89–98.

Fox, H. B. (1984, September). *A preliminary analysis of options to improve health insurance coverage for chronically ill and disabled children.* Paper prepared for the Division of Maternal Health, Department of Health and Human Services, Washington, DC.

Health Care Financing Administration. (1985). *Analysis of state Medicaid program characteristics, 1984.* (HCFA Publication No. 03204). Baltimore, MD: Health Care Financing Administration.

McManus, M., Newacheck, P., & Matlin, N. (1986). Catastrophic childhood illness. *Child Health Financing Report. American Academy of Pediatrics, III,* 1–2.

Office of Technology Assessment, United States Congress. (1987). *Technology-dependent children: Hospital v. home care.* Washington, DC: Author.

3

The Remolding of a National Program*

Henry T. Ireys, Ph.D.

The Crippled Children's Service (CCS), established by the Social Security Act of 1935, was America's first categorical health care program for children. In July 1985, federal legislation (PL 99–272) formally changed the title of the CCS to the Program for Children with Special Health Care Needs. This was important because it reflected an evolution in society's understanding of and approach to children with chronic health and developmental conditions.[†] The history and current functioning of the program reflect the general assumptions, practices, and policies that have governed the delivery of health care to handicapped and chronically ill children in this country. The program is also very much a part of the American medical system. Although many of the nation's health care programs for children have given physicians and hospitals the means to provide low-income families with remarkably sophisticated and expensive care, they have frequently failed to provide these same families with many other equally needed services. Indeed, too often the breadth and quality of care available through a public health program is shaped more by the

---

*Adapted from Ireys, H. (1980). *The Crippled Children's Service: A Comparative Analysis of Four State Programs.* Mental Health Policy Monograph Series, Number 7. Vanderbilt Institute for Public Policy Studies, Vanderbilt University, Nashville, Tennessee.

[†]Because this chapter largely concerns matters of history, and in order to avoid awkward constructions and cross-references, the author has elected to use the original name throughout.

interests of those who provide the care than by the needs of those it seeks to serve.

The CCS program is no exception to this pattern. Nevertheless, it is distinguished by an enduring concern for quality of care and an extraordinary pluralism among the states. The program's original legislative foundation has enabled some state agencies to create programs that provide excellent and comprehensive care to many children and families in need, while in many others various forces have ossified the CCS programs, turning them into inflexible mechanisms for the support of physicians and hospitals. Yet, in almost every state the CCS program is struggling: economic realities are forcing programs to curtail services; competition in the state political hierarchy is fierce; medical care costs continue to rise; old allegiances hobble innovation. The problems are familiar; they face most of the nation's health care programs. Nevertheless, the CCS program is different from these other programs in several important ways:

1. The diversity among state programs is extreme (Ireys, Hauck, & Perrin, 1985), a situation that has largely resulted from the states' widely divergent implementation strategies.
2. In no other health care program does the agency that provides or pays for care also set and enforce standards for the quality of that care, a circumstance that gives the state CCS agency the potential for considerable control over its delivery system.
3. The original legislation incorporated a progressive vision of care for these children and outlined a system for delivering that care. For example, it specifically incorporated concepts of prevention and comprehensive care. Unfortunately, actual practice has never matched initial promise.
4. Before the mid-1960s, the CCS and its companion program, the Maternal and Child Health (MCH) Program, were the major state and federal means for delivering health care to children and their families; since then, however, the programs have radically dwindled in visibility at both the federal and state levels (Lesser, 1985).
5. It is one of the very few publicly subsidized health care programs that has enjoyed substantive and consistent support from physicians, a circumstance that suggests the extent to which the program's mission has overlapped with physicians' needs and interests (Miller, 1980).

Despite the many social and political changes since its inception, the overall structure and function of the program have remained essentially the same for more than 50 years. The program's legislative mandate, now contained in the Maternal and Child Health (MCH) Block Grant of 1981, still empowers state CCS agencies to identify and evaluate "crippled" children, to provide prevention and treatment services, and to ensure follow-up care. States must still match a certain percentage of the federal grant, but many states contribute far more than is technically required. Within each state, CCS agencies still have great discretion in spending appropriations, in deciding what conditions will be covered, and in establishing financial eligibility criteria.

In its early years, the Reagan administration emphasized state control of health care programs—an emphasis that was novel for the health care programs that had begun in the 1960s and 1970s, when the federal government exercised a relatively large amount of control over state programs. The CCS, however, was begun at a time when federal oversight of state programs was negligible. In fact, federal regulations for the original Title V program were published only after several decades had passed. Although the MCH block grant resulted in significant changes for many CCS directors, it actually returned the program to its political roots (Ireys et al., 1985).

Because of its history and its distinguishing characteristics, the CCS program can provide valuable lessons concerning: (1) historical forces that have shaped priorities in the provision of health care services for handicapped children; (2) the implications of different organizational structures for the delivery and financing of health care services for children; (3) the nature and history of the relationship among local, state, regional, and federal agencies in the health care field; (4) the political and bureaucratic forces that both influence and are generated by differing implementation strategies; (5) the historical tensions between and within the health care professions in this country; and (6) the interrelation between the public and private sectors in the health care field. In this chapter, I focus primarily on the first issue.

HISTORICAL CONTEXT

As with most of the early child health and welfare programs, the history of the Crippled Children's Service began with the first White House Conference on the Care of Dependent Children in 1909. This conference led to the establishment in 1912 of the Children's Bureau, whose activities eventually aided the passage of the Sheppard-Towner Act (PL 67-97, the Maternity and Infant Care Act) in 1921. This legislation set several important precedents that, together with the continued efforts of the Children's Bureau and the newly formed American Academy of Pediatrics, shaped the form and implementation of the Social Security Act of 1935.

The purpose of the Sheppard-Towner Act was to improve the health of infants by conducting health education programs for mothers, particularly low-income mothers in cities. The program focused on the importance of adequate prenatal care and maternal health, on the means of preventing infant illness and handicap, and on the importance of periodic health examinations for both mother and child.

The Act's funding mechanism represented the first federal and state partnership in support of health care by providing federal grants-in-aid to the states, a portion of which they were required to match. The program was initially relatively small, but it proved to be an effective means for motivating states to develop maternal and child services within their public health departments. Although participation was voluntary, by 1928 all 45 states had formed some sort of separate maternal and child division, many of which would later play a role in implementing the MCH and CCS programs (Bremner, 1974).

It is likely that ratification of the women's suffrage amendment a year earlier influenced congressional passage of the Sheppard-Towner Act. According to Steiner (1976), "Anxious to tie down the voters, President Harding in his first message to Congress explicitly endorsed a maternal and child health bill and asked his party's congressional majority to pass it. Over vigorous medical association objections, Congress proceeded to enact one of the first federal grant-in-aid programs in the field of public health" (p. 209).

The AMA eventually prevailed, however, and in 1929 appropriations for the Act were not renewed. "In protest," notes Bremner (1974), "some physicians disassociated themselves from the AMA and formed the American Academy of Pediatrics" (p. 815). The purposes of the new organization were "to create reciprocal and friendly relations with all professional and lay organizations that are interested in the health and protection of children." Indeed, until the mid-1960s, the American Academy of Pediatrics (AAP) and the Children's Bureau were closely aligned.

In the years following the termination of the Sheppard-Towner Act, the Children's Bureau continued to collect information on the health and welfare needs of mothers and children. When President Franklin Roosevelt initiated the process that led to the passage of the Social Security Act, the Executive Director of the committee assigned to draft it consulted with members of the Children's Bureau, who, knowing well the needs of mothers and children and having data to document them, presented a proposal for the programs that was eventually incorporated into Title V (Witte, 1962). The CCS program, therefore, became a part of the Social Security Act not only because the Children's Bureau had helped draft the bill, but also because the Children's Bureau and other authorities (Apt, 1974) had earlier documented the significant numbers of children left orthopedically impaired by polio epidemics, for whom treatment was available, but often could not be afforded by their families.

Consistent with the political emphasis of the 1930s, the original legislation emphasized state control of the program. The intent was to allow states to develop their own plans for the program, and there were no well-articulated federal guidelines. Not surprisingly, once they had free rein in implementing the program and as they came to view the MCH/CCS funds as an entitlement, the states became resistant to any attempts by federal or regional offices to curtail their freedom.

Unlike the CCS section of Title V, the MCH section required the administrative responsibility for the program at the state level to be located in the state's department of public health. The Social Security Act never specified the means of linking the MCH and CCS programs, despite an assumption by those who drafted the Act that MCH nurses would work closely with the CCS program, providing at least some of the case-finding and aftercare services. Thus, in some states, the CCS is considered to be an MCH program, so that the CCS director reports directly to the MCH director; in other states, the CCS and the MCH programs are in completely different agencies.

This diversity reflects the fact that the CCS program was a personal, individualized, direct-service health care program—quite a different concept from the publicly-oriented approach of the Public Health Service (PHS). According to Altenstetter and Bjorkman (1978), the Children's Bureau stipulated that states administer the CCS and the MCH through different units. Furthermore, unlike PHS programs in many states, the CCS program depended heavily on the private sector for the provision of specialty services. These fundamental, but rarely recognized, differences in perspective still create difficulties when states begin to place the CCS program under direct control of local or district public health offices.

At the federal level, a single agency has always administered both the MCH and CCS programs. As Table 3.1 illustrates, the Children's Bureau was this agency from 1935 to 1969. Until 1967, there was remarkable stability: in 32 years, there were only three directors and four administrative relocations. During this time a strong network developed among the Children's Bureau, the AAP, the maternal and child health graduate programs in the schools of public health, and the state MCH and CCS agencies (Gershenson, 1980). In one sense, the Children's Bureau acted as a job placement agency, matching interested pediatricians with positions in state programs and placing social work graduate students in CCS and MCH programs for their field experience.

By the end of the 1960s, however, this network had unraveled. The Children's Bureau had lost its earlier stature and political muscle, and, in the wake of much political maneuvering, it also lost the child health

TABLE 3.1 Name, Director, and Location of the Federal Agency Responsible for Administering the CCS and MCH Programs, 1935–1980

Year	Agency	Director	Location
1935	Children's Bureau	Katherine Lenroot	Department of Labor
1946	Children's Bureau	Katherine Lenroot	Federal Security Agency
1951	Children's Bureau	Martha Eliot	Federal Security Agency
1953	Children's Bureau	Martha Eliot	Department of Health, Education, and Welfare (HEW)
1957	Children's Bureau	Katherine Oettinger	HEW
1963	Children's Bureau	Katherine Oettinger	Welfare Administration in HEW
1967	Children's Bureau	Katherine Oettinger	Social and Rehabilitation Service in HEW
1968	Children's Bureau	P.F. DelliQuadri	Social and Rehabilitation Service in HEW
1969	Maternal and Child Health Services	Arthur Lesser	Health Services and Mental Health Services, Administration in the Public Health Service (PHS) of HEW
1973	Office for Maternal and Child Health	Rex Ehling	Bureau of Community Health Services (BCHS), Administraton (HSA) in PHS in HEW.
1975	Office for Maternal and Child Health	Donna O'Hare	BCHS in HSA in PHS in HEW
1977	Office for Maternal and Child Health	Vince Hutchins	BCHS in HSA in PHS in HEW
1980	Office for Maternal and Child Health	Vince Hutchins	BCHS in HSA in PHS in the Department of Health and Human Services (HHS)
1987	Bureau of Maternal and Child Health and Resource Development	Vince Hutchins	HSA in PHS in the Department of Health and Human Services

care programs (Steiner, 1976). Eventually, in 1969, the Title V programs were placed in the Health Services and Mental Health Administration of the Public Health Service and became a part of the Bureau of Community Health Services in 1973.

Thus, despite having had the same federal administrative agency, the histories of the MCH and the CCS programs had already begun to diverge substantially by 1963, when the maternal and infant care (M&I) project grant authority was established. This was the first in a series of new projects [the children and youth (C&Y) project, the infant intensive care project, the dental care project, and the family planning project followed over the next five years] that the federal government initially administered but that were eventually given to state MCH programs.

Not until 1976, however, were the CCS programs given additional responsibilities. In that year, the Supplemental Security Income for Disabled Children Program (SSI/DCP) of Title XVI started an effort to develop individual service plans for children who were enrolled in the SSI program. The CCS program assumed responsibility for the administration of SSI/DCP in all but four states. From the perspective of many of the state CCS directors, the project increased financial pressures, largely because monies were insufficient to cover the costs of locating and providing services to the children and because of additional paperwork. The program in most states faltered under the burden of complicated and impractical regulations (Pratt & Bachman, 1979), and most states abandoned the SSI/DCP when its special appropriations were merged with the general funds of the Maternal and Child Health Block Grant in 1981.

Administrative chaos at the federal level during the late 1960s and early 1970s had a devastating effect on many state CCS programs. Although the Children's Bureau may not have had the best data collection system, and by the mid-1960s was no longer programmatically progressive, it still provided fairly strong leadership: it required yearly state plans; it kept in relatively close touch with the state programs; and it supported social work positions in many states. By 1969, this leadership had vanished. In the absence of clear regulations, many states dismissed their social workers. State programs had no technical assistance available to them, and many of the previously strong ties among state CCS agencies, the federal office, and the schools of public health were broken.

Furthermore, as part of former President Nixon's directives under his "New Federalism," the Health, Education, and Welfare (HEW) regional offices were vitiated in the early and mid-1970s: staffs were cut substantially, there were few incentives for experienced professionals to remain in the offices, and responsibilities became superficial because regional staff were prohibited from reading state plans. As a result, there was relatively little technical support available to the CCS programs. Moreover, the relationships between the state programs and the regional offices became adversarial (Miller, 1980).

Between 1977 and 1980 the central office in Washington sought to provide stronger guidance and ongoing technical assistance to individual states through the State Program Review, a mechanism whereby members of the federal and regional offices met with the MCH and CCS directors to review state plans, assess strengths and weaknesses, and develop specific, feasible strategies for the next few years. The federal and regional consultants' effectiveness was limited, however, by their lack of influence over a state's particular economic and political forces. About 30 state program reports were completed prior to 1981, when the new Administration curtailed federal participation in state reviews. Even at the height of their power, federal and regional offices stopped short of threatening states with a cutoff of funds if they did not comply with recommendations—a threat that the federal office viewed as unproductive in the long run. Yet state CCS agencies followed only those recommendations that were consonant with their state's political or economic view of what was needed or feasible.

THE PRESENT PICTURE

Despite chronic shortfalls and constant struggling for additional funds, the state CCS programs have continued to expand over the years, some more rapidly than others. They now resemble different species derived from a common ancestor, but their evolution has been shaped by the opportunities and constraints within each state. For example, because the initial legislation gave wide discretion in implementing the programs and establishing service priorities, different organizational arrangements have emerged over the years. Some state programs are essentially reimbursement programs that pay for specialized medical services and hospitalization; other programs support staff to organize and conduct clinics, often in areas that lack medical resources; a few agencies operate comprehensive multidisciplinary programs, with diverse health care services. Many programs combine different approaches, resulting in a remarkable pluralism among the 50 state agencies in their goals, functions, and service delivery arrangements, which itself has created difficulties in uniform recordkeeping and data gathering. Information relevant to program planning within each state and nationwide is often unavailable, and this may ultimately jeopardize funding for new programs (Peoples-Sheps, Siegel, Guild, & Cohen, 1986).

CCS agencies have also established different criteria for financial eligibility. In some states, for example, families are ineligible if their income is 100% above the national poverty level. In other states, the cutoff point may be 150% or 200%. In still other states, there are various cost-sharing strategies that may permit all families to utilize the program's services.

The Title V legislation that created Crippled Children's Services also allowed for broad interpretation of "crippling conditions." However, virtually every state CCS program was initially organized around the needs of a highly circumscribed group of patients: physically handicapped children for whom there existed some rehabilitative potential (Eliot, Bierman, & Van Horn, 1938). In the early years of the state programs, orthopedic problems were among the few handicapping conditions that could be treated to any extent. Thus, close to 80% of the children enrolled in the CCS programs nationwide were orthopedically impaired. Most of the other enrolled children had rheumatic fever (Lesser, 1985).

In the ensuing decades, rapid advances in medical knowledge and technology led to effective new means of treating previously intractable illnesses, and the CCS increasingly supported the care of children who could benefit from these developments. In the 1950s, for example, when techniques of cardiac surgery were refined, children with congenital heart conditions entered the program in large numbers. By 1954, orthopedically impaired children, around whom the CCS had originally been organized, constituted less than 50% of its patient population, and by 1966 they represented less than one-fourth of enrolled children (Children's Bureau, 1962, 1967).

Using the best available estimates (Children's Bureau, 1951; U.S. Bureau of the Census, 1971), in 1943 the target population (consisting principally of children with orthopedic problems and rheumatic fever) can be estimated conservatively to have been about 2% of the nation's childhood population, or about one million people under age 21. Although the growth in the range of diagnoses covered has proceeded at different rates in different states, findings from a recent survey (Ireys & Eichler, 1987) indicate that by 1979 orthopedic disorders, arthritis, craniofacial deformities, cystic fibrosis, hearing impairments, congenital heart defects, hemophilia, and myelomeningocele were covered to some extent by 90% or more of the state programs. In addition to these disorders, acute burns and convulsive disorders were covered by at least 50%, but less than 90% of the states. Juvenile diabetes, leukemia, severe asthma, and mental retardation were also covered by more than 25%, but less than 50% of the state programs.

Growth in diagnostic coverage was partially stimulated by a program, established by amendments in 1939, that designated funds for special demonstration projects. Demonstration projects, established at the state level with federal financing, frequently extended services to children who had previously been ineligible. While some of these projects were short-lived, many attracted a constituency of parents and physicians, and were voted state appropriations when initial monies were exhausted. As demonstration projects became permanently incorporated, the state CCS programs that were successful in gaining these demonstration projects often found themselves serving an expanded and increasingly diverse population.

AN ETHICAL PROBLEM

The specific intent of those who drafted the legislation was to initiate a health care program for handicapped children. The guiding principle for distributing funds was to concentrate limited resources on those children most likely to benefit from treatment. In an early description of the program, Eliot et al. (1938) noted that "children whose chief disability is incurable blindness, deafness, or mental defect, and those having abnormalities requiring permanent custodial care are considered beyond the scope of this program" (p. 688). Even though such explicit statements are rarely committed to writing, the priorities of many programs still reflect this principle. Unfortunately, it leaves the most severely disabled children, including mentally retarded individuals, without any resource for treatment. Furthermore, this principle is extremely difficult to implement in any consistent fashion. In many states, in practice, eligibility decisions are made more on the basis of the need as perceived by the provider than on the basis of well-articulated guidelines.

The criteria for allocating limited funds have remained problematic for most of the state programs. Some have adopted a conservative posture, in which outreach efforts are few in order to keep the patient rolls low. Other states have selected a limited number of conditions, provide full treatment coverage for children with these conditions, and hope that other children will find other programs. Still other states have a wide range of conditions for which they will provide partial coverage.

The core problem is an ethical one: By what criteria should limited funds be distributed to handicapped children, and who is to decide these criteria? Unfortunately, many state CCS programs may have answered these questions by default, by allowing those in control of the programs to decide and implement the criteria without careful thought or accountability to someone outside of the program. Most CCS programs have advisory groups, but the membership of these groups is overwhelmingly composed of physicians. Rarely do CCS agencies consult with parent groups or representatives of voluntary organizations in a sustained fashion (Hobbs, Perrin, & Ireys, 1985). As a general trend, CCS programs have avoided public scrutiny of their eligibility criteria and enrollment procedures. Traditionally, medical criteria for enrollment have been used: spend money on the technology and the services that will "cure" the child. Sometimes, financial criteria have been used: provide support services for children whose care is more expensive or, alternatively, support children whose care is less expensive. Other criteria—concern with the quality of the family's life, for example—are rarely invoked as guidelines for expenditures.

Ideally, there needs to be a well-articulated and carefully considered philosophy, informed and shaped by a variety of perspectives, that can provide reasonable guidelines for distributing limited funds within states. A pluralistic approach is essential in such a philosophy. Yet, most state CCS programs have lagged in integrating multidisciplinary perspectives into every level of decision making, from the direct-service to the policy-making level. In view of the multiplicity of services needed for the comprehensive care of children with chronic illnesses and handicapping conditions, a single disciplinary perspective is insufficient. Rather, diverse providers and consumers, working together in a relatively small group and representing varied interests, are likely to develop a more carefully considered and informed solution to the problem of distributing limited funds in the face of almost unlimited need.

At the moment, most directors of CCS programs are aware of the many unmet psychological, social, educational, and primary care needs of the children in their programs. Most would probably agree further that, ideally, the CCS programs ought at least to be responsive to these needs. But present realities narrow their vision.

Some state CCS programs can be useful models in the years ahead because they can teach many lessons. That the state programs have existed for so long, that they have been shaped by so many forces, and that they are both very sensitive and yet, in some ways, impervious to federal or national directiveness make them a rich field for study. In many states, the CCS program has provided truly excellent care to many children in need; in many others, it has never received the attention or support it deserves and has been unresponsive to the needs of the children and families it serves. Indeed, established in a decade very different from the present one and percolated through the grounds of history, the CCS programs reflect the best and worst of health care for children in America.

Acknowledgments: This work was supported by funds from the Division of Maternal and Child Health (Grants MCR 470444-02-1 and MCJ-473306-01-0), Bureau of Community Health Services, Public Health Service, Department of Health and Human Services, as well as by funds from the National Institute of Mental Health Grants (5-T24-MH15501-02 and IP50MH38280).

REFERENCES

Altenstetter, C., & Bjorkman, J. (1978). Policy, politics, and child health: Four decades of federal initiative and state response. *Journal of Health Politics, Policy and Law, 3,* (196–234).

Apt, H. E. (1974). *The care, cure, and education of the crippled child.* New York: Arno.

Bremner, R. H. (Ed.) (1974). *Children and youth in America, a documentary history* (Vol. 3, 1933–1973, Parts 1–4). Cambridge, MA: Harvard University Press.

Children's Bureau. (1951). *One in three hundred.... children served by the crippled children's program in 1948.* (Statistical Series, No. 10). Washington, DC: Federal Security Agency, Social Security Administration.

Children's Bureau. (1962). *Trends in crippling conditions, 1950–1960.* Washington, DC: DHEW, Social Security Administration.

Children's Bureau. *Crippled children's program: Statistical highlights, 1966.* Washington, DC: DHEW. Social Security Administration.

Eliot, J., Bierman, M., & Van Horn, A. (1938). Accomplishments in maternal and child health and crippled children's services under the Social Security Act. *J. Pediatrics, 13,* 678–691.

Gershenson, C. (1980). Personal communication.

Hobbs, N., Perrin, J., & Ireys, H. (1985). *Chronically ill children and their families: Problems, prospects, and proposals from the Vanderbilt study.* San Francisco: Jossey-Bass.

Ireys, H., & Eichler, R. (1987). The CCS revisited. Manuscript submitted, 1987.

Ireys, H., Hauck, R., & Perrin, J. (1985). Variability among state Crippled Children's Service programs: Pluralism thrives. *American Journal of Public Health, 75,* 375–381.

Lesser, A. (1985). The origin and development of maternal and child health programs in the United States. *American Journal of Public Health, 75,* 590–598.

Miller, C. A. (1980). Personal communication.

Peoples-Sheps, M., Siegel, E., Guild, P., Cohen, S. (1986). The management and use of data on maternal and child health and crippled children. *Public Health Reports, 101,* 320–329.

Pratt, M., & Bachman, G. (1979). *Evaluation of the implementation of the SSI/DCP. Final Report.* Silver Spring, MD: Information Sciences Research Institute.

Rice, G. (1980). Personal communication.

Steiner, G. (1976). *The children's cause.* Washington, DC: The Brookings Institute.

U.S. Bureau of the Census. (1971). *Historical statistics: Colonial times to 1970.* Washington, DC: Department of Commerce.

Witte, E. (1962). *The development of the Social Security Act.* Madison: University of Wisconsin Press.

4

Public Education:
New Commitments and
Consequences*

Deborah Klein Walker, Ed.D.

Vanderbilt University's recent policy studies and dissemination activities concerning chronically ill children and their families (Hobbs, Perrin, & Ireys, 1985) advocate a general public policy that is family centered, community based, flexible, and responsive to the generic needs of these children. Comprehensive and coordinated care should be available at the community level in a just and equitable manner so that all children with chronic illnesses can develop their potential and function optimally in society.

Since chronically ill children spend more time away from the family in school than in any other institution, school policies and programs for these children are critically important to their healthy growth and development. Services once thought to be clearly outside the responsibility of the public schools—for example, administering medications and complicated medical treatment regimens; providing physical, occupational, speech, and language therapy; transporting children from home to school

---

*Sections of this chapter are adapted from three earlier publications by the author: Walker, D. K. (1984). Care of chronically-ill children in schools. *Pediatric Clinics of North America, 31(1),* 221–233. Walker, D. K., & Jacobs, F. H. (1984). Chronically-ill children in schools. *Peabody Journal of Education, 61,* 28–74. Also a chapter in N. Hobbs & J. M. Perrin (eds.). (1985). *Issues in Care of Children with Chronic Illnesses: A Sourcebook on problems, Services and Policies.* San Francisco: Jossey-Bass.

and between school buildings; revising classroom curricula and routines to meet an individual child's physical and health-related needs—are now legally mandated by state and federal statutes for all children who need them. The passage of the Education for All Handicapped Children Act of 1975 (PL 94-142) has forced many school systems into previously uncharted territories with respect to the care and education of children with chronic illnesses. Prior to the passage of this landmark civil rights act, many of these children were excluded from school or given an inappropriate and incomplete set of education services; only those whose specific conditions (e.g., deafness, blindness, etc.) were covered by the states' narrow special education codes received education at the public's expense (Walker & Jacobs, 1984). This chapter summarizes school issues for chronically ill children, describes current special education and school health services, and makes recommendations for future policy and programmatic directions.

SCHOOL-BASED NEEDS OF CHILDREN WITH CHRONIC ILLNESSES

Children with chronic illnesses confront many potential problems in school, ranging from academic difficulties to psychosocial problems (Walker & Jacobs, 1984; Weitzman, 1984). In fact, many of these children perform at a low achievement level because of secondary psychosocial problems, not cognitive or physical impairments. Increased absences from school can also lead to a number of social, behavioral, and learning problems; this relationship has been best documented for children with asthma (Weitzman, Walker, & Gortmaker, 1986). Frequent absences from classroom routines and peer-group activities can lead to problems with self-esteem and motivation to learn new things.

How chronically ill children are handled in an educational program can influence their future success in school and in society. For example, teachers as well as peers may develop negative attitudes about particular children who have limited activity, mistakenly attributing lack of energy to laziness, lack of motivation, or a negative personality trait rather than to the effects of medication or a chronic physical condition. Special emphasis must be placed on classroom experiences that develop self-esteem and a feeling of competence in such children, rather than letting them become over-dependent on others in the school setting.

To prevent these potential problems, teachers and other school personnel need to be in close and ongoing communication with parents and health care providers about the child's health status and treatment needs. Pediatricians and other physicians can help immensely in the assessment of the child's needs and abilities by communicating crucial information directly to teachers, school health staff, and other school personnel. School personnel's lack of accurate information about the child may result in inappropriate educational placement, denial of a necessary service, or overprotective attitudes and behaviors (Walker & Jacobs, 1984).

In order to plan the educational program and daily management procedures for the chronically ill child in school, school personnel need to have physicians and allied health personnel answer the questions listed in Table 4.1 (Walker, 1984, 1987). Depending on the answers to these basic questions, almost every child with a chronic illness will need some form of special consideration by the school system at some point in his or her school career. The wide-ranging special services potentially needed by these children, listed in Table 4.2, include allied health support and psychologically oriented therapies, specially tailored career and vocational counseling, transportation, modifications in class scheduling and classroom environment, administration of medications and special medical procedures, and special staff training and support (Walker, 1984, 1987; Walker & Jacobs, 1984). In most school districts today the responsibility for the care of chronically ill children is shared by at least three main divisions within the school bureaucracy—the special education department, the school health services department, and the pupil personnel services department.

There is great variability among schools, school systems, and states in how the problems of educating chronically ill children are handled and how the state and federal special education laws and health codes are implemented. In many cases, providing an appropriate education for these children requires delicate negotiations among administrative, support, classroom, and school health professionals in addition to frequent communication and close collaboration of school personnel with parents, medical providers, and other involved health professionals.

EDUCATIONAL PLACEMENT OF CHRONICALLY ILL CHILDREN

Schools must provide an appropriate set of educational and supportive services for each chronically ill child, based on information about the child's developmental status, daily functioning capabilities, and perceived academic potential. Usually the parent notifies the school of the child's condition and capabilities when the child enrolls in school or subsequently when the child's condition occurs.

TABLE 4.1 Questions Educators Frequently Ask Physicians About Chronically Ill Children for Program Planning and Daily Management Procedures

1. Does the child's present condition require any specific physical restrictions?
2. Can the child participate in physical education and on any sports team without restriction?
3. Is there a need to shorten or modify the school day?
4. Is the child presently taking medication? How does it effect the child's behavior?
5. Are there special emergency procedures that should be learned by school staff?
6. Does the child need special protective equipment?
7. Does the child use special equipment?
8. Should the child have preferential seating?
9. Does the child need physical, occupational, or speech therapy?
10. Should the child receive special counseling?
11. Does the child require a special diet?
12. Does the child need assistance with toileting?
13. What is the prognosis for the child for the future?
14. What is the child's understanding of his or her condition? Are further explanations necessary?

SOURCE: Walker (1984, 1987).

Eligibility and Children's Rights

Many chronically ill and physically handicapped children are eligible for special education in every state. Public Law 94–142 became effective in 1978 for children aged 6–17 and in 1980 for children aged 3–21 in those states where existing codes provided services to chronically ill children of these ages or where nonhandicapped children of these ages were provided educational services (e.g., mandated kindergartens). Although PL 98–199 amended PL 94–142 in 1983 to encourage more services to children from birth through 3 years of age, only six states currently (Iowa, Maryland, Michigan, Nebraska, New Jersey, and South Dakota) have a state law mandating services from birth for children with special needs. A majority of the states (27) have special education mandates that begin at age 5 or later (Walker, 1986). It is anticipated that more states will serve children in the first three years of life in the future since the passage of the Amendments to the Education for all Handicapped Act (PL 99–457) in October 1986. This

TABLE 4.2 Related School Services Needed by Chronically Ill Children During Their School Careers

---

Support therapies
  Physical therapy
  Occupational therapy
  Speech and language therapy
Modified physical education
Schedule modifications
Transportation
Building accessibility
Toileting/lifting assistance
School health services
  Administration of medications
  Implementation of medical procedures
  Emergency preparations
  Case coordination
Counseling services
  School
  Career
  Personal
Sensitivity training and support
  Peers ·
  School staff

SOURCE: Walker (1987).

legislation created a discretionary program which enables states to provide services to meet the needs of disabled and at-risk infants and toddlers (birth through age 2) and their families.

The law covers services for a wide range of handicapped children, including those who are mentally retarded, hard-of-hearing, deaf, speech impaired, visually handicapped, seriously emotionally disturbed, and orthopedically impaired, as well as children with specific learning disabilities who, for that reason, require special education and related services (Education of Handicapped Children, 1977). Children identified, evaluated, and placed under the federal statute must be educated in the "least restrictive environment" or with their nonhandicapped peers to the maximum extent possible. Each child in special education must have an individualized education plan (IEP), which is based on the findings from the child's multidisciplinary assessments (Jacob & Walker, 1978; Palfrey, Mervis, & Butler, 1978; Walker & Jacobs, 1984).

Finally, the federal law mandates strong due-process requirements for protecting the rights of handicapped children and their families. It includes a well-defined process for parents' involvement that extends far beyond involvement in the health care system, where there is no mandate for services.

The highest priority for services is for those children who are eligible for and not receiving special education services. Most child identification activities in those states serving preschool children focus on the youngest eligible children; in these states pediatricians play a major role in identifying and referring eligible preschool-aged children to the schools (Cohen, Semmes, & Guralnick, 1979; Jacobs, 1979; Jacobs & Walker, 1978).

Placement Options

Depending on the determination of individual learning needs, the chronically ill child will receive one of the following placements, which are listed in order of integration from least to most restrictive:

    Regular school
        Regular class
        Special resource class
        Special class
    Homebound tutoring or hospital program
    Special day school
    Residential school

Since many chronic conditions are not strongly associated—or associated at all—with mental retardation (which would automatically be a reason for placement in some special education classes), the main determinant of whether a chronically ill child would benefit from something other than normal classes is the extent to which the illness impedes daily functioning and learning. Table 4.3 gives an overview of the levels of functioning and program modifications associated with various levels of severity of chronic conditions. In practice, only children with moderate and severe levels of impairment need to be considered for placement in a special education classroom; furthermore, some of these children could be placed successfully in regular education classrooms that meet their academic abilities if the necessary related set of services were provided (Walker & Jacobs, 1984).

For the most part, children with chronic illnesses in special education placements are classified by a local school system into one of two categories: "orthopedically impaired" or "other health impaired." Federal regulations (Education of Handicapped Children, 1977) define the eligible group of "other health impaired" as including:

> chronic or acute health problems such as a heart condition, tuberculosis, rheumatic fever, nephritis, asthma, sickle cell anemia, hemophilia, epilepsy, lead poisoning, leukemia or diabetes, *which adversely affects a child's educational performance.*

TABLE 4.3 Level of Functioning and Program Modifications Associated with Severity of Impairment

	Level 1: Mild	Level 2: Mild to moderate	Level 3: Moderate	Level 4: Severe
Is the child handicapped?	No	Possibly	Yes	Yes
How does it effect the child's functioning?	Health does not interfere with day-to-day functioning and learning.	Health impairment does not interfere with learning, but there is a possibility of unusual episodes or crises.	Health impairment either presents frequent crisis or so limits the child's opportunity to participate in activities that it interferes with learning.	Health impairment is so severe that special medical attention is regularly needed. The child's opportunity for activity is so limited that he or she may not be able to participate in a regular classroom.
Must the program be modified?	No	No change in program planning is necessary. Be aware of the potential for unusual reoccurances. Report them to the parents or doctor. Know any first-aid that might be required.	Activities will have to be modified to allow a health-impaired child to participate. Staff must know proper first-aid procedures and be prepared to deal with children's questions about crises.	Extensive staff and program alterations are necessary to accept child into program. Home or hospital-based programs may be more appropriate. Classroom support from medical services will be necessary if child is in classroom.

SOURCE: Healy, McAreavey, von Hippel, & Jones (1978).

In practice, however, there is neither a uniform definition nor clear guidance to schools on how to determine the functioning or severity criteria that make a child eligible for special education services. A further problem is that a child can be at different levels in terms of handicap, functioning, and need for program modification.

Thus local school systems and states vary in how they define the chronic illnesses that are serious enough to impede progress in a regular education program (Comptroller General, 1981 a, b). Furthermore, because the chronic conditions are basically medical or physical in nature, many states require a physician to determine the extent to which the condition interferes with learning.

With certain physical disabilities (e.g., cerebral palsy, muscular dystrophy, spina bifida), the physician can be quite certain that some type of special education placement—often in combination with some time in a regular classroom—will be necessary (Gearheart & Weishahn, 1976; Griffiths, 1975; Walker & Jacobs, 1984). But practitioners argue that the vast majority of children with chronic illnesses such as asthma, diabetes, cystic fibrosis, epilepsy, hemophilia, leukemia, congenital heart disease, and kidney problems will benefit most by placement in a regular classroom, although they may need some special considerations during the school day or year. To date there are no evaluative data available about the efficacy of various placements for certain types of chronically ill children.

Finally, all of these children could at some point in the course of their illness need homebound or hospital classes. Unfortunately, since most states require at least a two-week waiting period before homebound instruction can begin, some chronically ill children lose valuable instruction time as they change over from regular classroom placement to homebound instruction.

The number of children served in various special education placements by disability category is reported annually to Congress by the Office of Special Education. Over half of the children served are categorized as having a speech impairment or learning disability. In the 1983–84 school year the number of children aged 6–17 served under the federal education statutes in the "orthopedically impaired" category (34,941) and the "other health-impaired" category (41,767) represented about 2% of all children in special education placements in all states (3,664,628) (Office of Special Education, 1985). Thus only a small percentage of the children with a physical handicap or a health impairment who are in need of special education and related services are being served under federal mandates (Gortmaker & Sappenfield, 1984; Hobbs et al., 1985; Kaskowitz, 1977; Walker & Jacobs, 1984).

During school year 1982–83, 52% of the other health-impaired children aged 6–17 and 39% of the orthopedically impaired children were served in regular classes (Office of Special Education, 1985). About one-fifth of the other health-impaired and one-third of the orthopedically impaired were in separate classes; the remainder—29% of the other health-impaired and 24% of the orthopedically impaired children—were in separate school facilities or other educational environments. The appropriateness of these data on special education placements is difficult to interpret, since no information about the diagnoses, severity of condition, or functioning of each child in each placement is available.

The largest source of data about the educational placement of children with specific chronic conditions is the Community Child Health Studies conducted in three communities (Genesee County, Michigan; Berkshire County, Massachusetts; and Cleveland, Ohio) from 1977 to 1980. Data were obtained from random household surveys in Genesee County, Michigan, in 1977 and in Berkshire County, Massachusetts, in 1980 and from clinic samples in Cleveland, Ohio, in 1977. The expected placements for chronically ill children outlined above were observed (see Tables 4.4 and 4.5); that is, although most children with a chronic illness were in regular classrooms, the largest number in separate special classes had a physical impairment such as cerebral palsy or spina bifida. In addition, those children who were functionally impaired because of a specific chronic condition were less often in all regular classes and more often in special classes either full or part time than were all children with a chronic condition (Walker & Jacobs, 1984).

TABLE 4.4 Educational Placements for Children (Aged 6 to 17) with Selected Chronic Conditions

Condition		Genessee County, Michigan, 1977				Berkshire County, Massachusetts, 1980		
		Regular school				Regular school		
	(*n*)	% in regular classes	% in special classes	% in both	(*n*)	% in regular classes	% in special classes	% in both
Asthma	(148)	93.2	1.4	5.4	(21)	76.2	0.0	23.8
Kidney trouble	(68)	86.8	2.7	10.8	(5)	80.0	0.0	20.0
Heart trouble	(55)	80.0	9.1	10.9	(18)	61.1	5.6	33.4
Epilepsy	(28)	71.4	17.9	10.7	—	—	—	—
All children	(2,175)	94.4	1.9	3.7	(601)	84.0	2.5	13.4

SOURCE: Community Child Health Studies and Harvard School of Public Health in Walker and Jacobs (1984, p. 52).

TABLE 4.5 Educational Placements for Children (Aged 6-17) with Selected Chronic Conditions, Cleveland, Ohio, 1977

Condition	(n)	% Regular school/majority regular classes	% Regular school/majority special classes	% Special school/all special classes
Cystic fibrosis	(64)	96.9	3.1	0.0
Spina bifida	(63)	42.8	41.3	15.9
Cerebral palsy	(88)	30.7	31.8	37.5
Multiple handicaps	(84)	29.7	46.4	42.9

SOURCE: Community Child Health Studies and Harvard School of Public Health in Walker and Jacobs (1985, p. 53).

RELATED SCHOOL SERVICES NEEDED BY CHRONICALLY ILL CHILDREN

Regardless of whether children with chronic illnesses are placed in special education classes, a wide variety of daily and sporadic management issues surface (Tables 4.1 and 4.2). The real issue of whether children with chronic illnesses are eligible for special education revolves around the related services provision of the law, which has caused great controversy within local school systems across the nation. During their school careers, almost all children with a chronic illness will need at least one of the related services defined under the federal statute for inclusion in a child's individualized educational plan:

> transportation and such developmental corrective and other supportive services as are required to assist a handicapped child to benefit from special education . . . speech pathology and audiology, psychological services, physical and occupational therapy, recreation, early identification and assessment of disabilities in children, counseling services, and medical services for diagnostic and evaluation purposes . . . school health services, social work services in schools and parent counseling and training. (PL 94-142)

Because related services are defined as services required to help a handicapped child benefit from special education instruction, which many chronically ill children do not need, many children with chronic illnesses have been excluded by local school systems from receiving the related services they often need (Baird & Ashcroft, 1984). School systems vary in how they determine whether a child is in need of special education instruction; for example, a child who needs home tutoring during the school year may or may not be designated as a child in special education.

This related services provision under the law has caused great controversy (Davidson & Walker, 1983; Walker & Jacobs, 1984). In fact, the

Reagan administration tried unsuccessfully in 1982 to remove the responsibility of providing related services under PL 94-142 from local school systems. Much of the debate centers around the cost of providing these "extra" services; in addition, there are concerns about the appropriateness of educational institutions providing health and other services, many of which are available to child and family through Title V and other public- and private-sector specialized programs for chronically ill children.

Since historically many of these related services have been offered only at special school sites, related services have been specified more often in the plans for handicapped children in special schools than for those in regular schools. Although these segregated arrangements conflict with PL 94-142's goal of education in the "least restrictive environment," some school districts continue to place children needing several or highly specialized services in these special schools. Overall, the number of children receiving related services is less than the number who need them; independent studies and internal compliance reviews have noted that in some school districts the provision of related services is based only on what is needed for educational instruction (Walker & Jacobs, 1984).

The real dilemma surrounding the related services component of PL 94-142 occurs when a chronically ill child needs only related services and not a special program placement (Walker & Jacobs, 1984). For example, should the following children with chronic illnesses and normal intelligence be considered as special education students?

A child whose leukemia has been in remission for more than a year, but who continues to see a school social worker regularly for supportive counseling,

a child with asthma who needs daily medication administered in school,

a child with diabetes who needs a special lunch at a particular time in the schedule and needs to have the teacher prepared for changes in behavior related to insulin level,

a child with a shunt who needs some modified gym activities,

a child with juvenile rheumatoid arthritis who needs physical therapy and modified physical education, and

a child with epilepsy who needs medications on a specific schedule and needs to have the teacher prepared for possible attacks in the classroom.

In actuality, there is no standard mechanism to determine if these chronically ill children should be considered for special education across states and school systems. The tendency is not to classify the children listed above as special education students, since this would require labeling of the child as well as lengthy evaluation and due process procedures for the schools and parents. This policy is fine for children in school systems with adequate school health and ancillary services. The problem of not including all chronically ill children who need related services under special education is most acute for children in school systems with no (or inadequate) pupil personnel services. In some school systems, these children with chronic illnesses are ignored in the regular education system or are placed in inappropriate classes and settings. In these cases PL 94-142 could be used to advocate the necessary health and related services needed by chronically ill children.

The most current data available about the use of related services by children with special disabilities come from the Collaborative Study of Children with Special Needs (Palfrey, Singer, Walker, & Butler, 1986). Table 4.6 presents findings on three types of related services received during the previous year by 1,726 children in special education placements in the elementary grades in five large urban school systems: Charlotte-Mecklenburg, North Carolina; Houston, Texas; Milwaukee, Wisconsin; Rochester, New York; and Santa Clara County, California.

The districts varied in the scope of their commitment to speech and hearing therapy, reflecting differences in local traditions and programs. Not surprisingly, physical and occupational therapy was found to be concentrated on children in two major categories: special education students with a physical, sensory, or other health problem and special education students with mental retardation. Districts varied somewhat in their definition and eligibility, but it appeared that districts that limited these services to more severely impaired children also provided more depth of service (visits to the therapist) per child.

The receipt of child counseling was rather limited in all five school systems, ranging from 19% in Houston to 30% in Milwaukee. Parent or family counseling was much less frequently provided (only 10% of all students). The provision of counseling services, whether called psychotherapy for children or training for parents, has been the subject of much controversy since PL 94-142 was passed (Osborne, 1984).

The school systems themselves were almost always the source of payment for these three related services, or the focus of payment in cases where health department funds were used for care. Overall, 92.3% of reported speech and hearing visits, and 65.9% of child counseling visits were paid for via the schools. This pattern of expenditure suggests that insurance sources, both public and private, are not a very large part of the picture when it comes to support of related services.

In sum, there is great variability in how local educational authorities handle the special education and education-related needs of children with chronic illness. Those who need some type of special classroom instruction for learning are enrolled in special education. Those who do not need

TABLE 4.6 Related Services Received by Special Education Students in Elementary Grades in the Five Urban Study Sites During the 1982-1983 School Year ($n = 1,726$)

	Percent receiving related service		
	Speech therapy	Occupational & physical therapy	Child counseling
All special education students	48.5	7.8	32.3
Children with specific handicaps as defined by the school			
Speech	80.7	2.5	24.9
Learning	27.0	4.4	30.4
Emotional	27.4	2.8	62.8
Mental impairment	60.6	21.8	36.0
Physical sensory health	65.0	44.0	37.2

SOURCE: Collaborative Study of Children with Special Needs and the Children's Hospital, Boston, Massachusetts.

special classroom instruction on an ongoing basis but do need special health and other related services (which means virtually all children with chronic illnesses at some point in their school careers) are handled in three basic ways by school systems:

1. They are enrolled in special education and have an individual educational plan (IEP) which specifies their special health and other service needs as well as a contingency plan for homebound/hospital instruction.

2. They are treated as students who are entitled to services under Section 504 of the 1974 Rehabilitation Act, and thus receive all the services available to them under the special education laws.

3. They receive only the existing school health and other services (counseling, etc.) available to them in the regular school setting. Although this can be an adequate set of services in schools where there are responsive school health units and pupil personnel departments, such is not usually the case today, with schools facing community pressures to deliver basic education better with fewer dollars.

SCHOOL HEALTH SERVICES FOR CHRONICALLY ILL CHILDREN

Many of the needs of chronically ill children should be met by the resources of the school's health program. At the present time, there is a wide variation within school districts and among states in the way school health services are delivered (Guyer & Walker, 1980; Walker & Jacobs, 1984). Local school health policies and state school health codes also vary greatly; in addition, there is no federal statute or set of health codes that governs what occurs in schools. In most cases the school health program is administered by the local board of education or by school personnel; in a small minority of cases, it is administered by the local health board or by a dual arrangement (Lynch, 1977). Often the administrative staff of school health services at the district level is located in a different bureaucratic hierarchy from that of special education and, in many cases, from that of other pupil personnel services (e.g., counseling, social work, psychological services), thus compounding communication and policy problems among ancillary service providers within the district.

Specific health services sometimes needed by children with chronic illnesses are administration of medication, implementation of medical procedures, emergency preparations, and case coordination (see Table 4.2). Although there are limited studies about which school health services are delivered by whom to chronically ill children, the practice-oriented literature and discussions with school health personnel suggest that most schools view the school nurse as the case coordinator for chronically ill children (Wold, 1981). The nurse's role as the manager of the child's health care within the school includes communication with teachers and other school staff (e.g., principal, secretary, and physical education teacher) as well as with the child's physician and other relevant agencies in the community. In a well-organized school health program, the nurse keeps a confidential list of medical information on each child with chronic illness and shares it discreetly and as appropriate with all school personnel who interact with the child.

A major issue in schools that have chronically ill students is the training of school personnel who might be present when a child has a medical emergency (e.g., asthma attack, epileptic seizure, insulin reaction). Although school nurses or school physicians usually are responsible for this type of in-service training of individuals or groups, other demands on their time greatly reduce their level of involvement in such training. The importance of emergency-procedures training for all school personnel who interact with chronically ill children cannot be overemphasized, especially since the school nurse is often not present when an emergency arises. Most emergencies occur on playgrounds and usually involve the teacher on duty and the school secretary (Guyer & Walker, 1980).

Another major responsibility of school health services is the effective and safe administration of medical treatments and/or medication. Policies concerning medication are determined at the local level and/or by state codes. In a recent survey of all states' policies for eight nursing procedures (catheterization, seizure management, medication administration, respiratory care, tube feeding positioning, colostomy/ileostomy care, other), the majority of states had procedures for medication, fewer than a quarter had them for all eight procedures, and a quarter had no guidelines for any of the procedures (Wood, Walker, & Gardner, 1986).

Although there are guidelines and models for policies concerning medication (American Lung Association, 1980; *Medical Emergencies*, 1978), there is wide variation among schools in how they administer medication and whether they even have official policies (Walker & Jacobs, 1984). For example, in some districts only a qualified nurse is able to dispense medicines, whereas in others a designated nonmedical person can do so as long as a written note to that effect from the child's physician is on file. In some states, the requirement to have a nurse dispense the medication holds true for only certain types of drugs (e.g., psychotropics), while other medications can be dispensed by a variety of adults. In practice, it seems appropriate for a nurse to have this responsibility if the school has a full-time nurse available; however, in those districts where there is no full-time nurse (as is the case in many districts today) or where the nurse's training would be better used elsewhere (e.g., in health counseling and health education, participation on evaluation teams, etc.), designating someone else as the dispenser seems most efficient (Wolf & Pritham, 1965).

Finally, another important and often overlooked function of the school health staff is the training of teachers and other school personnel about chronic illness (Walker & Jacobs, 1984). This school-based training should include specifics about diagnoses as well as exploration of teachers' and staff's feelings about dealing with chronically ill children (especially those with terminal or catastrophic diseases). Much of this school-based training must be individually tailored to a specific teacher's needs concerning a specific child with a specific chronic illness. In addition, occasional supportive counseling for teachers needing or requesting it should be available in the community and supported by schools.

RECOMMENDATIONS

The special needs of chronically ill children in schools are served either through special education departments or through general education with supportive school health and pupil personnel services. There appears to be great local and state variation in the assignment of children with different conditions and functioning levels to either department; this lack of uniformity results from the varied interpretations of eligibility for special education and from the preference in some communities for using the well-established school health and support services. My recommendations, developed in collaboration with Dr. Francine Jacobs, therefore focus primarily on developing uniform jurisdictional policies within schools (Walker & Jacobs, 1984).

Eligibility Criteria

The intent of PL 94-142, state special education statutes, and Section 504 of the Rehabilitation Act need to be clarified to specify whether children with chronic illnesses are included. Children with moderate to severe impairments (as described in Table 4.3), that is, those whose illnesses may eventually result in school failure, chronic absenteeism, complicated scheduling, or architectural and adaptational requirements, should be evaluated and placed through the special education process. Most children with chronic illnesses such as asthma, diabetes, leukemia, sickle cell anemia, and arthritic diseases, which affect schooling mildly or infrequently, are most appropriately served by the regular education system, utilizing counseling and school health services. However, many such children do not receive these necessary support services and have been forced to turn to the often costly and potentially stigmatizing special education process to gain access to the services they need in order to function in school. Some states and local educational authorities have been interpreting PL 94-142 quite broadly to include as eligible chronically ill children with only mild impairments; they reason that the child needs an IEP to provide related services, such as emergency plans and therapies, and to facilitate access to homebound tutoring when the need arises. Clarification of the laws and regulations at the federal and state levels would ensure that this group of children is treated in a more uniform and just manner. If these children are not explicitly covered by these statutes, then other ways should be found (local school system budgets, public health funds, etc.) to provide them the necessary school-based services.

School Health Codes

To ensure that the chronically ill child with a mild impairment receives the necessary services within each school district, each state should adopt explicit school health codes, which do not presently exist, for this group of children. Although a parallel federal statute might ensure the maximum protection for these children, there is no precedent or mechanism for implementing such a mandate. State school health codes, which the local school systems would be required to adopt, should minimally include procedures and policies in the following areas:

1. *Medication procedures.* Each local school system should have an explicit written medication policy on record, allowing for the administration of

medication in schools, with orders from a physician on file, by a variety of persons—teachers, aides, and secretaries as well as school nurses. In addition, the school should provide an appropriate, safe place for the storage of medicines and a private area where medical procedures (e.g., insulin injections) can occur.

2. *Nursing procedures.* Each school system should have an explicit policy for the provision of various nursing procedures (e.g., catheterization, tracheostomy care, etc.) during school hours.

3. *Identification and tracking.* The school system should keep a listing of all students with chronic illness regardless of severity, so that all school personnel associated with those children can be notified and trained specifically if necessary. This system should include mechanisms for identification and tracking of children while in the school system. Discreet use of this information must be assured at all times.

4. *Emergencies.* Policies for handling potential medical emergencies should be detailed, as should the specific procedures for training all school personnel who come into contact with involved children.

5. *Inservice training.* Procedures for training school personnel for chronic illnesses should be incorporated into locally designed policies.

6. *Case coordination.* Each child with a chronic illness should have a designated school-based case coordinator; in most cases, this should be the school nurse. At a minimum, this person should help assure that the appropriate services are delivered and that effective communication between relevant school personnel (especially the classroom teacher) and community persons occurs.

Homebound Instruction

More flexible policies regarding the use of homebound and hospitalized instruction should be adopted. A waiting period of two to four weeks before homebound services can be provided is not in the best interest of chronically ill students, especially those who are absent frequently but for only a short period of time in each instance. Homebound instruction might also be provided to those chronically ill children whose school-based programs are shortened owing to limited endurance.

Role of Physicians

The physician's role in educating chronically ill children needs to be reexamined and clarified. The physician has health-related information on chronically ill children (general health status, medication needs and potential effects of medication, prognosis and limitations in activities) that the schools must have if proper placement and programming are to occur.

The transfer of this information to the schools and the fostering of two-way communication between schools and physicians are appropriate functions for the physician. The physician might also advise about placements and act as a patient advocate in instances where the child seems not to be receiving appropriate education. In general, however, the physician's role should be as a consultant rather than as a case coordinator or central educational program planner.

Provision of Training

There are many training needs within the school regarding chronically ill children, and efforts to educate and sensitize should be directed at both school personnel and other students. As stated earlier, training related to a child's specific condition should be required of all school personnel who come in contact with him/her; this more medically oriented task would best be undertaken by a school nurse or physician. Equally important is the development of specific curricula or techniques designed to explore and modify student and teacher attitudes about chronically ill and physically handicapped children. Supportive personal counseling may be required for school personnel involved with the education of children with terminal or progressive illnesses.

Communication

Finally, more communication among the schools, health practitioners, state and local agencies, and programs for these chronically ill children should be facilitated. Improved relationships would avoid duplication of services (e.g., counseling of child and family, support therapies, etc.) and help coordinate case management. Such cooperative arrangements are especially important in an era of diminishing support for public education and would ensure more careful use of public resources. Without this type of cooperation, children potentially best served by other agencies or the private medical sector might well be "dumped" on the schools, in the hope that their "free" services can be provided to these children. It is to be hoped that a more coordinated state and community approach for the chronically ill child will be forthcoming in the future.

Acknowledgments: The author would like to thank Francine H. Jacobs, Ed.D., for her insights and help in the conceptualization of issues covered in this chapter. Research reported in the chapter was supported in part by funds provided by the Charles Stewart Mott Foundation, the Cleveland Foundation, the Commonwealth Foundation, the Maternal and Child Health and Crippled Children's Services Research Grants Program, Bureau of Community Health Services, Department of Health and Human Services (#MC-R-250437), and the Robert Wood Johnson Foundation.

REFERENCES

American Lung Association of Massachusetts. (1980). There are solutions for the student with asthma. Boston: Author.

Baird, S. M., & Ashcroft, S. C. (1984) Education and chronically ill children: A need-based policy orientation. *Peabody Journal of Education, 61,* 91–129.

Cohen, S., Semmes, M., & Guralnick, M. (1979). Public Law 94-142 and the education of preschool handicapped children. *Exceptional Children, 45,* 279–287.

Comptroller General. (1981a). *Disparities still exist in who gets special education.* Washington, DC: U.S. General Accounting Office.

Comptroller General. (1981b). *Unanswered questions on educating handicapped children in local public schools.* Washington, DC: U.S. General Accounting Office.

Davidson, H., & Walker, D. K. (1983). National health line: Services for handicapped children. *Journal of Health & Social Work, 8,* 72–74.

Education of Handicapped Children: Implementation of Part B of the Handicapped Act, Rules and Regulations. (1977, August). *Federal Register, 43*(163).

Gearheart, B. R., & Weishahn, M. W. (1976). *The handicapped child in the regular classroom.* St. Louis, MO: Mosby.

Gortmaker, S. L., & Sappenfield, W. (1984). Chronic childhood disorders: Prevalence and impact. *Pediatric Clinics of North America, 31,* 3–17.

Griffiths, M. I. (1975). *Medical approaches in special education.* London: Wiley.

Guyer, B., & Walker, D. K. (1980). *School health services in Flint elementary schools.* Boston: Harvard School of Public Health.

Healy, A., McAreavey, P., von Hippel, C. S., & Jones, S. H. (1978). *Mainstreaming preschoolers: Children with health impairments.* Belmont, MA: Contract Research Corp.

Hobbs, N., Perrin, J. M., & Ireys, H. T. (1985). *Chronically ill children and their families.* San Francisco, CA: Jossey-Bass.

Jacobs, F. H. (1979). *Identification of preschool handicapped children: A community approach.* Boston, MA: Community Child Health Studies, Harvard School of Public Health.

Jacobs, F. H., & Walker, D. K. (1978). Pediatricians and the Education of All Handicapped Children Act of 1975. *Pediatrics, 61,* 135–7.

Kaskowitz, D. H. (1977). *Validation of state counts of handicapped children: Vol. 2. Estimation of the number of handicapped children in each state.* Menlo Park, CA: Stanford Research Institute.

Lynch, A. (1977). Evaluating school health programs. In A. Levin (Ed.), Health services: A local perspective. *Proceedings of the Academy of Political Science, 32* (special issue), 89–105.

Medical emergencies and administration of medication in school. (1978). *Pediatrics, 61,* 115–116.

Office of Special Education and Rehabilitative Services. (1985). *Seventh annual report to Congress on the implementation of Public Law 94-142.* Washington, DC: U.S. Department of Education.

Osborne, A. G. (1984). How the courts have interpreted the related services mandate. *Exceptional Children, 51,* 249–252.

Palfrey, J. S., Mervis, R. C., & Butler, J. A. (1978). New directions in the evaluation and education of handicapped children. *New England Journal of Medicine, 298,* 819–824.

Palfrey, J. S., Singer, J. D., Walker, D. K., & Butler, J. A. (1986). Health and special education: A study of new developments for handicapped children in five metropolitan communities. *Public Health Reports, 101* (4), 379–388.

Walker, D. K. (1984). Care of chronically-ill children in school. *Pediatric Clinics of North America, 31*(1), 221–233.

Walker, D. K. (1986). Chronically-ill children in early childhood education programs. *Topics in Early Childhood Special Education, 5*(4), 12–22.

Walker, D. K. (1987). Chronically-ill children in schools: Programmatic and policy directions for the future. *Rheumatic Disease Clinics of North America, 13* (1), 113–121.

Walker, D. K., & Jacobs, F. H. (1984). Chronically-ill children in school. *Peabody Journal of Education, 61*(2), 29–71.

Weitzman, M. (1984). School and peer relations. *Pediatric Clinics of North America, 31,* 59–70.

Weitzman, M., Walker, D. K., & Gortmaker, S. L. (1986). Chronic illness, psychosocial problems, and school absences. *Clinical Pediatrics, 25,* 137–141.

Wold, S. J. (1981). Tertiary prevention: Mainstreaming handicapped children. In S. J. Wold (Ed.), *School nursing: A framework for practice* (pp. 61–71). St Louis, MO: Mosby.

Wolf, J. M., & Pritham, H. C. (1965). Administrative patterns of school health services. *Journal of American Medical Association, 193,* 95–99.

Wood, S., Walker, D. K., & Gardner, J. (1986). School health practices for children with complex medical needs: A national survey of guidelines. *Journal of School Health, 56*(6), 215–217.

II

Underlying Questions and Critical Goals

5

Meeting the Needs of Individuals and Families*

Dorothy Jones Jessop, Ph.D.,
Ruth E. K. Stein, M.D.

Despite some premature announcements that the family is dead (Cooper, 1971), it seems to be enduring in a remarkable number of forms and shapes. There are single-parent families, headed mostly by women, many of whom are poor. There are stepfamilies, or "reconstituted" families, and families with adult relatives and extended kin networks. There are nonrelative household groupings, and, by now the minority, there are two-parent families in which the mother and father and their biological children live together.

In many families, even with young children, both parents work, sometimes by choice, more often by necessity. In other families, predominantly in disadvantaged areas, no one works, and the family subsists on public assistance. Each of these forms has its own strains. Superimpose on these demanding relationships and styles of life a child's chronic illness and the situations may become overwhelming.

*Based on a paper presented at a conference, "New Directions in Care of Children with Chronic Illness," sponsored by the United Hospital Fund and the Preventive Intervention Research Center of the Albert Einstein College of Medicine, in New York, May 31, 1985. Sections of this chapter have previously appeared in R. E. K. Stein and D. J. Jessop (February 1984). General issues in the care of children with chronic physical conditions. In R. J. Haggerty (ed.), *Symposium on chronic disease in children. Pediatric Clinics of North America,* 31; and R. E. K. Stein (1983). Growing up with a physical difference. *Children's Health Care,* 12, 53–61.

It is well known that the presence of a chronically ill child in the home has practical and emotional effects on the lives of all family members. Finances and work schedules are affected as illness-related costs mount and time is taken from work. The interaction of family members with each other and with those outside the home changes. There are psychological strains on the individual members of the family, both parents and siblings.

Family for some is a "haven in a heartless world" (Lasch, 1977). But even barring such an extreme situation, the family has become more and more a private arena in which the focus is on the person *qua* person and not as an instrument for attainment of goals. It is the arena for full development of the person. In other contexts, such as at work and in school, an aspect of the person is the focus, but in the family the wholeness of the person is emphasized. What happens to those total persons when a child has a chronic illness?

Daeschner and Cerreto (1985) have written that children with ongoing physical problems are "constantly part ill and part well—but never free of a problem that sets them apart. Their families, their social interaction, their educations and their daily routines are different from those of their peers" (p. 471). And Linda Hexter, herself the mother of a child with a serious chronic condition, writes that "birth and/or diagnosis of a chronically ill child is one of the most severe stresses that a family can sustain, because it involves not only the sudden shock and grief experienced when the child is diagnosed, but also years of multiple traumatic events, constant medical treatment, and continual worry and anxiety" (Hexter, 1980, p. 143).

The ongoing nature of the child's condition and changing status as he or she develops require a strong family presence and significant and central involvement in the child's care. Family issues and treatment issues cannot be separated as they are so often in a short-term acute illness. A child's medical condition and the technical care needs it imposes, as well as emotional characteristics, may place a great deal of extra strain on the family unit.

IMPACT OF A CHRONICALLY ILL CHILD ON THE FAMILY

Diagnosis of a major health problem in a child is a severe stressor, causing strain in a variety of areas. There are, in addition, often repeated hospitalizations, sometimes on an emergency basis. There may be unpredictable exacerbations of the condition requiring trips to the doctor or the emergency room.

Although there is no complete consensus about the effect of chronic childhood illness on a family, the bulk of the evidence seems to suggest that ongoing physical illness may disrupt the entire fabric of a family, especially during the crisis phase. Pratt (1976) suggests that:

> in general the limited evidence available indicates that severely disabling and stigmatized illnesses disrupt roles and relationships in many families, at least during the crisis stage of the illness, although the strenuous coping efforts that are stimulated by illness in the family often result in new patterns of adjustment within the families. (p. 131)

Psychological Costs to the Family

The initial emotional response to chronic childhood illness may be a mixture of fear, anxiety, anger, depression, and guilt. Drotar, Baskiewicz, Irvin, Kennell, & Klaus (1975) suggest there is initial shock, then denial, sadness, and anger, and only after time the reestablishment of equilibrium and the capacity of the family to reorganize and get on with the tasks of living. Although much clinical literature suggests this sequence of reactions, there is no solid research evidence for an invariant progression of states in families' reactions. Parents and patients talk more of going back and forth from one reaction to another. Individual family members may have different reactions and sequences of reactions, and these discordant responses may be a further source of strain. Exacerbations of the condition can lead to renewed confrontations with the implications of the disorder and bring buried emotions back to the surface. Additionally, many, if not most, parents feel some sense of personal failure or question their own adequacy in having produced a less than perfect child. Virtually every family member wonders what he or she might have done differently to prevent the child's condition, and many common themes run through their fantasies about possible causes.

Parents are confronted again and again by the ways in which their child's current function, special care needs, or future potential may differ from healthy peers. This occurs especially when the child reaches critical development stages, such as when peers are starting school or entering adolescence. Some families handle these worries with little mutual support, with each parent reacting to his or her own emotional needs by using coping mechanisms that may differ from the other parent's.

The Impact of Health Care

The needed treatments and home management may become very taxing. There may be a change in the physical aspects of daily living—in trips to health facilities, in special diets or medical procedures. Family members' roles may be affected both by the illness and by the demands placed on them by the health care system with respect to the care of the child's physical problem. There may be a realignment of family members; in most families the mother tends to bear the brunt of day-to-day responsibilities and medical care, spending the bulk of her time with the child who has a chronic condition, while the siblings manage relatively more independently or spend more time with the father or another adult. The mother typically has greater access to medical information and becomes the family's medical authority. Fathers and siblings are often left out of the medical care discussions, as may be the child him- or herself.

For child and family, ordinary events of life may have greater than normal impact. A move to a new home, away from familiar sources of care and community supports, may be very traumatic, or the potential disruption may be so severe that a family forgoes the move. Even commonplace events, such as the birth of a sibling or a family vacation, may pose special problems. Adaptation to these ordinary occurrences cannot be taken for granted but may require a good deal of planning and anticipation.

Financial Costs to the Family

Then there are the financial costs (see Rowland, Chapter 2). Most families are determined to get the best care they can for the child. Often, they expend great financial, as well as emotional, resources in the hope of finding a cure. Even for those who can find care nearby, the financial realities are enormous, with capricious insurance policies and eligibility requirements, as well as a pattern of generally inadequate public support, even for preventive services. There are also the hidden costs: lost opportunities, lost work time, lost chances to advance in one's career or to go back to school. The opportunity to change jobs may be missed because the parent fears loss of insurance coverage. There is the economic burden that derives from lack of energy to be a resourceful bargain hunter or homemaker and from the costs associated with the desire to find ways to "make it up" to the sick child.

Costs to Interpersonal Relationships

Another likely result is personal strain, fatigue, and intrafamilial tension. This is accentuated by, and contributes to, social isolation. Parents may be unable to find a babysitter in order to get away even for a few hours. It is often difficult to maintain friendships, and the constant worry and fatigue may detract from being "good company." All these problems lead to isolation, which may be coupled with resentment of the need to depend on the few remaining family, neighbors, and friends for favors without being able to reciprocate. There may be no time or money for vacations or recreation, as families use their job-allotted days off to meet medical emergencies.

It is important to note that the presence of a helpful social network can be a major predictor of successful coping with the care of child with a physical disorder. Yet a very common response to physical illness is withdrawal. People may pull away because they feel uncomfortable about how to act and about what to do or say. Caring may wear out, and social supports may become thin over time. In addition, serious illness may be threatening to families and friends, awakening their fears about their own vulnerability and that of their children. In a moving chapter of *Journey* (Massie & Massie, 1973), written by parents of a child with a chronic physical condition (hemophilia), Suzanne Massie writes that "people were always afraid of us. I could sense this. It is as though they felt we had been touched with a curse and that too close contact might contaminate them or give them a glimpse of an unpleasant reality they wanted to avoid having to face" (pp. 167–168).

A negative attitude may spill over to siblings. While siblings of chronically ill children often get less attention from their parents than other children, they may be quite conspicuous in their social world as the result of their brother's or sister's condition. For siblings, there may also be extra family responsibilities and the responsibility of being an intermediary between the outside world and their physically disadvantaged brother or sister. All the normal problems of sibling rivalry and conflicts are heightened and exaggerated. Additionally, siblings are often denied information about the nature and implications of the condition because it is falsely assumed that they can or should be protected.

EVOLUTION OF THE SITUATION

Problems faced by a sick child and the family very much depend on and must be dealt with in the context of a complex interaction among the illness, the family's responses, and the child's developmental status. The result of these complex interactions is that the situation of each child and family is unique. It may be helpful to think of several different types of change that are occurring simultaneously and are superimposed on one another. First, there is the evolving development of the child. Superimposed on this developmental change is the change in the chronic condition as it follows its own course. Then there is the change in the family as it evolves in its own lifecycle. Finally, there is the unfolding adaptation to the child's condition. The care of the growing child involves dealing with a dynamic process in which all those changes are occurring and requires continuous monitoring of an ever-changing situation.

Some health problems, such as asthma, can occur throughout the course of childhood, whereas others occur at particular ages and may cause more specific developmental disruptions. For example, the birth of a child with a congenital disorder causes stress during the important and critical period of bonding, and a serious change in the health of an adolescent can interfere with the development of adult autonomy. Many issues that span childhood have different manifestations and meaning in each stage of development. Hospitalization, with its attendant separation from the family, has different meanings for the infant, toddler, school-aged child, and adolescent.

DEVELOPMENT OF THE CHRONICALLY ILL CHILD

One controversial issue is whether development of a child with a serious, lifelong physical condition can be expected to parallel the development of a healthy child. Gliedman and Roth (1980) suggest that it may not be fair to apply concepts of normal child development to children with special physical problems and handicapping conditions because their life experiences may differ too greatly from those of their healthy peers.

In school and at home there is often uncertainty about how to treat the child, and people tend to spoil, baby, or overprotect. This deprives the child of important lessons in living and may result in significant social morbidity later on. Children who are isolated and not offered the normal range of give-and-take with peers do not master age-appropriate social skills or mature socially at the same pace as their age-mates. Household chores, normal sibling squabbles, and neighborhood and after-school activities are important growing experiences whenever they can be made available. These opportunities enhance social feedback and ultimately a sense of self-worth.

In addition to alterations in normal patterns of growth and development, a number of studies suggest that physical illness in childhood is associated with significant risk of mental health problems for the child and the mother, and possibly the siblings as well. A considerable body of empirical work documents that severely ill infants, children, and adolescents and their families are at increased risk. This may be a result of the actual physical symptoms of illness; the therapeutic regimens these children experience; the unpredictable outcomes or poor prognoses; the periodic medical crises; the potential trauma of hospitalizations and newer technologies; and the intermittent disruptions in family life. In general, these features can create stress for children and families, leading to emotional disorders of varying types, including depression, adjustment disorders, acute and chronic anxiety states, and family problems (Drotar & Bush, 1985; Eiser, 1985).

Epidemiological data indicate clearly that children with physical health problems have higher rates of mental health problems. Pless and Roghmann (1971) review three large-scale epidemiological studies and document an increased incidence of psychological problems among population-based samples of children with chronic health impairments. Data from the Isle of Wight, the national survey of the United Kingdom, and the Rochester (New York) Child Health Studies show that children with chronic conditions, in comparison to healthy children, exhibit higher rates of psychiatric disorders, abnormal behavioral symptoms, and school-related adjustment problems. More recent analyses by Pless of the British longitudinal cohort reveal more adaptational problems in school, work, marriage, and social relationships among children who have had chronic illnesses as they later enter adulthood (Pless, 1984) (see Pless & Wadsworth, Chapter 12). Walker, Gortmaker, and Weitzman (1981), in a population-based sample of children in Genesee County, Michigan, demonstrated that children with physical health problems have significantly more psychosocial difficulties, including behavioral, learning, social, and school problems. In a survey of patients seen in private practice settings in Monroe County, New York, Goldberg, Regier, McAnarney, Pless, and Roghmann (1978) showed that children with chronic physical illness have rates of emotional, behavioral, and school problems twice those of children without ongoing physical illness.

These findings have been confirmed in disease-specific studies. For example, children with leukemia have been found to be more anxious and isolated than the population of healthy children (Spinetta & Maloney, 1975). According to O'Malley, Koocher, Foster, and Slavin (1979), 59% of children who are long-term survivors of cancer have adjustment problems. Children with renal disease are more likely than healthy children to be isolated, withdrawn, and depressed (Fine, Malezadeh, Pennisi et al., 1978); juvenile-onset diabetes increases the likelihood of emotional disorder in children (Johnson, 1980). Many other disease-specific studies might be cited to document this increased risk.

It is worth noting that early case studies of individual children stressed the serious mental health problems that they faced (e.g., Bruch, 1948; Kubany, Danowski, & Moses, 1956; Toch, 1964; Turk, 1964). More recent studies, however, have shown that although seriously ill children and their families have more mental health problems than the general population, severe psychopathology is rare (Drotar, Doerschuk, Stern et al., 1981).

The differences between earlier and later studies may reflect basic improvements in medical outcome and the presence of comprehensive programs and preventive interventions in the model tertiary care children's hospitals, where many of these newer studies have been conducted (Hobbs, Perrin, & Ireys, 1985); they may also underscore the importance of identifying specific subgroups at differential risk for specific problems (Drotar, Doershuk, Stern et al., 1981).

Nevertheless, even very serious and debilitating illness does not preclude successful adaptation by the child and family and positive mental health outcomes. The challenge is to learn how to make successful adaptation and adjustment even more common.

ORGANIZATION OF SERVICES

There is recent evidence that the way services are organized can mitigate or prevent some of these problems (Stein & Jessop, 1984). The essence of chronicity is that the condition persists over time, sometimes years or an entire lifetime. People and resources can be mobilized around a self-limiting event, but do less well over long intervals. This is true of the personal resources of caregivers, which may become strained over time, as well as the social support of neighbors and kin. It is also true of the health care system, where providers may become frustrated at situations that yield no cure. Even health care financing is really geared to the acute, self-limiting condition, with policy limits per condition leaving families with large unpaid portions of care. This became most clear in the Prospective Payment System based on diagnosis-related groups (DRGs), where regulations may require sending a child home before the child or the family is ready.

The presence of a child with a chronic illness means living with illness and with the need for getting care for the child. The care may be necessary and helpful on one level, but often the lack of it with families and family needs produces its own problems. Many children have multiple, complicated medical problems that require their getting care from a variety of sources and providers. These families, far more than other families, need to interact with multiple institutions in our society: health care, special education, equipment vendors, social services, insurance companies, and so forth. There are medical subspecialists whose demands are sometimes conflicting, uncoordinated, and incomprehensible to the layperson. Families need help with concrete services, patient education, advocacy, health care maintenance, care for intercurrent crises, advice on special programs and what to expect in the future, explanations of illness, advice on genetic risks, coordination of health care both within the hospital and with other agencies, and someone to listen to their concerns. Work by our research group (Stein, Jessop, & Riessman, 1983) and others shows that most families receive traditional biomedical types of care, but few families receive psychosocial services. Optimally, families should receive biomedical and psychosocial assistance, and the data indicate they are especially not getting the latter.

Not every family can coordinate all the systems required to mobilize these services. They may need someone to put the pieces together, be an ombudsman. Ideally, this person should be someone with leverage with both the family and the system. It should not be another level of paper-pushing. The family also should be actively included in the care of the child if there is to be follow-through on a day-to-day basis and if the care is not to disrupt the bonds with the child by enforced separations, unworkable regimens, or technology.

And, in addition, even in the face of the child's special care requirements, the family should be able to remain independent and autonomous and not be subjected to undue supervision and paternalism. The nature of chronic illnesses may make it necessary for the providers to know about and have input into family lifestyles, work patterns, play activities, and relationships. This may strike some as "prying." However, there must be a balance between the privacy of the family and the desire to give or get help for the child. Physician hesitancy about intruding on individual privacy may run counter to the need to look into broader areas of family life. For some families, there may also be a reluctance to share family matters with professionals, especially if they do not perceive the pediatrician as a source of advice in these areas. Moreover, family information disclosed may in some cases create a choice for the pediatrician of either acting in a seemingly paternalistic fashion or closing his or her eyes to the child's needs. There are dilemmas involved in some of these issues.

It has been suggested by Moynihan (1986) that at a very fundamental level our society does not support families and children generally—much less those with serious health problems that go on over time. The burden of care is left to the family, who are on their own in many ways. The task is to determine how care can be delivered in a manner that empowers the family rather than rendering it inordinately dependent on the caregiving system. Bureaucratic encounters, whether in the school or in the health care setting, tend to reveal static snapshots of the child and family. They do not deal well with the multiplicity of family styles, the realities of development, the whole person, or other pulls in the family's life. They tend to focus on the disease rather than the whole child with a disease, and ignore the aspects of the disease that are important to families. For example, medical providers focus on diagnoses rather than characteristics of the condition, such as uncertainty or visibility, even though these characteristics may be critically important in family members' reactions to the illness and their ability to help manage the child and condition (Jessop & Stein, 1985). From the family members' point of view, their ability to help manage the child on a daily basis may be more important than the exact diagnosis or treatment.

The care of an ongoing condition is heavily dependent on the family, and the centrality of the role family members play cannot be sufficiently emphasized. The physician is not in control of the situation to the same degree as in the acute inpatient setting, in which most of medical training takes place. The majority of the responsibility for the day-to-day supervision of the child falls to the family members, who are the primary caretakers on a 24-hour basis. If the condition cannot be eliminated, and if there are a variety of possible interventions of potential, but uncertain value, individual preferences may play a role in the decision about whether a given intervention should be undertaken. This may be influenced by short- and long-term tradeoffs, by the sense of how much the problem is bothering the patient, and by how acceptable or unacceptable the intervention is in terms of family values. Moreover, in order for the family to function optimally for the child, the well-being of the family unit itself has to be taken into consideration. In chronic illness, the social context of the family and the psychological status and history of its members have central importance in the way the family interprets the illness and handles the situation.

Society benefits from having families that are strong and empowered, who are able to care for their children and get the kinds of help they need from a flexible system that is responsive to their individual needs, developmental trajectories, and diverse structures and styles. Reverend Robert Massie, Jr., writes (1985) that "chronic illness is a constant and sometimes overwhelming companion, a shadow both inseparable and eternal . . . [which] . . . creates a tremendous need in the patient—child or adult—for a group of supportive and caring human beings to show by their words and actions that they will stay with the patient through the physical and emotional roller coaster of disease..." (p. 14). "Only the power of a warm heart can alleviate the deep chill of a child's constant shadow" (p. 23). However, it is not enough for individual people to be warm—political, professional, and institutional programs and systems must be more responsive as well.

Acknowledgment: Work for this chapter was supported by the Preventive Intervention Research Center for Child Health, Albert Einstein College of Medicine/ Montefiore Medical Center under research grant #1 P50 MH38280 from the Branch for Prevention Research of the National Institute of Mental Health.

REFERENCES

Bruch, H. (1948). Physiologic and psychologic interrelationships in diabetes in children. *Psychosomatic Medicine, 11,* 200–210.

Cooper, D. (1971). *The death of the family.* New York: Random House. (Vintage).

Daeschner, C. W., & Cerreto, M. C. (1985). Training physicians to care for chronically ill children. In N. Hobbs and J. M. Perrin (Eds.), *Issues in the care of children with chronic illness: A sourcebook on problems, services, and policies.* San Francisco: Jossey-Bass.

Drotar, D., Baskiewicz, A., Kennell, J., & Klaus, M. (1975). The adaptation of parents to the birth of an infant with congenital malformation: A hypothetical model. *Pediatrics, 56,* 710–717.

Drotar, D., & Bush, M. (1985). Mental health issues and services. In N. Hobbs and J. M. Perrin (Eds.), *Issues in the care of children with chronic illness: A sourcebook on problems, services, and policies* (pp. 514–550). San Francisco: Jossey-Bass.

Drotar, D., Doershuk, C. F., Stern, R. C., Boat, T. F., Boyer, W., & Matthews, L. (1981). Psychosocial functioning of children with cystic fibrosis. *Pediatrics, 67,* 338–343.

Eiser, C. (1985). *The psychology of childhood illness.* New York: Springer-Verlag.

Fine, R. N., Malezadeh, M. H., Pennisi, A. J., Ettenger, R. B., Wittenbogaart, C. H., Aegrete, V. F., & Korsch, B. M. (1978). Long term results of renal transplantation in children. *Pediatrics, 61,* 641–651.

Gliedman, J., & Roth, W. (1980). *The unexpected minority: Handicapped children in America.* New York: Harcourt Brace Jovanovich.

Goldberg, I. D., Regier, D. A., McAnarney, T. K., Pless, I. B., & Roghmann, K. J. (1978). The role of the pediatrician in the delivery of mental health services to children. *Pediatrics, 63,* 898–909.

Hexter, L. J. (1980). A chronically ill child in the family. *Clinical Proceedings CHNMC, 36,* 133–145.

Hobbs, N., Perrin, J., & Ireys, H. (1985) *Chronically ill children and their families.* San Francisco: Jossey-Bass.

Jessop, D. J., & Stein, R. E. K. (1985). Uncertainty and its relation to the psychological and social correlates of chronic illness in children. *Social Science in Medicine, 10,* 993–999.

Johnson, S. (1980). Psychosocial factors in juvenile diabetes: A review. *Journal of Behavioral Medicine, 3,* 95–116.

Kubany, A., Danowski, T., & Moses, C. (1956). The personality and intelligence of diabetics. *Diabetes, 5,* 462–467.

Lasch, C. (1977). *Haven in a heartless world.* New York: Basic Books (Colophon).

Massie, R. (1985). A constant shadow: Reflections on the life of a chronically ill child. In N. Hobbs & J. M. Perrin (Eds.), *Issues in the care of children with chronic illness: A sourcebook on problems, services, and policies* . San Francisco: Jossey-Bass.

Massie, R., & Massie, S. (1973) *Journey.* New York: Knopf.

Moynihan, D. P. (1986). *Family and nation.* New York: Harcourt Brace Jovanovich.

O'Mally, J. E., Koocher, G., Foster, D., & Slavin, L. (1979). Psychiatric sequelae of surviving childhood cancer. *American Journal of Orthopsychiatry, 49*(4), 608–616.

Pless, I. (1984, November). *Childhood chronic illness as a risk factor.* Paper presented at Research Symposium of the Preventive Intervention Research Center for Child Health, Albert Einstein College of Medicine/Montefiore Medical Center, Bronx, New York.

Pless, I. B., & Roghmann, K. J. (1971). Chronic illness and its consequences: Some observations based on three epidemiological surveys. *Journal of Pediatrics, 79,* 351–359.

Pratt, L. (1976). *Family structure and effective health behavior.* Boston: Houghton-Mifflin.

Spinetta, J. J., & Maloney, L. J. (1975). Death anxiety in the outpatient leukemia child. *Pediatrics, 56,* 1034–1037.

Stein, R. E. K., & Jessop, D. J. (1984). Does pediatric home care make a difference for children with chronic illness? Findings from the pediatric ambulatory care treatment study. *Pediatrics, 73,* 845–853.

Stein, R. E. K., Jessop, D. J., & Riessman, C. (1985). Health care services of chronically ill children. *American Journal of Diseases of Children, 137,* 225–240.

Toch, R. (1964). Management of the child with a fatal disease. *Pediatrics, 3,* 418–427.

Turk, J. (1964). Impact of cystic fibrosis on family functioning. *Pediatrics, 34,* 67–71.

Walker, D. K., Gortmaker, S. L., & Weitzman, M. (1981). Chronic illness and psychological problems among children in Genesee County. Boston: Harvard School of Public Health, Community Child Health Studies.

6

The Roles of Professionals and Institutions

Antoinette P. Eaton, M.D., Daniel Lee Coury, M.D., Richard A. Kern, M.D.

Medical advances through research and new technology have created an increased demand for health care services, and professional and institutional resources are a critical aspect of the plan of action to serve children with chronic illness. This chapter examines the needs for such services by considering (1) what we had in the past, (2) what we currently have, and (3) what we need in the future.

SERVICES IN THE PAST

The health care system of two or three decades ago was focused on the treatment of killing and crippling infectious diseases; it gave little attention to children with chronic illness. Gaps and deficiencies in the provision of services in the past abounded across all categories—medical, psychosocial, educational, vocational, and recreational. If the child lived in a rural area, it was reasonably certain that the full complement of resources required would not be available, and in many instances even the most elementary program did not exist. The health care professional, usually the pediatrician, worked alone to assess and treat a child, and often was forced to throw the burden of identifying appropriate special services back onto the child's parents. There was little or no emphasis in medical training on dealing with this population and a scant amount of theoretical or clinical research.

Two vignettes of patient experiences illustrate these deficiencies. They are impressive because the advice frequently given to parents was to serve as their child's advocate themselves and demand the necessary services from the appropriate professionals and institutions.

Case 1. Tom was six years old when referred by his community pediatrician to the tertiary level medical center with significant visual impairment and developmental delay. He lived in a small town in southeastern Ohio with no programs geared to meet his special needs. Following the initial comprehensive evaluation by a multidisciplinary team at the children's hospital, the pediatrician, psychologist, and social worker successfully combined efforts with the family to design an educational program that would begin to meet his needs in his own community. His mother then was encouraged to find a way to implement it.

The next interaction with the mother of this child occurred a few years later at a meeting of the State Department of Education Special Education Advisory Council. She had been appointed a member and had undertaken as her mission the establishment of a parent advocacy group to lobby for all children in the state with special educational needs. Her leadership resulted in the formation of an effective statewide advocacy organization of parents, whose initiatives later expanded nationally.

At that time, she stated that her commitment to and achievements in advocacy were directly related to the advice given to her at the children's hospital. This mother had been instructed to go out and seek—rather demand—what was best for her child from professionals and institutional providers. Based on her successful endeavors, she was recently honored for her contributions at the state level.

Case 2. Robbie was first seen in early infancy for evaluation of multiple congenital malformations. He was the first child of well-educated and highly caring parents who lived in a small, semi-urban community. Here too, however, there were no community resources such as an infant stimulation program or a home visitor for this child, nor were there adequate family support services. Robbie's mother crusaded for and eventually created an appropriate infant preschool intervention program to meet not only her son's needs but also those of other children with chronic illness/disability as well.

Successes like these were hard-won and unusual. Many parents simply did not have the educational, financial, or emotional wherewithal to advocate effectively for their children, and pediatricians, working singly, could often do little better.

These examples demonstrate the need for services and the deficiency of qualified health care professionals to assure the provision of these services. They also portray the physician in the pivotal role as gatekeeper to the health care delivery system. Although lacking the competence to totally manage these patients, the physician can still be an effective medical provider by advocating for necessary services and supporting legislative efforts, as well as coordinating multidisciplinary management (Coury & Eaton, 1984).

THE CURRENT SITUATION

To assess the present system of professionals and institutions devoted to the care of chronically ill children requires an evaluation of the documented need for services in this special population. It is important to recognize that the composition of this special population group is changing as a result of successful medical prevention and intervention strategies in many infectious disorders, such as paralytic poliomyelitis and rheumatic heart disease. The present era of scientific medical advancement and technological sophistication has given rise to a new group of chronically ill children—those who are ventilator-dependent, or on chronic renal dialysis, or who have treated or stabilized malignancies or metabolic disorders. In addition to changes in the spectrum of chronic diseases, therapeutic achievements have resulted in survival into adolescence and early adulthood of children with more "traditional" chronic diseases, such as cystic fibrosis and cerebral palsy, thus creating new demands on professionals and institutions to consider such questions as job training and placement and sexuality. (See Richardson, Chapter 11.)

Children with chronic illness require primary care as well as special services. The delivery of preventive health care to this population is an important corollary to the provision of the specialized medical, psychosocial, educational, and recreational components of comprehensive care. There is also a critical need to be intimately familiar with community resources to guarantee access to and continuity of care for these patients. The importance of community-based services is evidenced by increasing involvement by hospital-based providers with community professionals and agencies to create a network of services. This may include alternatives to hospitalization, such as home health care and respite and preventive care, as well as other family support systems.

Coordination of professionals from many disciplines to provide high quality, comprehensive health services to address the complex special needs of these children and their families is the most important component of successful management. This is not an easy task, since involvement of an interdisciplinary team in medical management, care coordination, family support, primary care, and education may result in an overlap in some areas of responsibility while other needs are neglected. A variety of approaches have been suggested for reducing this potential role conflict—changes in the health care delivery system, revision of professional training or enhancement of inservice education, and improved financing for services that are required but not provided (Klerman, 1985).

The hallmark of the present system is a limited network of interdisciplinary teams that emphasize continuity of comprehensive care and address the medical, psychosocial, educational, vocational, and recreational needs of the child with chronic illness/disability. These teams are usually based in tertiary level centers with academic affiliations. The need for more such teams has been frequently reiterated. As the Select Panel for the Promotion of Child Health of the Department of Health and Human Services (1981) stated in its report to Congress:

> Routine collaboration between diverse professionals remains the exception rather than the rule . . . consequently the interests of children are not as well or efficiently served as they might be. Economies of joint effort are likely to occur over time only if training opportunities, organizational structure, financing incentives and consumer education are designed to promote them. Because the cost of failing to promote joint effort is so great—in terms of both dollars wasted and low quality of care—the Select Panel for the Promotion of Child Health believes that high priority should be given to promoting better collaboration among professional and service sectors in the future.

A critical requirement for the health care team to accomplish this list of responsibilities is a caring attitude toward the child and his/her family. This population of patients, perhaps more than any other, requires a professional commitment not only to be knowledgeable about the patient's illness but also to understand the impact of the chronic illness on the family. There is little doubt that the current care system for chronically ill children has a number of characteristics that interfere with the provision of health care that reflects a caring attitude by health professionals. This is evidenced by a medical care system that is still focused on a disease entity, is fragmented and categorical, and revolves around institutional imperatives rather than the needs of families (Kohrman & Diamond, 1986).

A major focus on this population by federal and state governmental institutions occurs through the Title V Maternal and Child Health Block Grant, especially the Services for Children with Special Health Needs* (CHSN) Program. State CSHN agencies have made a significant, although variable, commitment to serving children with chronic illness. For example, the Ohio CSHN agency served 28,000 children in 1984 through a system of team and individual health care providers. This compares with services to only 2,000 children in the mid-1960s. This is a real indication of the increased commitment to this special population by one state agency.

---

*Formerly known as the Crippled Children's Services (CCS) program.

Overall, Title V continues to be an important national program thrust not only in facilitating service provision but also in setting high standards for quality of care and fostering increasing coordination between all local, state, and federal programs essential to health care for chronically ill children. In addition, the CSHN agencies have had extensive experience that can serve as the basis for health policy and financing changes necessary to improve the plight of this population and their families. These and related programs, including Title XIX (Medicaid), are described in Chapter 3.

The Early Periodic Screening Diagnosis and Treatment (EPSDT) program of Medicaid is also important because it offers the opportunity for prevention or early identification of children with chronic illness. Despite the tremendous potential value of this program, with its focus on prevention, it is generally felt to have been less effective than intended. Expenditures for EPSDT currently constitute a minuscule portion of the overall Medicaid budget. Making it a higher priority would clearly be a great advantage for all children, including those who have a chronic illness.

Other governmental programs, particularly special education agencies responsible for administering PL 94-142, and rehabilitative and vocational services, play a significant role in serving children with special needs. Since they are described elsewhere in this book (see Walker, Chapter 4), they are only mentioned here.

University Affiliated Centers for Developmental Disorders, initially developed in the mid-1960s by the federal government, continue to provide care to the individual patient and family through the team approach. They emphasize training of professionals to deliver comprehensive, ongoing, multidisciplinary care in a university setting to one subgroup of children with chronic illness. Further, they educate health professionals in the value of the other disciplines necessary to the care of children with chronic illness/disability. Unfortunately, restrictions placed on these programs through governmental funding have often separated these training programs from physician education and kept them outside the mainstream, significantly reducing their impact on the health care system. "Full integration of these programs into the [medical] education curriculum could heighten attitudes and skills needed for care for chronically ill or handicapped children and their families" (Daeschner & Cerreto, 1985).

FUTURE NEEDS

It is well known that the service system for chronic illness/disability is fragmented, services are duplicated, and eligibility criteria restrict access

to them. Therefore, considerable effort should be directed to the improvement of services through interagency collaboration for children with
chronic illness. This may occur at various governmental and community
levels, in a variety of organizational models, and through the provision
of a spectrum of health services (Eaton, Pepper, & Bajo, 1985).

In addition to refinement of the health care delivery system, numerous well-trained interdisciplinary teams are necessary to coordinate,
manage, and integrate community-based, family-centered services for
each child with chronic illness. It has been suggested that the major
responsibility for coordinating this effort be assigned to the pediatrician
(Kanthor et al., 1974; Klerman, 1985).

The person who serves as coordinator of the team of diagnostic and
therapeutic specialists meeting routine and emergency health care, and
who counsels the family, has been described as the "ombudsman" (Battle,
1972). To assume this important professional obligation, the pediatrician
must have the required knowledge and skills, and this requires a shift
in pediatric training from the purely biologic to include the psychosocial.
Training must move from the old model of the physician as sole medical
provider to the new model of physician as problem solver, aware of the
multiple factors influencing wellness and illness, cognizant of the need
for the expertise of other disciplines in the care of children with chronic
conditions, and able to obtain appropriate information or to consult as
the need arises (Coury, in press). Concern must be for care as well as
cure. Achieving this laudable goal will require a supervising faculty with
a commitment to these values who can serve as role models for students.
These teachers must emphasize not only the management of disease, but
the coordination of services, the utilization of other health professional
team members, the availability of community resources, and the emotional and financial impact of chronic illness on families.

These multiple roles for the pediatrician were delineated by a group
of national experts in a conference on "Education of the Pediatrician for
the Ongoing Care of Children with Special Health Needs" at Harriman,
New York, hosted by Ruth E. K. Stein (Stein, 1983) and are shown in
Table 6.1.

To prepare pediatricians adequately to assume the multiple roles needed
to serve this target population effectively will require improvement in the
training programs for residents and fellows. In response to this perceived
need, a model for fellowship training has been developed by the Department of Pediatrics, The Ohio State University/Columbus Children's
Hospital (OSU/CCH), with the aid of a grant from DHHS/Division of
Maternal and Child Health Special Projects of Regional and National Significance (SPRANS). The primary goal of the OSU/CCH Fellowship in
Behavioral-Developmental Pediatrics is to train pediatric subspecialists

TABLE 6.1 Responsibilities of the Pediatrician Caring for Children with Chronic Conditions

1. Coordinating care, which requires a knowledge of community resources, subspecialists, and the interdisciplinary approach

2. Assessing child development and utilizing this data in management for:
   a. early identification of the problem
   b. family assessment, especially the parent's psychological functioning
   c. evaluation of the patient's behavioral status, gross motor functioning, and temperament

3. Assessing family development and adaptation regarding:
   a. response to the medical care environment
   b. response of family members to each other
   c. response of family members to illness
   d. counseling

4. Being a leader in identifying and providing for the child's and family's needs, both normal and special

5. Advocating and teaching advocacy:
   a. for the patient and family, so that the patient can be a more effective participant in his or her own health management
   b. in the community, to promote early identification of at-risk children and service to them
   c. among colleagues
   d. for self-education (CME)

who can serve as members of medical faculty, conduct original research in the area of behavioral-developmental pediatrics, and serve as role models for medical students and residents in the delivery of patient care, exemplary teaching, and research (Coury, Mulick, Eaton, et al., 1986). The subgoals of the fellowship are outline in Table 6.2.

As a first step in the attainment of these goals, an interdisciplinary faculty was selected that included a psychologist, a social worker, a special educator, a speech pathologist, an audiologist, and a nutritionist. An education consultant was also recruited and proved to be a valuable resource in the development of a *written* curriculum for the fellowship. The initial twelve-month period was utilized to prepare the curriculum, with goals, objectives, and reading lists for each topic included. Designed to train future academicians in the field, the curriculum addresses not only behavioral and developmental issues, but other areas in which academicians must be knowledgable. These include health legislation and policy, health planning, psychosocial aspects of chronic conditions, and the development of research and teaching skills. This curriculum (Table 6.3) is presently being used in the three-year fellowship program in behavioral-developmental pediatrics at The Ohio State University, and similar fellow-

TABLE 6.2 Goals of the OSU/CCH Fellowship in Behavioral-Developmental Pediatrics

A. Training in the knowledge and principles of normal child development, including:
   1. Knowledge of child development theory and its translation into clinical judgments
   2. Description of the basic capabilities of newborns, infants, preschoolers, school-aged children, and adolescents

B. Training in clinical issues in behavioral pediatrics, including:
   1. Knowledge of common behavioral complaints and disorders, such as psychosomatic disorders, stress-induced disease, depression, conduct disorders, sleep problems, enuresis, anorexia, school learning problems, coping and adjustment problems, and substance abuse
   2. Instruction in the skills and knowledge necessary for the practice of behavioral pediatrics, including: effective communication, behavioral and pharmacologic therapies

C. Training in issues relevant to the practice of developmental pediatrics, including:
   1. Knowledge of mental retardation/developmental disabilities, parent-child interaction, learning disabilities, cerebral palsy, communication disorders, common developmental problems, and their early identification and prevention
   2. Training in developmental testing, educational testing, consultative skills, and counseling

D. Supervised patient contact experiences and instruction from the core faculty on the application of behavioral/developmental pediatrics to treatment of children with chronic illness, including: facilitating normal social, intellectual, and emotional development; effects on family functioning; coping with stresses of development related to the illness; behavioral management techniques for improving compliance; crisis intervention, anticipatory guidance; self-care and self-medication; and identification of predictable stress and crisis points in the course of chronic illness

E. Supervised training experiences and instruction in the interdisciplinary process

F. Supervised training experiences and instruction in research methods

ship training programs in ten other centers are being implemented through an expansion of the DHHS grant initiative in 1987.

The curriculum has been designed using educational goals and objectives. The knowledge base identified through this curriculum is presented through direct clinical experience, tutorials with the core faculty, readings, and accredited course work at The Ohio State University. An innovative aspect of this fellowship training program is its involvement with existing Title V agencies. The Ohio Department of Health, Bureaus of Maternal

TABLE 6.3 Curriculum Content

1.0 Mission statement
2.0 Behavior, development, and learning
    2.1 Basic knowledge and clinical skills
        2.1.1 Behavioral assessment and behavior modification
        2.1.2 Counseling
        2.1.3 Educational assessment
        2.1.4 Family structure and dynamics
        2.1.5 Interdisciplinary process
        2.1.6 Interviewing
        2.1.7 Normal growth and development
    2.2 Learning and behavior disorders
        2.2.1 Common behavior disorders
            2.2.1.1 Antisocial behavior
            2.2.1.2 Encopresis
            2.2.1.3 Enuresis
            2.2.1.4 Fears
            2.2.1.5 Habit disorders
            2.2.1.6 Hyperactivity/attention deficit disorder
            2.2.1.7 Noncompliance
            2.2.1.8 Sleep disturbance
            2.2.1.9 Tantrums
        2.2.2 Eating and feeding disorders
            2.2.2.1 Feeding disturbances in infants
            2.2.2.2 Obesity
            2.2.2.3 Vomiting and rumination
        2.2.3 Prevention of behavioral disorders
        2.2.4 School performance and educational problems
            2.2.4.1 Assessment
            2.2.4.2 Learning disability
            2.2.4.3 School phobia
    2.3 Problems of adolescent
        2.3.1 Adolescent pregnancy
        2.3.2 Adolescent sexuality
        2.3.3 Adolescent suicide and depression
        2.3.4 Eating and feeding disorders
            2.3.4.1 Anorexia and bulimia
        2.3.5 Substance abuse
    2.4 Special issues
        2.4.1 Abuse and neglect
            2.4.1.1 Family violence
            2.4.1.2 Nonorganic failure
            2.4.1.3 Rape
        2.4.2 Compliance with medical advice
        2.4.3 Death and dying
        2.4.4 Dysmorphic child
        2.4.5 Ethics
        2.4.6 Genetic counseling
        2.4.7 Hospitalization
        2.4.8 Injury control (accidents)

(continued)

TABLE 6.3 *continued*

         2.4.9 Pain and stress management
                2.4.9.1 Abnormal pain
                2.4.9.2 Headache
                2.4.9.3 Severe pain
3.0 Developmental disabilities
     3.1 Handicapping conditions
          3.1.1 Autism
          3.1.2 Communication disorders
          3.1.3 Mental retardation
          3.1.4 Motor disabilities
          3.1.5 Multiple handicaps
          3.1.6 Sensory impairments
     3.2 Living alterations
     3.3 Special education
     3.4 Vocational education and programs
     3.5 Prevention—primary and secondary
4.0 Chronic illness/conditions
     4.1 Generic problems in children with chronic illnesses
     4.2 Specific illness
          4.2.1 Asthma
          4.2.2 Cleft palate
          4.2.3 Congenital heart disease
          4.2.4 Cystic fibrosis
          4.2.5 Epilepsy
          4.2.6 Hemophilia
          4.2.7 Juvenile diabetes mellitus
          4.2.8 Leukemia
          4.2.9 Muscular dystrophy
          4.2.10 Renal diseases
          4.2.11 Sickle cell anemia
     4.3 Prevention—primary and secondary
5.0 Health adminstration and public policy
     5.1 Advocacy
     5.2 Community organizations resources
     5.3 Finance
     5.4 Health planning
     5.5 Interagency coordination
     5.6 Legislation process
6.0 Research skills
     6.1 Biostatistics
     6.2 Epidemiology
     6.3 Grant writing skills
     6.4 Methodology
7.0 Teaching skills
8.0 Evaluation of the fellow
9.0 Epilogue
     9.1 Glossary
     9.2 Indexes
     9.3 References

and Child Health, and Children with Medical Handicaps provide the
fellow with training in the realm of public health, public and private interagency coordination, health administration, and health legislation. The
Nisonger Center, the University Affiliated Facility for Developmental Disorders, provides a training site for comprehensive evaluations of children
with developmental disabilities and for exposure to the interdisciplinary
team process. These two agencies work in conjunction with the Department of Pediatrics, OSU/CCH, to form a unique training ground for an
academic fellowship in behavioral pediatrics.

This type of broad interdisciplinary training needs to be replicated for
pediatricians at other sites and in other stages of training. It must also
be supplemented by broader training of nonphysician team members
whose own disciplines currently emphasize a single disciplinary approach
to the care of children with special needs.

SUMMARY

The focus of this chapter is what we need from institutions and professionals to improve the delivery of health care for children and adolescents
with chronic conditions. Medical education programs have the responsibility for educating and training physicians so that they are equipped with
the necessary knowledge and skills to meet the needs of this special population. They must emphasize the provision of high quality, comprehensive health care that is coordinated and family centered. Effective
participation in the interdisciplinary teams must be stressed. Intimate
familiarity with community resources and governmental programs must
be achieved to facilitate an appropriate plan of management for each
individual in this special population. Knowledge about health issues for-
mulation and active involvement in those decisions affecting the pediatrician and other health professionals are essential. Advocacy for appropriate
governmental and private third-party financing of necessary health care
services and systems is critical to the survival of this special field.

A model for fellowship training in behavioral-developmental pediatrics
has been described, with the major goal being to facilitate the development of faculty with expertise in chronic illness/disability. It will be their
responsibility to educate and train future health professionals to meet the
special needs of these children and adolescents. It is hoped that the example described will be replicated or appropriately adapted for and at other
academic centers. The new initiative recently undertaken by the Department of Health and Human Services/Division of Maternal and Child
Health to fund ten additional special projects of regional and national significance (SPRANS projects) in behavioral pediatric fellowship training

will significantly enhance this important training mission. It will have the added effect of delineating other models of training that may be equally as effective, since it is unlikely that a uniform approach in every center would be successful. Evaluation of these projects will be critical to objectively define the best approaches to training fellows in this field. Delineation of the "ideal" model remains a challenge for the future.

REFERENCES

Coury, D. L. (in press). Needs and directions in pediatric medical education. In P. Karoly, (Ed.), *Handbook of child health assessment*. New York: Wiley.

Coury, D. L., & Eaton, A. P. (1984). Children with special needs: A priority. *The Ohio State Medical Journal, 80*, 767–769.

Coury, D. L., Mulick, J. A., Eaton, A. P., et al. (1986, May). *Structure and implementation of a fellowship curriculum in developmental-behavioral pediatrics.* Paper presented at the annual meeting of the Ambulatory Pediatric Association, Washington, DC.

Daeschner, C. W., Jr., & Cerreto. M. C. (1985). Training physicians to care for chronically ill children. In N. Hobbs & J. Perrin (Eds.), *Issues in the care of children with chronic illness* (pp. 458–478). San Francisco: Jossey-Bass.

Eaton, A. P., Peppe, K. K., & Bajo, K. (1985). Integrating federal programs at the state level. In N. Hobbs and J. Perrin, (Eds.)., *Issues in the care of children with chronic illness* (pp. 758–771). San Francisco: Jossey-Bass.

Gortmaker, S., & Sappenfield, W. (1984). Chronic childhood disorders: Prevalence and impact. *Pediatric Clinics of North America, 31*(1), 3–18.

Haggerty, R. (Ed.). (1984). *Pediatric Clinics of North America. 31*(1), 1–3.

Kanthor, H., et al. (1974). Areas of responsibility in the health care of multiply handicapped children. *Pediatrics, 54*, 779.

Klerman, L. (1985). Interprofessional issues in delivering services to chronically ill children and their families. In N. Hobbs & J. Perrin (Eds.), *Issues in the care of children with chronic illness* (pp. 420–441). San Francisco: Jossey-Bass.

Kohrman, A. F., & Diamond, L. (1986). Institutional and professional attitudes: Dilemmas for the chronically ill child. *Topics in Early Childhood Special Education: Chronically Ill Children, 5*(4), 82–91.

Public Health Service, U.S. Department of Health and Human Services. (1987). *Better health for our children: A national strategy. The report of the select panel for the promotion of child health to the United States Congress and the Secretary of Health and Human Services: Vol. 1. Major findings and recommendations* (DHHS [PHS] Publication No. 79-55071). Washington, DC: U.S. Government Printing Office.

Stein, R. E. K. (1983, July). Education of the pediatricians for the ongoing care of children with special health needs. Conference at Harriman, NY.

Task Force on Pediatric Education, American Academy of Pediatrics. (1978).

7

Ethical Views and Values

Alan R. Fleischman, M.D.

Children play a special role in our lives. They are at the same time among the most vulnerable and the most precious members of our society. In a real sense, they represent our future. Children who are ill elicit a feeling of sadness from us, while children with a chronic illness affect us even more profoundly. When we address ethical issues concerning children with chronic illness we question our own values and the values of our society. The ethical dilemmas that must be raised include the following: (1) Do we as a society value children with chronic illness? (2) How should children with chronic illness be treated and how should decisions be made for them? (3) What should the role of families be in the care of children with chronic illness?

The first issue to be addressed in considerations of ethical dilemmas in the care of chronically ill children is the question of whether our society values children with a chronic illness. Immanuel Kant said "man is not valued as a mere means to the ends of others or even to his own ends, but as an end in himself. He possesses a dignity, an absolute inner worth by which he exacts respect for himself and for all other rational beings in the world. He can measure himself with every other being of this kind and value himself on a footing of equality with them." This learned philosopher believed that each person has an inherent worth, but that the most critical and important part of human dignity is the person's ability to make judgments for him or herself—to be autonomous. Children in general are not autonomous individuals. They are unable to weigh the risks and benefits of their actions and make reasoned decisions concerning appropriate alternatives. Children, however, are protected by the assumption that they will develop autonomy and therefore deserve the respect and protection of our society.

VALUING CHILDREN WITH A CHRONIC ILLNESS

Some chronically ill, disabled, and handicapped children may never become autonomous members of our society. They may be viewed as a burden, a drain on resources, and a threat to many societal values. Respect for this group of individuals who may never be able to make decisions for themselves must revert back to the basic idea that human beings have an absolute inner worth irrespective of their relationships to others.

The National Commission on the Protection of Human Subjects of Biomedical and Behavioral Research (1977) issued what has become known as the Belmont Report, in which it addressed the issue of respect for persons with diminished autonomy. It stated that "respect for persons incorporates at least two basic ethical convictions: first, that individuals should be treated as autonomous agents, and second, that persons with diminished autonomy are entitled to protection" (p. 14). Children have diminished autonomy and are entitled to protection. Children with a chronic illness have diminished autonomy based not only on childhood, but also on the disabling or handicapping condition with which they must cope. Even if such children are unable ever to make autonomous decisions, there is a need to value their worth and their unique contribution to our society based on the principle that each living person has an inherent worth and dignity. However, children with a chronic illness will have to challenge our society for many years before they are accepted as integral members.

Demographic Factors

How do we measure our societal value of children? If our society undervalues our children, it will certainly undervalue children with a chronic illness. Unfortunately, children in our society have begun to compete with the elderly for societal resources (Preston, 1984). From 1960 to 1982, the number of children under age 15 in the United States fell by 7%; at the same time, the number of people over age 65 increased by 54%. One might expect such a change in age structure to help the young and hurt the older. Fewer children might mean less competition for resources and social services; however, it appears that the well-being of the elderly has improved greatly, whereas that of the young has deteriorated. Recent legislation (PL 99-457) suggests that there may be some increasing response to the needs of very young children with special conditions. If so, this is only a minor reversal of the trend.

In 1970, 16% of those under age 14 lived in poverty, compared to 24% of those over age 65. By 1982, the situation had reversed—23% of children lived in poverty, compared to 15% of the elderly (Preston, 1984).

There is some evidence suggesting that chronic illness in childhood is disproportionately distributed among the poor. Thus the changing status of the elderly and, in comparison, the decreasing status and well-being of children in our country create an ethical dilemma of major proportions and directly impact on the ability to deliver quality health care services to the child with a disability or handicapping condition.

Because there is a disproportionate distribution of chronic illness among the poor, the financing of care for these children is extremely complicated, particularly in the present economic climate. In a time of fiscal constraint, limited resources, and inadequate insurance coverage and reimbursement mechanisms (see Rowland, Chapter 2), there is an obvious need to develop an equitable and efficient delivery system.

Obligations of Society

In order to be assured that the society wishes to accept its obligation to provide excellence in health care for disabled children, one might look to another President's Commission for its analysis. The President's Commission for the Study of Ethical Problems in Medicine and Biomedical and Behavioral Research published its volume, *Securing Access to Health Care*, in March 1983. This Commission described health care as having a special place in American society and concluded (President's Commission, 1983):

> The society has an ethical obligation to ensure equitable access to health care for all. This obligation rests on the special importance of health care which derives from its role in relieving suffering, preventing premature death, restoring functioning, increasing opportunity, providing information about an individual's condition, and giving evidence of mutual empathy and compassion. . . . Equitable access to health care requires that all citizens be able to secure an adequate level of care without excessive burden. Discussions of a right to health care have frequently been promised on offering patients access to all beneficial care, to all care that others are receiving, or to all that they need or want. By creating impossible demands on society's resources for health care, such formulations have risked negotiating the entire notion of a moral obligation to secure care for those who lack it. In their place, the Commission proposes a standard of "an adequate level of care" which should be thought of as a floor below which no one ought to fall, not a ceiling above which no one may rise. (p. 4)

What is clearly missing in the Commission's recommendations is the acceptance of society's obligation to provide for each individual the amount of health care that will be required to allow that individual to develop to a reasonable, if not optimal, potential. Since the provision of health care for the chronically ill child is extremely expensive and must be provided over a long period of time, the Commission's concept of adequacy is an inadequate standard upon which to base the future potential of vulnerable children with handicaps. Perhaps the President's Commission, when thinking about chronically ill individuals, reflected on the plight of the elderly, for whom the goal of health care is to provide comfort and prolong a reasonable existence. The goals for the chronically ill child in our society, on the other hand, must be to normalize their lives, optimize their functioning, and enhance their future productivity.

Allocation of Resource

Not only has society set certain limits on the amount of money that will be spent for health care, but the entire evolving approach to health care financing has placed the physician in the role of arbiter of which treatments are too expensive and which are appropriate or beneficial. Increasingly, physicians will either benefit directly from decreased expenditures for health care based on their participation in a health maintenance organization (HMO) or be under institutional pressures to save dollars through the new diagnostic-related group (DRG) approach to financing hospital care. Kapp (1986) suggests that

> the day of physician's exclusive loyalty to the individual patient is probably behind us . . . it is no longer sufficient for the physician to judge the propriety of a possible medical intervention solely by considering the potential benefits to the patient directly involved. The modern physician must for the sake of society and the individual patient ponder costs as well as benefits and must factor cost/benefit and cost/effectiveness ratios into treatment calculations. (pp. 247–248)

We have created a system of decreased resources for health care and of physician arbiters who, at least in the HMO setting, may benefit from decreased allocation of dollars to the chronically ill child, who may be the most expensive patient in the hospital and, furthermore, may be a patient with diminished autonomy and a potential for diminished future productivity. All such allocation decisions will inherently tend to discriminate against chronically ill children. Protection of this most vulnerable group in our society will not be easy. It will have to include advocacy by professionals and parents, because it may take many years before our society will sufficiently value these children to provide appropriate resources.

Among chronically ill children there is a small group of patients, perhaps increasing in number, who are dependent on technology, such as respirators, intravenous feeding, or dialysis machines. These infants and children are often graduates of our neonatal and pediatric intensive care units and beneficiaries of new, life-saving technologies. Because these children will require technological assistance for many years, or perhaps for the duration of their lives, some have argued that they would be better off at home. Thus programs have been created around the country to allow the home care of such technology-dependent children.

Parental Obligation

Heroic and pioneering families have fought courageously against the system and sacrificed their homes and their family lives to enable their children to be cared for within the nurturing environment of the family. These families were motivated by a clear desire to have their children at home as part of their families, and for the most part, the family itself provided the majority of care for the child. It has become increasingly clear that the cost of caring for a technology-dependent child at home is less than the cost within an acute care hospital, and this realization has created an interesting dilemma: in order to allocate fewer dollars to the care of this child, the family may be asked by health care providers to assume a tremendous level of care, with consequent family disruption.

Our society needs to address and define the limits of parental obligation to a chronically ill child. We ought to praise those who make great sacrifices, but at the same time should we condemn those who do not wish to or cannot provide this extraordinary level of commitment to their child? Should society, as has occurred in the setting of a poor or disrupted family, take custody of a child away from the parents because they cannot provide adequate home care for a technology-dependent infant? Does "can" imply "ought" when it comes to the family responsibility for a chronically ill, technology-dependent child?

It is fair to ask a great deal of parents concerning their obligations to their child, but there must be a limit on our expectations. Society has an obligation to support the family in its task, both financially and psychologically. If the family cannot meet the challenge, society must step in as caregiver while facilitating the parents' role as parents.

DECISION MAKING

This brings us to the next major ethical issue in the care of chronically ill children—the question of decision making.

For adults who are competent to make decisions we respect their autonomy—their right to decide for themselves. Even, when we disagree and, more importantly, perceive that an adult's decision is not in his or her best interests, we still respect that autonomy. The concept of autonomy derives from the principle of respect for persons. The new emphasis on autonomy in medicine is in contrast to the concept of paternalism, which holds that interference with a person's liberty is justified when done for the person's own good. Medicine, particularly pediatrics, is often paternalistic; we constantly recommend treatments and courses of action to our patients, but frequently we do not share the decision-making responsibility with the patient or the patient's family. Sometimes physicians arrogantly impose treatment decisions rather than discussing them. Often there are alternatives that are not shared with families out of a desire to protect them, a concern that they would not understand, or the attitude that a full explanation is just too time consuming.

Informed Consent

Respect for a person's fundamental right of self-determination has resulted in the medical doctrine of informed consent. Informed consent assumes that the patient is capable of understanding the risks and benefits of alternative treatments and can make an informed choice. When the principle of informed consent relates to children or to any individuals who lack the capacity to decide for themselves, it invokes the use of a proxy or surrogate. A proxy consent is based not on the involved individual's choice but rather on another's perception of the appropriate choice.

There are two possible standards for surrogate decision making: the substituted-judgment standard and the best-interests standard. In the substituted-judgment standard, regardless of the surrogate's perception of what is the right decision, he or she is obligated to make the decision that the patient would have wished. The patient may have explicitly voiced his or her desires or may have lived a life consistent with the choice the surrogate is obligated to make. With children we often have little if any prior history that would give us a good idea of their wishes. We can preserve the child's future right to autonomy only by making a decision that is clearly in the best interests of the child—sometimes, although rarely, even when it conflicts with parental beliefs.

The principle of informed consent has limited application to children, since informed consent presupposes an autonomous decision maker. When a parent is a surrogate decision maker for a child, the principle of informed consent might better be replaced by a collaborative principle of combined parental permission, child assent, and physician agreement.

The principle of informed consent for autonomous adults is extremely powerful in that it allows capable adults to refuse treatments despite negative consequences. However, parental refusal of treatments deemed in the best interests of their infants does not hold the same weight as refusals by competent adults of treatments on themselves. Parental refusal of a needed therapy does not relieve the physician of an ethical duty to the child, particularly if the refusal of such treatment puts the child at significant risk. This is why a principle of parental permission with collaborative decision making among physician, parent, and child is preferable in the case of children. It presupposes a different role for the parent.

Parental refusal may be based on a belief that the refusal of treatment for the child is in the best interests of the family, but the best-interests standard is a *child-centered* one. When the child's best interests are in conflict with family autonomy, the child's best interests must prevail (Macklin, 1982). The best-interests standard presupposes that the decision makers are able to consider a judgment as to the interests only of the child, negating all interests of the decision makers, including the family. It is not the intent of the best-interests standard to invoke a disinterested decision maker who would have no relationship to the child for whom the decision is being made. It is hoped, however, that the interested decision maker will make the child's well-being the most prominent determinant of the decision. It is also of note that for children with chronic illness, interests may change and evolve over time.

In examining the cognitive and psychological capabilities of children, it is obvious that long before their 18th birthday, the legal age of maturity, children have the ability to abstract and to decide what is in their own best interests (Piaget, 1969). Similarly, from an ethical standpoint, it seems obvious that older children are quite capable of sorting out risks and benefits and knowing what is in their own best interests (Gaylin, 1982). However, the law is fairly clear that only minors who have been emancipated or are totally independent of their families hold the right to make autonomous decisions, except in certain specific medical circumstances (Capron, 1982). The role of the child in decision making concerning chronic illness seems even more important than in the acute setting. Many of the decisions have lifelong implications concerning commitment, compliance with treatments, and future quality of life. This is all the more reason to respect the judgment of the child and to take his or her wishes into account whenever possible.

Roles of Society and Family

It is obvious, however, that decisions concerning the care of children with chronic illnesses directly affect and impact upon the family. Unlike decisions for acutely ill children, decisions concerning long-term treatment for a chronically ill child often involve the parent—not only as decision maker, but also as caregiver. Many studies support the idea that the family plays an important if not vital role in determining whether the child will flourish. When the decision being made by the family impacts not only on the child but also on the family, the limits of parental obligation to the chronically ill child must be decided. However, even if the family does not have an unlimited duty to provide a certain type of care, if it is deemed in the child's best interests to have that care it seems incumbent upon society to provide it. The problem, of course, with providing care outside of the family setting is that it is both difficult and often not nearly as beneficial to the child. The psychosocial aspects of the family environment may play a major role in determining the success of a treatment regimen.

An alternative to society's providing treatment is providing appropriate social support that will predispose the family to consent to be the primary caregiver. Although respite care, in-home services, and psychological and social support to the family can help them act in the child's best interests, these are frequently unavailable.

It seems, therefore, that the best-interests standard for a child must include societal commitment to providing the resources that will allow the family to make decisions that are truly in the child's best interests without imposing an undue burden on the family.

CONFLICTS

Multiple conflicts may rise among health care providers and between health care providers and families concerning the right decision and the right treatment plan for a chronically ill child. Decisions must take into account the personal needs of the patient and the family, community resources, and the strengths and weaknesses of various programs and facilities. Health care providers cannot assume that a treatment that worked for one patient will work unmodified for every similar patient. It is becoming increasingly clear that multidisciplinary team discussions, as well as total involvement of the parents, will optimize decision making for an individual child. This will also help to insure that decisions are collaborative rather than prescriptive.

This collaborative approach to decision making is somewhat foreign to the style of acute care physicians. It attacks the traditional paternalistic assertion of the physician that only he or she knows what is right, and it asserts that there are multiple approaches to accomplishing the same goal. Physicians must learn to accept that the goal of acute care medicine—to cure—is not adequate in dealing with children with chronic illnesses or handicapping conditions. Chronic illness must be viewed in the contextual framework in which restoration of function, normalization, optimization, and sometimes just caring replace the acute care goals of curing.

Many personal value conflicts express themselves in the care of the chronically ill child. The physician may be ambivalent about a child's worth and potential, instead of being interested in all aspects of care and caring. He should focus first on the medical facts of an individual case, and should know the possible and the most probable outcomes in order to assess the patient's potential and formulate a recommendation for a treatment plan. There is little room for cursory "Gestalt" approaches and general feelings about prognosis. Rather, there is a need for accurate information, communicated in a clear manner. The professional may have value conflicts concerning for whom he is the advocate—for the patient, the parents, the institution or program, or for himself. He must become involved in the psychosocial aspects of care, realizing that these dimensions are perhaps even more critical to the success of treatment than the specific prescription.

There are value conflicts also within the family itself, with family members frequently angry and ambivalent about the child. Parents may react differently, and may often wish to deny the reality of the illness, be unable to face the serious nature of the diagnosis, the complexity of the treatment, or the uncertainty of the ultimate long-term prognosis. Physicians, nurses, teachers, therapists, and others caring for the child may view these troubled parents as difficult, noncompliant, or uninterested, but many of the seeming value conflicts between caregivers and families are really based on psychological issues within the family. A thorough understanding of the dilemma facing the family is imperative if real communication to enhance the care of the child is to occur. The family may need help in accepting the child's illness, coping with planning for the future, or overcoming anger, guilt, and denial concerning the illness.

WITHHOLDING OR WITHDRAWING TREATMENT

A final ethical issue concerns whether it is ever appropriate to withhold or withdraw medical treatment from a child with a handicapping or disabling condition. For many years, society has devalued children with disabling or handicapping conditions and has lacked appropriate resources and programs for their rehabilitation. This has resulted in the feeling by some that it is appropriate to opt for death through withholding or withdrawing medical treatments from newborns, infants, and children with serious or potential chronic and disabling illnesses.

Many physicians believe that withdrawing a treatment is legally and morally less justified than withholding it. But this seems an erroneous distinction. In the real world, bad deeds seem more often to occur because of someone's action rather than from lack of action. In the physician–patient relationship, with its implied contract to help and to provide appropriate treatment, there is no moral difference between withholding and withdrawing a treatment. If there is good reason to withhold a particular treatment from a particular patient, then it is equally defensible to withdraw it after it has been begun. Conversely, if a treatment is morally indicated, it is as wrong to withhold it as it would be to withdraw it. There is no question that it is psychologically more difficult to withdraw a treatment than to withhold it, but that does not create an ethical distinction. Many physicians also believe that there is a legal difference between withholding and withdrawing treatments. In the opinion of most legal scholars, nothing in the law makes stopping treatment a more serious legal issue than not starting it.

Some would argue that withdrawing a treatment that proves to be ineffective is morally superior to withholding a treatment because of its uncertain efficacy. Decisions to withdraw a treatment may be based on more information and may also be able to be discussed with patients or parents. Decisions to withhold a treatment are often made in emergent situations in which contemplative discussion is impossible and for which uncertainty of outcome is quite great.

In an attempt to protect infants with handicapping and disabling conditions from inappropriate withholding or withdrawing of treatments, the federal government and many advocacy groups have called for mandating treatments for seriously ill infants, allowing few, if any, quality-of-life criteria to be invoked to rationalize nontreatment.

In order to protect infants, one might state an absolute vitalist principle that all children should be treated at all times for all illnesses with all possible interventions until the last heartbeat, with the hope that by miracle, magic, or medical marvel the disease process will be reversed and the child will be restored to some level of functioning. This vitalist, or sanctity of life, approach implies a disregard for the patient who is truly dying, for the patient who is in severe pain with little hope for that pain and suffering to diminish or relent, and for the patient with little ability to interact with society or the environment or little hope of attaining the basic human quality of knowing one's caregiver and of interacting with one's environment. This sanctity of life approach would protect some infants for whom treatments might be inappropriately withheld or withdrawn, while at the same time causing other infants to suffer inappropriate treatments. Although some individuals believe in the sanctity of life principle, it should be noted that no organized religion holds unequivocally to a sanctity of life doctrine. Orthodox Judaism and Catholicism believe in the inherent worth of each human being and the value of life itself. However, both of these religions provide for withholding or withdrawing treatments through invoking the optional nature of extraordinary treatments or the belief that individuals who are dying need not be burdened with unnecessary prolongation of suffering.

Unfortunately, some of our families and some of our health care providers believe that their religions preach a vitalist approach to the sanctity of life. It is a principle to be respected; and if a family or health care provider truly believes in the absolute sanctity of life, then decision making for that patient is clear. All available medical treatments must be provided until the last heartbeat. And once we move from a sanctity of life position, we are making quality of life judgments, whether or not it has become fashionable to say that there are decisions short of sanctity of life which do not involve quality of life determinations.

Many have pointed out that any use of quality of life determinants for withholding or withdrawing treatments may place us on a ''slippery slope,'' such that once we take the first step we will be unable to stop and will make decisions that will hurt many children. This fear of wholesale infanticide is without foundation. It is mandatory that we consider quality of present and future life, so that we can fairly judge whether children are suffering severely, whether our treatments are merely prolonging dying or in fact have life-enhancing potential, and whether children and infants for whom we are making decisions have the capability of interacting in society in even the most minimal manner. As for all infants and children, decision making for those with chronic illnesses must be based on protecting their best interests. This is not inconsistent with withholding or withdrawing technological interventions and medical treatments that may only prolong dying, will not relieve pain and suffering, or will leave the infant with such impaired potential that he or she will never be able to interact in society.

In making quality of life judgments for children with handicapping conditions, we must utilize the best interests principle (Macklin, 1982). This standard, however, has certain limitations. If a child is neither dying nor in severe pain, but nevertheless has no capacity for social interaction, how can it be in his best interests from his point of view to be better off dead than in his present state of unresponsiveness? For such a severely impaired child, can life have much significance or value? Might the child have few interests at all to which a best interests standard might apply except the interest in maintaining comfort and alleviation of pain? In these devastating cases, the best interests standard requires a supplementary standard geared to the presence or absence of basic human capacities. Arras (1985) states that

> the ethical principle that justifies this standard is the proposition that biological human life is only a relative good in the absence of certain distinctly human capacities, e.g., for self-consciousness and relating to other people.

> The usual connection between biological life and our notion of the good is effectively severed. Just as the presence of unrelievable pain can preclude the attainment of those basic human goods that make life worth living, so the absence of fundamental human capacities can render a life valueless both to its possessor and to others. (pp. 121–122)

When this point is reached, treatments ought to become optional and left to the discretion of families and physicians.

Because decisions concerning withholding and withdrawing treatments from infants with handicaps and disabilities are so complex, there is a need for procedural safeguards in implementing these judgments. Physician and family ambivalence may lead to inadequate valuing of children with disabilities and may result in biased decisions not in the infant's best interests. Furthermore, we must accept that there have been some wrong decisions for individual children in which physicians and families have agreed to withhold or withdraw treatments inappropriately, with the resultant death of the child.

How, then, should we protect the best interests of the child, allow maximal involvement of parents in decision making, and still prevent "wrong" decisions? Institutional ethics committees would be of significant help in decisional review, particularly for children with handicapping conditions. Ethics committees should not take upon themselves all of the authority to make such decisions but should have respect for the autonomy of the family and for the fact that most parents and physicians have the interests of the child at heart. As much of the decision-making authority should be left in the hands of parents and physicians as is compatible with protecting those very few infants for whom bad decisions might be made. The ethics committees should focus on ascertaining and supporting the best interests of the infant, while making a determination in each case as to whether the best interests of the infant require treatment, nontreatment, or are ambiguous.

We must admit that we often do not know which modes of treatment will be beneficial and which are in the patient's best interests. In these ambiguous situations, we need not impose treatments on infants merely because they are available. Thus the ethics committees should support the collaborative wisdom of the physicians and parents in treatment choices in these difficult decisions.

Alternative protections of the infant include the use of governmental supervision or the courts for making specific determinations in individual cases. But in addition to being time consuming and expensive, both of these approaches are too distant from the infant to be sensitive to the child's and family's needs. Nor is there any compelling reason to believe that such decisions are better ones.

The government might choose to mandate treatment of all infants as a vitalist procedural safeguard against inappropriate withholding or withdrawing of treatments. The natural outcome of mandated treatments for all neonates would be the creation of a class of citizens with fewer rights than any other group: their right to have treatments withdrawn would be forever limited, regardless of the extent of the pain and suffering endured.

CONCLUSIONS

In conclusion, the ethical dilemmas facing chronically ill children as well as their caregivers and family are multiple. All children, including those with a disabling or handicapping condition, have inherent worth, which must be respected and valued by our society. It will, however, take another generation until our society accepts on an equal basis individuals with decreased potential for autonomous decision making and decreased ability to interact within society.

Health care decisions for children with chronic illnesses must be made based on their best interests, incorporating regard for their families, their communities, and their environment. Decisions must be collaborative rather than prescriptive, utilizing all disciplines, all resources, and intimately involving the family.

Society's obligation is not only to the children themselves, but also to their families; there is a responsibility to provide the social services that will allow families to care for and support these children without incurring undue burdens.

As sad as it sounds and as unfortunate as it may be, there must be a time when we can and should consider withholding and withdrawing treatments from some infants and children with chronic illnesses. We can still make these decisions based on the best interests standard, at times supplementing that standard with a look at the capability of the infant to interact at a basic human level. We must involve families in these decisions, and we must develop alternative criteria and procedural safeguards so that the best interests of the child will be maintained and so that the fears concerning slippery slopes and wholesale infanticide will not be realized. At the same time, we can decrease pain and suffering, we can refrain from prolonging dying, and we can allow for humane care and caring by not mandating technological intervention and by not creating a class of citizens with fewer rights than the rest of us.

And finally, although the President's Commission and others have voiced belief of the entitlement of all to equal access to health care, until we value optimizing the outcome of all our children—those who are healthy, those with acute illness, and those with chronic illness—we will fall short of setting a standard that will allow for the development of an optimal society.

REFERENCES

Arras, J. D. (1985). Ethical principles for the care of the imperiled newborns: Toward an ethics of ambiguity. In T. H. Murray & A. Caplan (Eds.), *Which babies shall live?* (pp. 83–136). Clifton, NJ: Humana Press.

Capron, A. (1982). The competence of children as self-deciders in biomedical interventions. In W. Gaylin & R. Macklin (Eds.), *Who speaks for the child?* (pp. 57–114). New York: Plenum.

Fleischman, A. R. (1986). An infant bioethical review committee in an urban medical center. *The Hastings Center Report, 16,* 16–18.

Gaylin, W. (1982). The competence of children—No longer all or none. *The Hastings Center Report, 12,* 33–38.

Kapp, M. B. (1984, December). Legal and ethical implications of health care reimbursement by diagnosis related groups. *Law, Medicine and Health Care,* 245–253.

Macklin, R. (1982). Return to the best interests of the child. In W. Gaylin & R. Macklin (Eds.), *Who speaks for the child?* (pp. 265–302). New York: Plenum.

National Commission for the Protection of Human Subjects of Biomedical and Behavioral Research. (1978). *The Belmont report.* (DHEW Publication No. (05) 78–0012), Washington, DC: U.S. Government Printing Office.

Piaget, J. (1969). *The moral development of the child.* New York: Free Press.

President's Commission for the Study of Ethical Problems in Medicine and Biomedical and Behavioral Research. (1983). *Securing access to health care.* Washington, DC: U.S. Government Printing Office.

Preston, S. (1984). Children and the elderly in the U.S. *Scientific American, 251,* 44–49.

8

With a Parent's Eye

Julianne E. Beckett, M.A.

As parents and professionals, we have come a long way from the tradi-tional patient–therapist relationship. We have become partners—equal partners—in the care of our children. It has not been an easy sharing of responsibility, but with the complex world around us and the expansion and growth of new technology, it is the only way we afford our children the opportunity to grow in the least restrictive environment possible, while meeting their optimal needs in a world outside an institution. We have also grown to recognize that if the child is to survive, the family must also survive.

This new world of catastrophic care is no longer composed of just the health professional and the parents, but also the educator, the funder, and the legislator, each with an integral part to play in our lives. In short, such chronic medical care has evolved into a team effort, with each member playing a vital role.

How has this new world affected families? To answer this question, I would like to relate our story and tell how it has affected our lives.

KATIE'S STORY

Mary Katherine Beckett, better known as Katie, was born March 9, 1978, at St. Luke's Hospital in Cedar Rapids, Iowa. Although premature and weighing only 2 pounds, 3 ounces, Katie had very few medical problems. She required an oxygen hood for the first 48 hours, but continued to grow at a rate that allowed her to come home on May 6, 1978. She was a normal baby in every sense of the word.

Fewer than four months later, on September 1, 1978, Katie was back in St. Luke's, only this time in the pediatric unit for observation. It was soon determined that she was suffering from viral encephalitis, unrelated to her prematurity. On September 2, Katie aspirated as a result of a grand mal seizure, and severe respiratory distress complicated an already serious illness. It was a beautiful Sunday morning, the sun was shining—I entered the hospital not knowing what had occurred. I'd gone to church first and had called just prior to leaving home. Things had been fine; Katie had taken her first bottle in three days. I was elated. I thought the worst was over: Katie would soon be home. Little did I know it would be three very long, very trying years before that event became an actuality.

Katie struggled throughout the morning and for most of the afternoon. By 3:00 P.M., she just could not fight both the encephalitis and the pneumonia. We were sitting in the parents' lounge when we saw Katie's respiratory therapist, Mark, run by, followed closely by Katie's doctor, Jim Ziska. We were half way down the hall when we heard the code. Hustled away to a room, my rosary beads in hand, a nurse praying with us, we received minute-to-minute updates from a nurse on the floor. The only words I can remember are "her heart never stopped, her heart never stopped." This was our first battle in what would be years of battles.

I could dwell on those years: through the weeks of Katie's coma, her waking to find herself totally paralyzed and completely dependent on a ventilator as a result of the viral encephalitis, her countless pneumonias, the surgeries. But those are times of sadness. There were also times of joy—Katie's first tooth, her first birthday, her first steps—all taking place in an intensive care unit. Each of these milestones gave us a glimmer of hope and helped to take us through each crisis, seemingly making our bond stronger.

Not only we, but everyone at St. Luke's was touched by Katie. When she became ill an alert went out and everyone prayed. They just would not let anything happen to their little girl. When Katie took her first steps, just shortly after her second birthday, I was greeted at the door by the security guard who could not wait to tell me, and he was not the only one I encountered on my journey to the fourth floor pediatric intensive care unit.

When Katie's doctors told us we could take her home, it seemed as if all our prayers had finally been answered. All the crises and learning processes seemed minute compared to the joy of our being together. You don't have much of a family life in an institution, even one as caring as St. Luke's.

It was at this time that we were notified that Katie's Medicaid coverage would not extend to home care costs. We had always carried insurance to protect ourselves, but it is impossible to foresee a catastrophic illness with its soaring medical costs using all of your private insurance. Having exhausted all lifetime major medical coverage on a Blue Cross/Blue Shield policy *with a million dollar cap*, Katie had been placed on the Medicaid roles shortly after her second birthday. This meant a child with a wonderful potential for a full life at the age of three years was left with no health insurance coverage and no governmental insurance should we take her home where she belonged. Katie's home care costs would run $2,500 to $3,000 per month. We did not earn nearly enough money to pay $36,000 per year to keep her at home. Few people do, and no other options existed for us. Katie had to remain in a pediatric intensive care unit even though she was costing the Medicaid program $12,000 to $15,000 a month.

The next few months were exhausting—fighting governmental red tape, reviewing the brushes with death that had occurred over the last few years, and facing rejection after rejection. Private funding was another road we sought, but each organization examined explained that we did not fit into their guidelines. They had been established mainly for educational and informational purposes. We even attempted to apply for grants, but were rejected because Katie was an individual and the grants were designed for group aid. Their purpose was mainly for research in an area that would benefit a greater number of the general populace. There was no broad base for support; therefore, we were nonessential to their programs.

In June 1981, we turned to our Congressman, Tom Tauke. Here we met a willing response to our plea for help. He judged that it would be difficult to get Congress to schedule a private bill to alter the present regulations. It would take two or three years before such a bill would even come up for debate, so he encouraged us to apply for an "exception to policy." These efforts and analysis of the problem took months, with much correspondence with state agencies. It was agonizing, and by the end of the summer our frustrations were high.

It was at this time that Congressman Tauke sent our case to Richard Schweiker, then Secretary of Health and Human Services. On November 4, 1981, Congressman Tauke received a letter rejecting our "exception to policy" because of what President Reagan later termed "hidebound regulations." Then Congressman Tauke turned to Vice President Bush, who was at the time head of the Regulatory Reform Commission. Tom had met Katie earlier in the year and just could not understand leaving an essentially healthy child with severe medical complications living in a pediatric intensive care unit when her parents could care for her medical needs appropriately at home if only the government would pay for home care costs. He voiced his frustration with the current regulations in a letter to the Vice President who, in turn, discussed his deep concerns with President Reagan. On November 10, 1981, the President discussed our dilemma with the nation, saying:

> Recently we received word of a little girl who has spent most of her life in a hospital. . . . The doctors are of the opinion that she could receive the same treatment at home, it would be better for her. . . . Staying away from the home atmosphere is a detriment to her, but Medicaid cannot pay the $1,000 a month it would take to send her home. Instead Medicaid pays $6,000 a month to keep her in the hospital. By what sense do we have a regulation in government that will pay $6,000 a month to keep someone in the hospital when they could receive better treatment and be better off at home?

Using the phrase *senseless bureaucracy and hidebound regulations*, the President clearly revealed that government had become tied up in bureaucratic red tape. My heart stopped as he spoke; there were tears in my eyes. But he had not actually said that something could be done. Then, at the end of the news conference, Daniel Schorr stood up to ask the last question: "Mr. President, getting back to that little girl. Do you believe Medicaid should be paying for home care?"

The President smiled and said the word I had been waiting to hear: "Yes." My first thought was, "There must be a way—the President believes it should be done—there must be a way." Little did Mark and I know that the Surgeon General and several members of the Health Care Financing Administration (including Administrator Carolyn Davis) were searching for the loophole. It came in the Omnibus Reconciliation Act of 1981. On Thursday, November 12, Secretary Schweiker read a statement releasing Katie from the present regulation. This waived our income in meeting Katie's eligibility requirements. Henceforth, the program would be called "the Katie Beckett waivers."

Through the efforts of the President, the Vice President, Congressman Tauke, and Secretary Schweiker, Katie was able to come home. Many other children have also benefited, but hundreds of others still remain institutionalized and their number is expanding. I hope that, because of our experiences, home care will become a reality and life enriched for those children and their families.

Katie Beckett's unusual life has served as a model for home health care because she has overcome the serious after effects of encephalitis. This has made her a miracle child. No one could have foreseen how well Katie would do at home. But her future after leaving St. Luke's has had to be lived one day at a time, and it has not been without worry and strain.

Before she left the hospital in December 1981, all efforts were mobilized by state and private professionals to help Katie improve at home. These efforts have been truly successful. Medically, Katie has improved remarkably. Serious illnesses have become less and less frequent since our initial discharge. We have been able to wean her from the respirator for naptimes, and the little girl who was previously strapped to its tubing 16 to 18 hours a day presently uses it only on an intermittent basis.

Katie was able to attend preschool within her first year home, and it was the consensus of the other parents that Katie grew more than any of the other children. Her need for socializing skills was very evident in the beginning of the school year, but by spring she was just "one of the kids." It was a time when we saw peer pressure work in a very positive way.

Much of Katie's ability can be credited to her speech therapy, which began even before she left the hospital. Katie has had speech therapy three times a week since she was one-and-a-half years old. For her, learning has become a fun experience. Her therapist, Ann Briggie, brought the world to Katie through pictures and words.

Katie's speech therapy continues to help her grow in various ways. It was believed before her discharge that Katie would have to sign to be communicative. This is no longer the case. Her growth in the last few years and her exposure to other children in a learning situation have improved Katie's speaking to a level where she no longer needs to sign and is not even asked to repeat to be understood. Shortly after Katie's fifth birthday her vocabulary was tested as average for 7 years, and her level of understanding was that of a 6-year-old.

The initial insult from the encephalitis concentrated in an area that controlled Katie's breathing, her swallowing, the tip of her tongue, and her left shoulder girdle. Paralysis resulted from this nerve damage. Some nerves have regenerated; however, the muscle tone in these areas is very poor. The need for coordination of mouth and tongue for swallowing has limited Katie to liquid or blended supplements, mostly from a high-calorie formula, but there is hope that she will eventually eat normal foods, even if only in smaller portions. She is continuing speech therapy for more tongue control, with the hope of improving her ability to eat by mouth. April 1984 saw the removal of her gastrostomy tube, which had been her sole means of nutritional support for 7 years. There is a light at the end of the tunnel.

The only educational drawback Katie seems to have is in the fine-motor skills, but after working with a tutor from the Grant Wood Area Education Agency since her discharge, she has been able to gain tighter control and to guide her hands through writing, cutting, and other fine-motor activities. She also receives physical therapy through Grant Wood in the school she attends. Her inability to crawl as a normal toddler and her lack of mobility because of paralysis again resulted in deprived muscle tone and lack of proper coordination. How has this deficit affected her participation in various school activities? Katie has an innate sense of teaching other children about handicaps: she participates, and they accept what she can and cannot do; she has had to develop a strong sense of self-esteem, but she has an overwhelming understanding of human nature and adjusts to the circumstances surrounding her. Clearly Katie's experience demonstrates that when a sense of limitation is imposed on a disabled child she will approach difficulties with those same limitations. Even though caution was always used to guide her, limitations were not imposed in Katie's case, and she faces difficulties with the attitude with which she faces life—"somehow I'll be fine."

FIGURE 8.1 Katie—happy and healthy.

SUPPORT NETWORKS

All of these success stories occurred because we work together as a team. Speech therapists, physical therapists, respiratory therapists, nurses, teachers, school officials, psychologists, sociologists, suppliers, and our entire community became committed to one goal—helping one particular child to grow.

Mark and I are not trained medical professionals, but the years we spent watching Katie grow and the support we received from doctors, nurses, and therapists while she was in the hospital reinforced our belief that we could care for her at home. The first time we took Katie home for a visit, we were both apprehensive about taking on the sole responsibility—Katie had been breathing on her own only for an hour or two, three times a day, for about a month. I can remember asking Dr. Ziska if we were taking a nurse with us. His response was, "Julie, if you go home, you go home alone." I knew that he would never jeopardize Katie's life; therefore, he must have believed we could take care of her outside the hospital. His was our first vote of confidence—the seed had been sown.

We knew also that once we left the hospital setting, we had a network of community-based support to rely upon. This support network permeated the community. People whom I had never met would stop and ask how Katie was getting along. Just knowing they cared helped us enormously. Being able to face our troubles with extra hands and extra hearts somehow lightened our load, and it just did not seem so great. We felt a sense of community that supported us through our bad times, and our sense of isolation lasted only for short periods of time. Not being afraid to share our needs and to educate others about those needs promoted understanding and awareness. We have learned to adjust to limitations in a positive way and have developed a sense of normality and a sense of pride—indeed, we've come a long way.

HOME CARE FOR DISABLED CHILDREN

Can other children progress so at home, and can parents learn to care for their children, even technologically dependent chronically ill children at home? I would say, very definitely, Yes! We need to convince our society that these children can and should experience normal growing. They should be allowed the opportunities we afford any human being. We must be cautious, however, for not every parent is able to cope physically or emotionally with having a chronically ill child at home. Safe, alternative placement facilities must be developed to meet the needs of these children. I do believe that with the right training, proper coordination of services, and great public awareness, many fears can be negated.

We must also be aware that every child's case is different. We need a strong case management program and assessment as follow-up to the release of children into their parents' care. This helps in sharing the responsibility and takes a supportive effort by trained professionals. It provides a psychological boost to parents and allows for quality assurance guarantees, both of which could easily be provided through current state services with realignment and training. Such a procedure would encourage development of interagency cooperation while allowing the family eventually to assume the total role of managing their child's case.

Parents should be empowered by those services involved to develop a strong sense of responsibility for their children. People generally want that responsibility once they are allowed to participate and are educated to become decision makers, educated about the maze of systems that will enter their lives and the most appropriate services to help their child grow. Professionals in service systems should not feel threatened by parents' yearning for this knowledge or intimidated as parental coping abilities expand to open up new alternatives that could replace them. Parents of disabled children tend to build up a trust in the professionals who first show them respect and encouragement. All parents have this in common, and the community only becomes stronger through this process of education.

The community then carries the ongoing burden of continual emotional support. But it is a burden shared by many people, and therefore the personal load becomes easier. These others share in the families' successes as well as their failures. They become a part of the problem-solving team, aware of the emotional bonds that pull the family together in times of crisis. Their role is essential if the family is to survive. These health care professionals are forging a new frontier in health care delivery: it is a role whose time has come.

This role, abruptly thrust on our family, resulted from the growth of modern technology. However, preparation for this "new generation" of children dependent on technology for survival is still being expanded. We were fortunate to have had such wide, community-based support to develop a program tailored essentially to Katie's needs. Therefore, we know programs can be developed throughout the country, pulling together all resources currently available to meet the unique needs of handicapped children.

PARENT ADVOCACY GROUPS: SKIP (Sick Kids Need Involved People)

The organization my husband and I were instrumental in building is a prime example of a community-based support model. It is now one of a large number of similar state programs throughout the country that may be used to serve as an example of the various "parent models" developed to share knowledge learned through hands-on experience.

However, it must be noted first that although parent advocacy models have for many years infiltrated systems dealing with specific diagnostic categories, they are just now being recognized for the unique expertise in training programs and systems building they can provide. For many years, parents and professionals coexisted in an adversarial relationship, arguing instead of cooperating. To change systems and attitudes takes a joint effort, and both groups have gained knowledge and confidence by working together. Parents need not be looked at as "those who cannot cope," but as strong, direction-setting individuals accepted on their merit; and professionals should be viewed as resources, not as gods. They learn to relate as people set in separate categories, but at a level beyond ego and territory. Much like the parent–educator model that it took PL 94-142 (and beyond) to establish, they have learned to share their expertise as individuals engaged in problem solving to achieve a better life for "their" children.

Organizations such as the Alliance for Genetic Support Groups carry their expertise further by recognizing the importance of this coalition building. We know also that by looking at the generic needs of all families of children with disabilities, we can cooperate to achieve the same rights any citizen in our country has to life, liberty, and the pursuit of happiness in the least restrictive environment possible.

Our organization, SKIP of Iowa, acts as a parent resource group to support programs for home health care for the technology dependent. Our goal is threefold. First, we educate parents, health care professionals, public and private funders, community-based agencies, and the general public on the advantages of and the need for home health care for technology-dependent children. Second, we act as a resource for families and providers to assist in expanding programs and developing new resources to meet the needs of this "new generation." Lastly, our goal is to identify and access resource services necessary for family support.

In meeting this final goal we have established a 24-hour hotline that provides persons, not only in Iowa but all over the nation, with a sensitive ear and a creative outlet to establish new paths in meeting the needs of all chronically ill/technology-dependent children. Parents of these children have learned to be crisis oriented. We are hoping through this hotline to create a link with established service systems, so that times of crisis become less frequent because the knowledge base has become broader for dealing with the everyday circumstances of this chronically ill population.

We feel this will lessen the handicaps imposed on the children and families whose lives center on medical technology and "will promote child and family self-sufficiency and autonomy in the least restrictive environment possible."

SKIP of Iowa is unique because it is run by parents who have overcome enormous hurdles. They are parents who have children living at home on medical technology. They have afforded their children the opportunities of family, home, and love that cannot be realized in an institution. But more importantly, they are parents who are willing to share their children with society. Because of this, our population has grown remarkably in its short life span. Knowledge and acceptance have broadened our base to several hundred families, from all walks of life, who at one time or another shared the fears and anxieties of having a child in an intensive care unit, dependent on some sort of life-saving technology. Because they are willing to share their knowledge, we have created a process for channeling negative circumstances into positive action.

Katie did not lead a deprived life in the hospital. She was happy, loved, and stimulated, but the reality of home and family have changed and enriched her life so much more. Through SKIP of Iowa, more children can live the reality of home care.

HOME CARE NEEDS AND PLANS

Achievement of Goals

How do we achieve the goals of home care? How do we know what families' needs are? First, we must ask questions. Some parents are able to articulate their needs very soon after the initial crisis has occurred; others will take longer. We must be there and be supportive of whatever decisions they are forced to make. We must continually reinforce: "together we can do what needs to be done for your child."

Next, professionals must recognize the parent as an integral part of the care team. As soon as it is feasible, the family must be united and helped to participate in their child's care while he or she is hospitalized, helping the bonding take place. Often, because they have relied on the professional to "make their child better," parents feel they no longer can add anything to their child's life. They need help to realize that this is not so. They need to be taught *how* to play their new role of primary care provider. They must be helped to make educated decisions. It is important to reinforce the fact that the child is *their* child. This will only help to strengthen them through the years to come. If they feel supported from the outset, they can become strong, loving parents. We must be honest, but be supportive as well. We must come to realize, if the child is to survive, that we must treat the family as a whole, not separate the weak from the strong, but improve the whole cluster.

Post-Hospital Care

How do we meet the needs of both patient and family when they leave the hospital? How do we make the transition easier?

First, we must make sure that the child's care plan is written with the home and community in mind. Medical needs of the child must be answered through appropriate community agencies. These may include public health, education, social services, proprietary home health care, nursing, support, and advocacy, to name a few. Then, we must meet with hands-on care providers. We must ask the family how workable the plan is *for them* and what they feel is necessary to meet the reality of home life. Remember, the child is *their* responsibility. They need to be involved in the decision making. So often when a problem arises the professionals come together to solve the problem and then explain to the parent what to do. If they, together with the parent, come to a resolution, then the parents will have had an opportunity to be discriminating in choosing the solution. It is a process of growing that can be achieved easily through cooperation and support.

When the medical plans have been met and the community care plan has been written, the families' other needs should be concentrated on. Funding must be secured to make sure the child is coming home to a family whose biggest fear is not giving up every worldly possession to pay for home care. There is a need to protect family well-being when identifying funding resources. An excessive burden should not be placed on parents and siblings to meet the needs of home care for their son or daughter, brother or sister. Long-term financial planning must be examined when discussing future needs for these children and their families. The feasibility of home care rests heavily on the funding element. Home care can be cost effective, but constant monitoring and assessments must be done to assure that quality care is provided and to define appropriate services needed for child and family support. Remember that the child does better at home. As a result home care can be less expensive.

At the same time, we must be cautious not to force children out of hospitals before the family and the community have been prepared to deal with them. If needs are not met prior to discharge, the family is set up for failure. The result can be disastrous for everyone involved.

Funders need to be extremely cautious because of the growth of proprietary home health care agencies. We must have standards and guidelines established and monitored by appropriate state agencies with experience in monitoring home care for disabled children. To do this, training must take place for those individuals charged to provide hands-on care as well as asse ssment and monitoring functions. Least costly care is a criterion, but quality must not suffer. Each child's case is different, and home circumstances must be examined. In other words, life with a ventilator-dependent child requiring two-person care in a single-parent family will be different from life in a two-parent home with that same child. Resources can be made available to both, but the extent to which added services will be necessary will need to be determined by the primary physician and the family.

Who is most appropriate to deliver that service must also be examined. Home health and nursing care agencies should be made aware that a person's experience in dealing with technology-dependent children in an intensive care unit in a hospital does not necessarily guarantee expertise delivering that care in the home setting, and vice versa. There are many newly identified community players who can fulfill roles with the proper training.

A second needed area to plan for is some type of relief for the parents. Because they will be taking on the many and varied facets of the child's care previously fulfilled by a variety of health care professionals, they will need to be relieved. This is especially necessary if extended-family members are not available to provide this relief. They will never totally forget their responsibility for the child they brought home, but they need the opportunity to get away for a while to be who they are. With a chronically ill child, the family's life revolves around the child's care. I wear my watch on Iowa time whenever I travel so that I know where Katie is every minute. As long as the team Mark and I have put together for her do their job, she will be fine. But we still need the time to get away to be who we are, not just Katie Beckett's parents, even though that role has given us the greatest pleasure in our lives.

I know that parents and professionals can work together as equal partners in developing care plans. We have had the opportunity to do that, but it all goes back to our first few months after Katie's initial crisis. We knew we were supported and listened to and sought out to make decisions; therefore, we can continue to do that for the rest of our lives.

ONGOING HOME CARE

After national attention focused on Katie's problems, we hoped that things would have improved substantially for other families. However, it became clear from hundreds and hundreds of phone calls for months after that this was just not the case. Often we were able to help others on a one-to-one basis by using federal contacts we had made, but it soon became clear that overall, consistent program development needed to be created. It was then that we began to work within our state to expand a network of services by helping to develop the Home Care Monitoring Program (see Table 8.1) through the Iowa Child Health Specialty Clinics (CHSC), formerly State Services for Crippled Children, a Title V agency headquartered at the University of Iowa. Separate child health centers in 12 statewide areas, each run by a pediatric nurse practitioner, became the focus for a coordinated, regionalized system of care for our more acute technology-dependent children.

With the advent of a nursing coordinator who can help the hospital unit develop a discharge plan with the home and community in mind (see Figure 8.2), many children who currently are locked in to the tertiary and secondary level care centers can return to their rural homes and still be assured of quality care. The pediatric nurse practitioner acts as a case manager, providing leadership for the community care team made up of the local physician, hospital, educational system, home health care agencies, social service agencies, funder, vendor, supplier, and any other support personnel necessary. Each takes on a responsibility for the specific child's care. Parent input begins even before the discharge plan is written. Families are continually supported by all members of the team, including a member of our SKIP of Iowa network. A process of interagency agreements establishes the communication link across disciplines to provide comprehensive, quality care. We feel this will prevent children from falling through the cracks.

We hope that someday these community care teams will provide coordination of services to all chronically ill children. We believe that by individualizing the care plans, providing case management and assessment guarantees, and developing a support network through realignment of services currently offered, these children, their families, and the citizens of our state will benefit from less duplication and, therefore, less costly care being provided. It will strengthen the bond of caring, making each person more acutely aware of what we can truly do together to be successful.

Mark and I feel strongly that plans similar to these can be developed throughout the fifty states. Through establishment of such programs, we will be supporting a stronger family bond and in turn stronger state and national bonds built on sharing and caring for one another. That is the ultimate goal for SKIP of Iowa: a coalition crossing diagnostic categories to look at children as children first and as children with disabilities second. We can, we should, and we must work together as people who care about the future.

TABLE 8.1 CHSC Home Care Monitoring Program

HOSPITALS

UNIVERSITY OF IOWA HOSPITALS & CLINICS NICU/PICU

Responsibilities
1. Assist in conducting continuing education program(s) for regional nurse.
2. Assist in education of regional nurse for specific patients/clients.

HOSPITAL CARE TEAM

Responsibilities
1. Identify children who are candidates for home care. (a)
2. Identify and prepare family/alternate caregivers to provide home care. (a) (b) (c)
3. Refer to CHSC home care monitoring program. (a) (b) (c)
4. Develop hospital plan of home services in cooperation with program coordinator, parent consultant, and regional nurse. (a) (b) (c) (d)

(a) Physician(s)   (b) Nurse(s)   (c) Support Services   (d) Child's Family

IOWA REGIONAL HOSPITALS NICU/PICU

Responsiblities
1. Assist in education of regional nurse for specific patients/clients.

Child Health Specialty Clinics (CHSC)

Program coordinator

Patient care responsibilities
1. Cooperate with staff of referring NICU/PICU in creation of hospital plan of home services.
2. Serve as liaison between referral hospital care team and community services network team.

Administrative responsibilities
1. Monitor the reporting & evaluation system to maintain quality assurance.
2. Conduct continuing education program(s) for regional nurses to assure they will have the skills needed to assure quality care.
3. Supervise regional nurse's activities in developing and implementing the hospital plan of home services and the community services network plan.
4. Develop standards for home care.

Regional center nurse

Patient care responsibilities
1. Assist in development and implementation of hospital plan of home services.
2. Organize the community services network plan.
3. Serve as liaison between members of the community services network team.
4. Serve as case manager to coordinate and monitor hospital plan of home services and community services network plan.

Administrative responsibilities
1. Identify local personnel and resources needed to provide home care as recommended in the hospital plan of home services.
2. Convene case planning conferences of local providers to create community services network plan.
3. Designate who will be responsible for providing "hands-on" care to maintain quality assurance.
4. Monitor records that are kept for reporting and evaluation system.

(continued)

TABLE 8.1 *(continued)*

Program parent consultant

Patient care responsibilities	Administrative responsibilities
1. Assist families to examine home care options.	1. Parent advocacy.
2. Provide direct family support.	2. Review and monitor financial status of referred families.
3. Assist families with financial planning.	3. Assist in development of hospital plan of home services and community service network plan.
	4. Identify and monitor activities of SKIP of Iowa personnel.

COMMUNITY

COMMUNITY SERVICES NETWORK TEAM*

Responsibilities

1. Provide for child's daily physical, emotional, and social needs.	Child's family
2. Provide primary medical services for acute care, crisis intervention, and health maintenance.	Child's local physician
3. Make acute hospital care available and be lifeline for patients from home to appropriate hospital.	Community hospital
4. Supervise or provide "hands-on" patient care in the home.	Home care program
5. Pay for services provided child eligible for public/private financial assistance.	Funding agency
6. Assure that transportation and required services as electricity, etc., will be available on a 24-hour basis.	Emergency support personnel
7. Provide a variety of intervention, educational, and related service programs in the home.	Education system
8. Provide support to family with advice and counseling.	Family support group
9. Be available on 24-hour call to provide or service equipment used in home care.	Equipment vendors
10. Provide services such as respite care and special transportation.	Service programs

---

*Not all of these individuals/agencies will be necessary for each child.

FIGURE 8.2 Child's coordinated plans of home care.

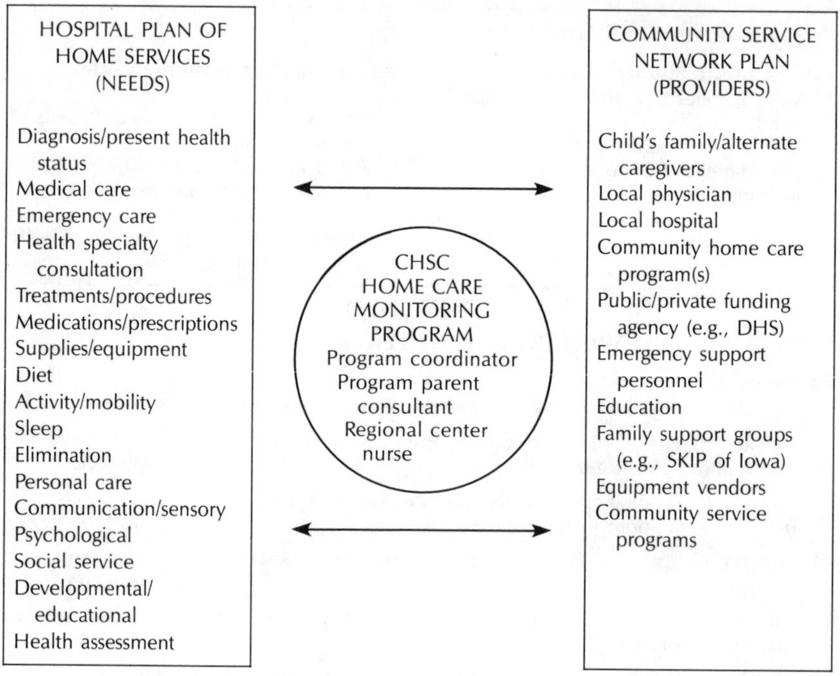

HOSPITAL PLAN OF
HOME SERVICES
(NEEDS)

Diagnosis/present health
  status
Medical care
Emergency care
Health specialty
  consultation
Treatments/procedures
Medications/prescriptions
Supplies/equipment
Diet
Activity/mobility
Sleep
Elimination
Personal care
Communication/sensory
Psychological
Social service
Developmental/
  educational
Health assessment

CHSC
HOME CARE
MONITORING
PROGRAM
Program coordinator
Program parent
  consultant
Regional center
  nurse

COMMUNITY SERVICE
NETWORK PLAN
(PROVIDERS)

Child's family/alternate
  caregivers
Local physician
Local hospital
Community home care
  program(s)
Public/private funding
  agency (e.g., DHS)
Emergency support
  personnel
Education
Family support groups
  (e.g., SKIP of Iowa)
Equipment vendors
Community service
  programs

III

New Challenges

9

Children Without Homes

Elaine Lugovoy, R.N., M.A.

The problem of caring for children whose families are unable to provide for them when they are ready for hospital discharge has been with us for a long time. Infants born to families with complex social problems, serious parental medical conditions, or low family coping resources are at high risk for ultimately requiring foster-care placement even if they themselves are physically healthy. Children with serious health conditions, however, have needs that place an extra burden on their families—a burden sufficient to tip the scales and render a family unable to care for the child at home. For a long time, this added burden has led children with handicaps or chronic conditions to need foster care at a rate that exceeds foster-care placement of the physically healthy. The increasing complexity of home health care needs of children with special health conditions has produced considerable growth of the population of children whose care cannot easily be absorbed within their own homes. Additionally, those without homes of their own cannot always have their needs met by traditional foster care. In New York City, as in other places, there are children who remain in hospitals for weeks, months, and even years awaiting placement. They are truly a new group of homeless children.

Many of these children, hospitalized with severe chronic medical conditions that have stabilized, could be cared for, with special medical assistance, in a home setting. The needs of these children and their families do, however, require a wide range of interventions, including supplemental services to already existing homes, traditional and enhanced foster care, and medical foster care or specialized programs such as deinstitutionalized group homes.

This chapter reviews the history of the problems in New York of developing a system of care that is responsive to the needs of children who are hard to place because of their physical health conditions.

HISTORY

The records document peaks and valleys of public policy efforts in New York City to develop a system of care that is able to meet the needs of hard-to-place children effectively (King, 1985). In the mid-1960s, welfare agencies, hospitals, and public agencies formally joined together, changing practices, procedures, and policies to develop a more responsive system of providing appropriate care for "boarder children." Boarder children are those who are forced to remain in the hospital without a medical basis for their continued hospitalization. For those with chronic illness, this is the period of time after their medical situations have been stabilized when discharge is delayed because there is no home available to receive them and/or to provide adequate care. In response to the problem, two child care agencies stationed social workers in a few of the larger municipal hospitals to expedite the placement of children and developed nearby satellite foster homes to assure rapid rehospitalization of the children if this were required. A study was made of the boarder children problem in five hospitals, and a computer tracking system was designed to provide early identification of potential boarder babies and to follow up on these children. As an incentive to secure homes for boarder children with special needs, the agencies began paying foster parents an additional rate for caring for children with special health needs. Hospitals began to be more alert to anticipating which children might need placement and to initiate appropriate referrals at the time of admission. Finding foster homes for hospitalized children with special needs became a high priority of the child welfare system.

In 1972, officials from the New York City Health and Hospitals Corporation and the Bureau of Child Welfare announced that "132 children had finally been placed in foster homes . . . some after three or more years in hospitals" (King, 1985, p. 3). Many of these were children with fairly routine ongoing health problems, such as asthma and epilepsy, and those with developmental delays. Although slow and inefficient, the system did work for some of these children.

Over time, however, the movement to aid boarder children lost its momentum, and the computer tracking system was abandoned. In 1977, a report of a New York State Select Committee on Child Abuse, *Forgotten Children: The Plight of Hospital Boarder Children*, warned, "if one could read all of the relevant statutes, administrative rules and regulations, and descriptions of programs, one would probably think that there is no reason for keeping children in hospitals unnecessarily. On paper the systems seem to exist, but [they do] not work" (cited in King, 1985, p. 5).

RENEWED ATTENTION

More recently, there has been an acute rise in concern about the issues of children languishing in hospitals. Superimposed on the chronic concern about the adverse effects of hospitalization on child development have been three new forces: (1) concern about the medically fragile child who is dependent on technology, (2) the emerging pediatric population with AIDS, and (3) the placement of caps on hospitalization costs.

These three forces have brought new issues into focus. They have resulted in a new awareness of the delicate balance between the burden of the illness and the family's available resources to handle that burden (Stein & Jessop, 1984). In this framework, extraordinary resources may have to be mobilized in order to handle the technology-dependent child at home, while even children with inactive disease, such as those who are positive for the human immunodeficiency virus (HIV), may not be able to be managed in very marginal homes.

A significant action on behalf of hospitalized handicapped children took place in 1982, when the Surgeon General convened a workshop on "Children with Handicaps and their Familes." This meeting gave formal recognition to the existence of a large population of technology-dependent children who were spending most of their childhoods in hospitals, and it helped to establish a visible force in support of home care as an option for these children and their families. A strong movement has evolved that advocates keeping disabled children in their own homes, with strategies developed to remove all barriers, whether physical, social, or financial. (See Adam, Chapter 13; Freedman & Pierce, Chapter 14; Bilotti, Chapter 15.)

Renewed attention to the problem of hospitalized boarder children was also triggered by requests received in 1983 for foster home placements for hard-to-place children with a newly identified disease, pediatric AIDS. In March 1985, confronted with the rising numbers of children with AIDS, Pauline Thomas, M.D., Director of AIDS Surveillance, New York City Department of Health, and her staff gathered data by telephone survey from 45 New York hospitals during a three-day period. Two percent of the estimated total census, or 56 boarder children, were identified, not including healthy children awaiting placement. The children ranged in age from 4 weeks to 16 years, and they had been medically ready for discharge for from 1 week to 6 years. Diagnostic categories included cancer,

diabetes, epilepsy, severe mental retardation, tuberculosis, and technological needs such as nasogastric feeding and ventilator use. Fewer than
half of the children actually had pediatric AIDS. Of the total, 43% could
have been cared for at home by the children's parents with special medical help, and the other 57% were clearly in need of foster care. It was
estimated that at an average cost of $500 per day per child, inpatient care
of these 56 boarder children was costing $28,000 daily. In 1985, Bernard
Guyer, M.D., then director, Maternal and Child Health, Massachusetts
Department of Public Health, reported a $1 million cost reduction by
changing the care of six ventilator-dependent children from hospital to
home.

Today, New York City is once again facing a boarder baby crisis. The
Citizen's Committee for Children (1987) reported in March 1987 that there
were 300 boarder children in New York hospitals. The sharp increase has
been attributed primarily to the large number of infants born to drug-
using mothers. Some of these are healthy babies, with no problems requiring hospitalization, for whom foster homes cannot be found. They are
mentioned here to dramatize some of the difficulties encountered in finding new foster homes even for well children; these problems are, of
course, compounded for children with special health needs. Presently,
foster parents receive minimal monthly allotments—in New York, this
ranges from $340 to $460. This subsidy is for food and other needs of the
foster child, exclusive of clothes and medical expenses. But recruitment
of foster parents has become increasingly more difficult in recent years
as more women have entered the job market outside their homes.

Finding traditional foster homes for well children, however, is a relatively easy issue compared to the problem of finding homes for medically needy children. Despite the many difficulties in finding such homes,
foster care agencies in New York, as stated earlier, have been able to find
some suitable homes for disabled children with chronic conditions. In
some instances, families may receive extra financial incentives for their
care.

However, there is a growing number of children whose complex medical needs cannot be met by their own families or by traditional foster
care. In the last decade, the partial solutions to the boarder babies' problem found in the 1960s and early 1970s have not kept pace with the medical advances and increasing complexity of home management for a new
class of children. Some of these are children whose homes would be adequate if the technical demands for care were less extreme. These children
represent a new class of youngsters who have become dependent on the
hospital environment, but whose best long-term interests cannot be met
there.

STRATEGIES FOR ADDRESSING THE PROBLEM

Two strategies that can be used to address the problem of children with extensive health care needs are (1) increasing home health care and supplemental outreach services to the children's own families, and (2) providing placement and outreach services, where necessary, outside their own homes.

Services in the Home

The problems of caring for medically needy children in home settings prompted the conference on "Home Care for Hospitalized Children with Chronic Medical Conditions, Including Pediatric AIDS," in April 1985. Conference participants, including representatives from hospitals, home care programs, and social welfare agencies, as well as officials from New York City and State child welfare and health departments, called for steps to actively pursue the development of a program for home care, medical guardianship, and foster care for children with chronic medical problems.

As part of the workshop on "Children with HIV Infection and Their Families," convened on April 6, 1987, by Surgeon General C. Everett Koop, the problems of finding appropriate homes for all HIV-infected children when ready for hospital discharge were deliberated at length. Participants all recommended increased supports for the natural family of the HIV-infected child, including, but not limited to, improved housing, home care, or respite care. Despite these supports, however, conference participants emphasized that some families will not be capable of caring for their children because of social problems, parental illness, or parental death. Traditional, individual foster care represents the best of possible alternatives. In this respect, in addition to increased funding, foster care families will also need such additional supports as daycare centers and home health care. Finally, conference participants proposed an innovative model program of nurturing homes for a small number of HIV-infected children. In these community-based homes, the children would be cared for by appropriately trained and supervised caregivers who would bond with and care for the children.

Initially, the pediatric AIDS children were viewed as a group separate from other chronically ill children. As the AIDS children live longer, however, their needs for socialization, education, and respite have become similar to other chronically ill children. Mary Boland, R.N., M.S.W., Director, Children's Hospital AIDS Program of United Hospital, Newark, New Jersey, speaking before the plenary session of the Surgeon General's Workshop, discussed the importance of a chronic disease model in managing children with AIDS and their families (USDHHS, 1987). An additional recommendation made to the Surgeon General was that existing systems for handicapped and disabled children . . . be accessible to HIV-infected children.

Unfortunately, enhanced support services are not always available for natural families. Sometimes the assessment that a child with a chronic illness cannot go home is based on a less than optimal evaluation of the family and home or on the basis of accepting the status quo, rather than on creative problem solving in a flexible system that emphasizes partnership and collaboration with the family. It is a sad irony that, on occasion, extra supports (e.g., a visiting nurse, respite care, or transportation) can be made available to a foster family that are not available to natural families.

Changing the System

Recently the New Jersey Division for Youth and Family Services (DYFS), the state agency responsible for foster care services, adopted a new set of initiatives in an attempt to solve some of the problems specific to children with AIDS. The experiences encountered and issues raised in the process provide a focus for discussion of concern around the provision of services for children who have other special health needs. In April 1988 in New Jersey there were 146 children with pediatric AIDS. Forty-one were in foster care, 5 were in a special group home, and 11 were hospitalized for medical reasons. The remaining were at home with their families. The absence of an "AIDS boarder–baby" hospital problem is attributed to the close working relation begun early on between DYFS administration and the Childrens Hospital AIDS Program (CHAP) staff at United Hospital, Newark, where most of these children receive their care. DYFS has provided CHAP with the funding for an additional full-time social worker, and DYFS staff and foster parents have been trained by the program staff, who are available for frequent case consultations. This is important in order to ensure the children's medical safety, but it is not a universal feature of placement programs for medically at-risk children. In addition, foster parents have been provided with such supports as home health aide services, transportation, and counseling. Most important, a "difficulty of care" rate has been established that gives foster parents who care for children with AIDS $700 monthly beyond the $200–$300 monthly base rate.

Unlike New York City, where most of the direct foster care is contracted out to voluntary care agencies, in New Jersey DYFS has chosen to provide all of the foster care services itself. Although each model has some advantages, it is essential that some agency within the system has explicit responsibility for services.

In New Jersey, when children who cannot return to their own homes are ready for hospital discharge, DYFS is under considerable pressure to find foster homes as quickly as possible. However, if a child has a serious medical problem, it is often difficult to locate an appropriate foster home. As a result, children are sometimes placed in distant locations out of the county. Occasionally, children remain hospitalized for several weeks, but ultimately DYFS is under pressure to find some solution that will allow the child to be discharged from the hospital. The result is not always a good placement. It may be a children's rehabilitative hospital, skilled nursing facility, or residential school that is far from optimal for the child's needs.

There are a small number of foster parents who can manage the care of medically needy children, but their number is limited, and increasing demands are being made on them. Their homes are frequently overused, and sometimes inadequately supervised or monitored. As many as four or five medically needy children have been placed in one foster home, a situation that can overwhelm even the best of families. Often, foster parents suffer from burnout and leave the system.

Frequently, foster parents who accept children with health needs are ill-equipped to care for them adequately, in terms of both their training and their emotional ability to handle the situation. In New York City foster care agencies, community health nurses supervise the health of foster care children, but in New Jersey, DYFS district office staff have no easily available health professional for consultation. Neither the foster parents nor the caseworkers have received training in understanding the medical needs of many of the children in their care.

One important positive move to address this problem was the establishment, in 1983, of a Pediatric Consultant on a state level by DYFS. This pediatrician travels broadly throughout New Jersey, consulting with DYFS workers and health professionals and helping to resolve difficulties and establish appropriate care plans for children with difficult-to-manage medical problems. But for most day-to-day medical problems, social workers are forced to cope alone.

The system, therefore, remains somewhat of a patchwork. For example, in Newark, if the hospital discharge plan includes a referral for the pediatric home health care services provided by the local visiting nurse service (Community Health Care for North Jersey), pediatric community health nurses will visit these homes. They try to teach the foster parents appropriate home health care and monitor and coordinate the child's health care. Frequently, however, the nursing services are not coordinated with DYFS foster care casework services.

Several new initiatives have grown out of the identification of these issues. For example, DYFS administration has recognized the immediate need for a body of foster parents who are adequately trained to care for children with special medical needs and who can be rapidly accessed when a special need arises. One of the Newark District DYFS offices has recently obtained funding for a collaborative project with the local visiting nurse service. Pediatric home health nurses will train a group of foster parents and social workers in home health care of children with handicapped conditions. The pediatric nurses will also be available for frequent home visiting and case-management consultations and discharge planning with DYFS caseworkers and hospital staff (NJDYFS, 1986).

Novel Approaches to Medical Foster Care

When natural parents cannot manage even with supports, novel approaches are needed. Two innovative programs that have responded to this situation are discussed below. The first is still in the planning phase; the second has already been implemented.

Henry L. Barnett, M.D., and his colleagues at the Children's Aid Society have a medical foster care program that would provide a range of comprehensive foster care, home health care, and medical services to children now hospitalized and in need of such placement. This specialized program would recruit as foster parents qualified individuals who have had some related health experience and can demonstrate that they can make knowledgeable health decisions if needed, can understand and manage complex equipment, and have the maturity and stability needed to cope with children who may have life-threatening illnesses. Medical foster parents would receive an "exceptional rate" above that ordinarily paid for foster care.

The overall program would be directed by a M.S.W. social worker experienced in child welfare and medical social services. A caseworker would provide casework services to the child and both the biological and foster parents, work closely with the nursing staff in coordinating the child's care, and participate in the training of medical foster parents. A pediatric nurse clinician, assisted by a public health nurse, would provide extensive home health care training, monitor and coordinate the child's care, and make frequent home visits to assist the medical foster parent in providing health care in a home setting.

To ensure a high quality of medical foster care, the children would be under the medical supervision of the system specialists presently responsible for their care in a tertiary center and of a local primary care pediatrician who would provide ongoing pediatric care and important liaison with the hospital staff.

A second program of medical foster care is already operating successfully through the Children's Crisis Center in Jacksonville, Florida. This program focuses on severely abused and neglected children with ongoing medical problems who are placed in foster homes where the foster parent is a nurse (Davis, Foster, & Whitworth, 1984). The program began in 1980 as a pilot project, when the Children's Crisis Center recruited three foster medical homes to care for children who would have been hospitalized indefinitely because of burns, a gastrostomy, and a tracheotomy. Two of the children returned to their parents in 24 months, and the third was subsequently placed in regular foster care.

The rationale for using nurses as foster parents is based on their licensure, their scope of practice, which includes physical assessment skills and patient teaching, and their accountability for nursing practice. Unlike traditional foster care, biological families are encouraged to visit these homes in which the foster parent provides health education, role modeling, and advocacy. Medical foster families need and receive extensive counseling and support, including respite care.

Nurses must hold a current license in Florida and have their own professional liability insurance. Based on legal advice, respite care or babysitting may be provided only by an approved registered nurse. Access to the child's medical records by the foster mother/nurse is legally sanctioned. Successful recruitment appears related to the employment market for nurses. When there is an increase in job opportunities in health and hospitals, recruitment becomes more difficult.

The program was made fiscally possible by coordinating funding streams from two existing programs. Licensed as foster parents, the nurses receive the state foster-care payment rate. In addition—and what is unique—the nurses also receive $400 to $1,000 monthly for their nursing services, as determined by a "complexity of care" scale (Davis, Foster, & Whitworth, 1984). This subsidy for nursing care is provided through the State Children's Medical Services (previously known as Florida's Crippled Children Program). Patient care dollars, which would have paid for hospitalization care, were used to fund the nursing care subsidy. In one year, the placement of seven children in Medical Foster Care saved an estimated $245,000 (Davis, Foster, & Whitworth, 1984).

CONCLUSION

Over the last two years, some progress has been made in solving the problem of finding homes for boarder children with chronic illness. A large number of programs have been put in place to strengthen natural families, such as those described in this volume by Beckett (Chapter 8), Adam (Chapter 13), Bilotti (Chapter 15), and Freedman and Pierce (Chapter 14). Other programs, such as New Alternatives for Children, a recently established organization, are helping families who alone cannot meet the complex demands of bringing chronically ill children home. This group acts as a bridge between the hospital and the home. By providing intensive support services, including a van for transportation, the hospital discharge of about 25 children into their own homes has been made possible. One child care agency in New York, Leak Watts, addressing the problems of finding homes for pediatric AIDS children, has also been able to place about 25 children in foster homes in its first year and continues to seek more of such homes. However, many boarder children with severely handicapping conditions still remain in hospitals in New York and elsewhere for longer than they should because of our inability to establish viable mechanisms for providing the specialized care they need.

At the 1985 home care conference, Eulala King, M.S.W., Director, Foster Care Services, The Children's Aid Society, described the history of the boarder baby problem over a 25-year span. She concluded her presentation by stating, "If there is a mission for this conference, it must be that we pool our collective wisdom and not repeat our past history of assuming that the boarder baby population is a one-time problem, ready to yield to intervention in time of crisis" (King, 1985, p. 7). That advice is as true today as it was then. We need, instead, to develop flexible and creative solutions to maximize the natural family's ability to make an adequate home for a child with a chronic medical condition and, if that fails, to provide an appropriate alternative.

REFERENCES

Citizen's Committee for Children of New York. (1987). *The New York City child welfare crisis.* New York: Author.

Davis, A. B., Foster, P. H., & Whitworth, J. M. (1984). Medical foster family care: A cost effective solution to a community problem. *Child Welfare, LXIII*(4), 341–349.

King, E. (1985, April). *Boarder babies 1960–1985.* Paper presented at the Conference on Home Care for Hospitalized Children Including Pediatric Aids, New York.

New Jersey Division for Youth and Family Services, Newark West District Office. (1986, November). *Newark foster care health project.* (unpublished proposal)

Stein, R. E. K., & Jessop, D. J. (1984). Does pediatric home care make a difference for children with chronic illness? Findings from the pediatric ambulatory care treatment study. *Pediatrics, 73,* 845–853.

U.S. Department of Health and Human Services. (1987). *Report of the Surgeon General's Workshop on Children with HIV Infection and Their Families.* DHHS Publication No. HRS-D-MC 87-1.

10

Community-Based Self-Help Efforts

Leslie E. Borck, Ph.D

Chronic illness in a child is a severe stressor for families, and there is accumulating evidence to suggest that such an ongoing physical illness may lead to financial, marital, social, and other health problems within the family. Families can become socially isolated, frequently unable to hire babysitters or get any respite from their 24-hour care responsibilities.

The concept of social support has become increasingly popular. Research in such diverse fields as medicine, epidemiology, sociology, and psychology has documented the relationship between social support systems and an individual's vulnerability to physical and mental problems. An individual's social relationships not only play a role in the determination of health status, but seem to be directly related to mortality risk (Berkman & Syme, 1979).

Albee (1980) has pointed out the positive correlation between social support and physical and mental well-being. He has suggested that the incidence of emotional distress and the severity of emotional disturbance can be reduced by enhancing coping skills, raising self-esteem, and establishing social support groups. A major form of social stress involves the feeling of powerlessness. Community efforts aimed at assisting people during a period of crisis can prevent despair and suffering.

Although friends and extended-family members may provide significant amounts of support, information, and concrete assistance, there are other supportive interventions that can be developed. Community-based efforts should be designed to maximize the adjustment and psychological well-being of each member of the family system involved in the care of the child. This requires an orientation toward prevention through a community-strengths model (Rappaport, 1977), which builds on the strengths already found in the individual or community rather than on apparent weaknesses.

Among interventions designed to maximize community strengths, there are three strategies that represent community-based efforts to help families cope with the stress of a chronically ill child. Two are designed to enlarge a family's social support network: the creation of self-help/mutual support groups and the strengthening of informal natural helping networks. Both underscore the potential of nonprofessional resources. The third strategy is respite.

ENLARGING THE SOCIAL SUPPORT NETWORKS: SELF-HELP GROUPS

Gottlieb (1981) reviews two types of planned interventions intended to expand the social support available to people. One type is aimed at bringing people into contact with similar peers. Joined together in a mutually supportive way, this type of self-help or mutual aid group encourages the sharing of information, resources, coping strategies, and friendship.

As defined by Katz and Bender (1976), self-help groups are

> voluntary small group structures for mutual aid and the accomplishment of a special purpose. They are usually formed by peers who have come together for mutual assistance in satisfying a common need, overcoming a common handicap or life-disrupting problem, and bringing about desired social and/or personal change. The initiators and members of such groups perceive that their needs are not, or cannot be, met by or through existing social institutions. They emphasize face-to-face social interactions and the assumption of personal responsibility by members. (p. 9)

Membership is voluntary and is restricted to those who either presently or in the past have suffered a stressful situation. Common activities of membership include fellowship, crisis assistance, mutual aid, self-development, and social action.

Groups stress experiential rather than professional knowledge. Group members become role models for each other, through direct demonstration of coping skills and problem-solving strategies gained by direct experience. Each member is ultimately recognized as having some expertise in the particular problem situation. Promotion of self-help groups or an agency designed to create and support these groups can encourage their social support-strengthening potential.

In the case of the relatively rare situational crisis, such as the diagnosis of a serious illness in a child, it is likely that members of the family's existing social network will not be sufficient sources of support. Additional information and contact with others who have shared similar experiences can provide problem-solving strategies and reduce the sense of uniqueness.

There is a misconception that support groups provide a forum in which "misery loves company." The principles of self-help groups are that their members are a group of peers. Since they share homogeneous problem situations, they afford people an instant sense of being connected to others who understand, of not being alone. Families of chronically ill children report a sense of impotence because decisions about their child are being made by others (e.g., doctors, school system). Active helping roles of participants in support groups can help restore a sense of control and competence. Group meetings tend to be upbeat, positive, and inclined to stress the importance of hope. It is an approach that stresses the emotional assistance that is greatly needed by families adjusting to a chronic illness.

Gottlieb (1982) documents how self-help groups bring about changes in the members' social network. More than one-third of the members of each type of self-help group in his study maintained either daily or numerous weekly extra-group contacts with co-members. The same proportion reported several monthly contacts with other group members.

Self-help groups are proliferating nationwide. A conservative estimate is that there are more than 15 million people throughout the country participating in self-help groups of some sort.

Until recently the majority of participants in problem-focused self-help groups have been white adults, primarily middle-class in economic status; but the self-help group approach is a viable one for a wider audience of participants. To expand this nonprofessional source of support beyond the white middle class will require more culturally individualized models of support and creative new outreach efforts.

It will be necessary to duplicate the existence of many self-help groups so that a network of groups exists in which leaders and participants speak languages other than English. It may be that the historically most frequently chosen meeting site, a church or synagogue, would not be the most wisely chosen site for dealing with common problems in a group with more heterogeneous membership. New forms of community organizing, eliciting the support of community helpers, become important in attempting to involve families of different cultural values in the self-help group movement.

Mutual aid strategies can also be designed as one-to-one peer-monitoring networks. Two such programs are a peer counseling project being conducted by the Preventive Intervention Research Center (PIRC) for Child Health at Albert Einstein College of Medicine–Montefiore Medical Center (see Halper & Ireys, Chapter 18, for a discussion of the PIRC) and a program begun at the Westchester Self-Help Clearinghouse through funds given by the William T. Grant Foundation. They are both programs that provide a buddy system for chronically ill adolescents. The purpose of these projects is to make available emotional support from a role model who has successfully adjusted to a chronic physical illness. Based on the self-help/mutual support group model, adolescents who are successfully coping with a chronic illness can be trained as mentors for others more newly diagnosed with a disorder. Not only can these mentors offer enourgement and support and decrease the patient's loneliness and fear, but the mentor offers a concrete example of successful coping. He or she becomes living proof that a satisfactory level of coping with a physical problem can exist. The newly diagnosed patient is typically more likely to ask questions and express concerns to a peer, since the sense of inhibition or embarrassment is decreased in such situations. For children who are chronically ill, other children can also be helpful in showing how to maintain some level of independence from parents who may become overprotective.

In addition, the PIRC model demonstrates the beneficial effects of the training and counseling on the peer mentors themselves. The PIRC program has also found that the younger adolescents seem to gain a great deal from the counselors in terms of support for nonillness-related issues that are normal concerns for adolescents and that support in these arenas may be as important as modeling illness coping.

Although there are considerable data suggesting a noncategorical approach to chronic childhood illness (i.e., one that is not disease-specific) (Stein & Jessop, 1982), the decision was made for the Westchester Self-Help Clearinghouse mentoring network to match adolescents with others diagnosed with the same disease. Five chronic childhood illnesses were selected: asthma, juvenile arthritis, epilepsy, diabetes, and renal disease. The program is known as Buddies for Health.

In both models, the training needs of the volunteer buddies providing the support to the newly diagnosed children were deemed generic across the diagnostic categories (e.g., communication skills, the qualities of a good mentor, making the initial phone contact, logistics of the peer counseling system network) and were integrated into one common curriculum.

ENLARGING THE SOCIAL SUPPORT NETWORK: NATURAL HELPERS

The second type of community-based intervention is the strengthening of natural community helping networks. Most of the families being addressed in the context of this book will ultimately have their children at home. Most of the help and support that these families receive in their day-to-day needs comes from their neighbors, co-workers, clergy, school nurses, librarians, pharmacists, and other such natural helpers.

As documented by Gottlieb (1981), the mobilization of natural helpers improves the supportive quality of an individual's network. This can be done by teaching helping skills to categories of people, such as those listed above, known to be informal helping agents, or natural helpers (Borck, Fawcett, & Lichtenberg, 1982; Danish, 1978; Weisenfeld & Weis, 1979). These natural helpers are generally sympathetic people within the individual's social network. The concept of a natural helper is not an easy notion to communicate. Those who reach out a helping hand to others often do not see themselves as having a special role. Interventions to optimize the quality of help and information they can provide represent a second way to improve the quality of support available to stressed families. Various curricula have been designed to sharpen the helping skills of informal helpers (Borck & Fawcett, 1982). Most include practice in effective listening, understanding feelings, and problem solving.

The Natural Helper Training Program at the Westchester Self-Help Clearinghouse began in 1981. Its desired outcome was to identify people within designated communities who reach out to others and to structure an educational series for them to sharpen their ability to listen, share, and be better helpers. The goals were to create a heightened sense of caring about neighbors and to enable acting in more supportive ways in order to reduce feelings of isolation within their communities.

Six training sessions were offered. Besides sharpening listening skills, natural helpers were taught to recognize when professional intervention was needed and to make appropriate referrals. Individuals were not asked to act in any official way or to take on a specific role as a result of their participation in the training sessions. They were selected because they naturally reach out to others in the course of their everyday lives, and it was hoped that these enhanced skills would be woven into use as they interacted as natural helpers.

RESPITE

The third community-based effort that will be described is respite, a mechanism to allow caregivers to take time out from their care responsibilities. It is unique because it is a service for the entire family, not just for client or parents. It is one of the few family-oriented services that is designed to support people living in their home communities. As mentioned previously, the burdens of grief and stress upon a family in which a child is diagnosed with a chronic illness or physical disability can precipitate family breakdown. It is believed that respite care helps maintain family stability by improving interpersonal relationships and decreasing family stress.

Various models of respite care are available throughout the country. In out-of-home models, the dependent family member is cared for in a residential facility or another family's home on a short-term basis. The in-home model offers the advantages of providing the service in the family's own home. A sample of such an in-home respite program is Project Time-Out.

Project Time-Out is a community-based family support program administered by the Westchester Self-Help Clearinghouse. It is designed to provide in-home respite services to families caring for a developmentally disabled member at home. Sitters/companions are trained in the specific care needs of the dependent family member. Families typically use their free time to attend to personal business, participate in recreational activities, or simply interact with other family members without the burden of care responsibilities.

Training of respite providers depends on the population for whom they will care. Included in training are basic first aid and home safety, an overview of the relevant physical or developmental disability, and an understanding of the impact of an illness or disability on the family.

There are many models of in-home respite care. Some models recruit and train volunteers as respite providers. Others use nonprofessional community members who are trained and then paid as respite providers by either the family or the sponsoring agency. Still others use certified homemakers or visiting nurses. The decision rests on the care needs required by the child and by the financial resources of either the family or social service system.

CONCLUSION

The common denominator of every community-based project described is the use of nonprofessional helpers. The empowerment of nonprofessionals calls upon professionals in the health care arena to define a new set of roles for themselves.

In the case of self-help groups, many are self-initiating and self-sustaining. They are frequently autonomous of professional leadership and receive no external funding. This is not to imply that there are no roles for the professional; rather, the roles are different from the traditional ones of group leader, expert, and initiator.

Promoting community support programs requires professionals to recognize that the roles of referral agent, trainer, consultant, and researcher are the new ones needed. Access to agency resources (e.g., a meeting room for the group, photocopying, bulk mailing) is what nonprofessional groups need of the professional helping system. These are not typically services that are deemed "professional," and yet, without this form of support, frequently self-help groups cannot exist within the community.

It is ironic that at a time when the role of social support is being documented as important to help individuals buffer stress, there is a decreased amount of such support available in modern society. The traditional nuclear family of two parents is no longer necessarily the norm. Families today often consist of only one parent. The multigenerational family living within the same community also no longer exists to the extent it once did. This requires the design of other systems to approximate the stability and calming reassurance the extended family once provided.

Even the definition of community has changed. Where once families living in close proximity to one another looked out for each other's interests and families, this is not necessarily true today. Many of these responsibilities have been replaced by social service agencies and programs.

In response to all these variables, it is imperative that the creation of community-based efforts for families be given high priority. Funding and resources will always be limited, but we must remember the quality-of-life issue for families in helping them adjust to the stressful experience of caring for a chronically ill child.

REFERENCES

Albee, G. W. (1980). *The third annual Gisela Konopka lecture*. St. Paul: Center for Youth Development and Research, University of Minnesota.

Berkman, L. F., & Syme, S. L. (1979). Social networks, host resistance, and mortality: A nine-year follow-up study of Alameda County residents. *American Journal of Epidemiology, 109* (2), 186–204.

Borck, L. E., & Fawcett, S. B. (1982). *Learning counseling and problem-solving skills*. New York: Hayworth.

Borck, L. E., Fawcett, S. B., & Lichtenberg, J. W. (1982). Training counseling and problem-solving skills with university students. *American Journal of Community Psychology, 10* (2), 225–237.

Danish, S. J. (1978, August). *Facilitating natural care-giving as a means of improving a community's quality of life*. Paper presented at the meeting of the American Psychological Association, Toronto, Ontario, Canada.

Gottlieb, B. H. (1981). Preventive interventions involving social networks and social support. In B. H. Gottlieb (Ed.). *Social networks and social supports* (p. 211). Beverly Hills, CA: Sage Publications.

Gottlieb, B. H. (1982). Mutual help groups: Members' view of their benefits and of roles for professionals. *Prevention in Human Services, 1* (3), 55–68.

Katz, A. H., & Bender, E. I. (1976). *The strength in us: Self-help groups in the modern world*. New York: New Viewpoints.

Rappaport, J. (1977). *Community psychology: Values, research and action*. New York: Holt, Rinehart & Winston.

Stein, R., & Jessop, D. (1982). A noncategorical approach to chronic childhood illness. *Public Health Reports, 97* (4), 354–362.

Weisenfeld, A. R., & Weis, H. M. (1979). Hairdressers and helping: Influencing the behavior of formal caregivers. *Professional Psychology, 7,* 786–792.

11

Transition to Adulthood

Stephen A. Richardson, Ph.D.

There is little systematic knowledge about the transition to adulthood of young people with chronic conditions. To some extent the kind of chronic condition, whether it is an illness, disorder, or disability, will have some influence on this transition. The studies presented in this chapter deal primarily with young people who have physical disabilities but may serve as a model in the study of transition for those with other forms of chronic disorders. The extent to which the transition will be different for those with other forms of chronic disorders will require comparable studies.

Although the two studies used here followed up children with cerebral palsy into adulthood, it is important to stress that their findings are not confined solely to cerebral palsy patients. In both studies the young people had received good medical care. The authors of the studies summarize their findings as follows:

> The most striking feature, shared to some extent by all those who require prolonged training, is immaturity. . . . It does seem, however, that these children have been denied experience in many activities, which given encouragement, they could have enjoyed. Many behave as though they had gone through their childhood on a "conveyor belt" system which involved no real responsibility or need for awareness of life around them. (Ingram, 1964, pp. 93–94)
>
> Cerebral palsied adults who are potentially employable and capable of social activity are typically unemployed and socially isolated. (Klapper & Birch, 1966, p. 655)

CHILDHOOD EXPERIENCES OF CHRONICALLY ILL CHILDREN

At an annual meeting of the American Academy of Cerebral Palsy, a panel of young adults with cerebral palsy was asked to talk about their experiences while growing up in the 1960s (Richardson, 1972). The following are some of the points they made.

1. Professionals in the health services who were responsible for them were preoccupied with what was biologically wrong with them and with treatment for their physical problems. These treatments took precedence over their schooling and their social development.

2. They were often as children segregated with others who had cerebral palsy, and this later made it more difficult to relate to peers who were not disabled.

3. Other people assumed they should always be receiving help and that others should take responsibility for them. They resented not having opportunities to give help to others and to take responsibility. Similarly, because they were so closely supervised as children, they did not have sufficient freedom and independence to make their own mistakes and learn from them.

4. They felt pressure to conform with the cultural stereotype of how a sick person should act—to be passive, compliant, and dependent.

5. Because others were preoccupied with what was wrong with them, their talents, abilities, and other personal attributes were often ignored.

These young adults attributed their difficulties during adolescence not to what they were unable to do, but to the restrictions placed on them by the way others perceived them and behaved toward them, especially health professionals. To understand why professionals unwittingly restricted the social development of these young people, we can examine the thought patterns learned in the course of becoming a physician. In medicine, the conceptual approach to disease is codified in the *International Classification of Disease* (ICD) (WHO, 1980). Starting with the manifestation of the disease or disorder, the physician is trained to examine the symptoms and pathology and make inferences about the cause of the disease or disorder. The ICD classifications deal with manifestations, pathology, and etiology (WHO, 1980, p. 10).

MEDICAL ATTITUDES AND TREATMENT

This approach has provided a valuable methodology to disorders that can be prevented or cured, but is limited in value for conditions that are chronic and cannot be cured. The limitation of the classical medical model is that it pays no attention to the *consequences* of the disease or disorder for the patient—either the biological or social consequences or the social context in which the patient lives.

The World Health Organization recognized these limitations and in 1980 published an *International Classification of Impairments, Disabilities, and Handicaps,* a manual of classification relating to the consequences of disease. It contains three sets of categories that take into consideration the consequences of impairment for disability and handicap. These three terms are defined as follows:

> *Impairment:* "Any loss or abnormality of psychological, physiological or anatomical structure or function" (p. 46).
> *Disability:* "Any restriction or lack (resulting from an impairment) of ability to perform an activity in the manner or within the range considered normal for a human being" (p. 143).
> *Handicap:* "A disadvantage for a given individual resulting from an impairment or a disability, that limits or prevents the fulfillment of a role that is normal (depending on age, sex, and social and cultural factors) for that individual" (p. 183).

The term *disablement* was suggested by Wood and Badley (1978) as "collective description referring to any experience identifed variously by the terms impairment, disability and handicap" (p. 17).

The medical focus of attention on the impairment and disability is appropriate because this is where medical knowledge may reduce or remove the disorder. The unintended consequence of this focus, however, may be that it increases the handicap of the patient. This can come about by prescribing treatments that interfere with patients' carrying out roles appropriate for their age and sex. These treatments include long periods of hospitalization, segregation of patients with others who have the same disease or disorder, and requiring treatments or clinic visits that take them away from settings and experiences they would otherwise be exposed to. For all these "treatments," there is an assumption that treatment is more important than the experiences the patients would have had if they had not been treated.

The term *patient* is a label that conveys a set of behavioral expectations that were originally described by Parsons (1958) under the term *sick role.* The expectations include exemptions from normal activities and responsibilities and assumption of a compliant and obedient stance toward prescriptions for medical treatment. From those who are socially important to the patient, there is the expectation of providing sheltering from stress and responsibility, tolerance for and patience with behaviors that otherwise might not be acceptable, and performance for the patient of caring activities that would not otherwise be expected. All this may seriously limit experiences that are important for the patient's social development and are needed to enable a young person to become an effective, functioning member of adult society.

Apart from treatment, the disabilities that stem from the disorder may place direct restrictions on the ability of the disabled person to obtain the kinds and varieties of social experience that would have been obtained were it not for the disability. The disabled person may tire more quickly, not be able to engage in certain physical activities, have to spend time in bed or resting, and have difficulty in getting about. When parents have to spend time caring for their child whose activities are restricted, this takes away from other experiences they could provide. The dilemma of parents is well illustrated by Hewett, Newson, and Newson (1970) in writing about parents of children with cerebral palsy:

> Their . . . effort to treat the child as 'normal' has to be realistically related to the extent to which he is capable of behaving (and reacting to their behavior) like an unhandicapped child. . . . The parents and later the child himself must walk a tightrope between acceptance of the fact that he is different from other children and insistence that he should be like them in as many ways as possible. If they emphasize his differences continually, making allowances for his disability, and learn a habit of helping and shielding, they may be branded overprotective. If they minimize his handicap, treat him as an ordinary member of the family and speak with optimism of his mental attainments or physical prospects, they may be judged to have failed to accept the situation. (p. 202)

It is easy for the parents' natural concern over the physical problems of their child to be reinforced by the focus of medical attention to the point that it interferes with what they would have been able to do for the social development of their child had they not had a preoccupation with the physical disorder.

VIOLATION OF EXPECTATIONS

The young person with a chronic disorder or disablement may encounter a barrier to social relationships that stems from being perceived as different from others in appearance. I have reviewed the research on these barriers elsewhere (Richardson, 1976, 1983). The concept of "violation of expectation" is one way of summarizing some of the results of the research.

Throughout our upbringing we develop an increasingly complex set of expectations about how people ought to be, about their physical appearance, dress and manner, behavior, speech, movement, and how they think, although depending on our experiences, we are accustomed to some range of variation. If we meet someone whose appearance or manner of behavior exceeds the variability of our expectations, we respond with emotional arousal, anxiety, and fear. Such a response was important for our early ancestors and was a biological response preparing us to fight, freeze, or flee. Violation of expectation can have serious consequences for interpersonal relations with the person who caused the violation.

The following summarizes some of the evidence for the concept of violation of expectations.

1. The attribute of appearance or behavior that caused the violation of expectation dominates the attention of the person who perceived the violation. This domination causes inattention to the other characteristics or attributes of the person who caused the violation, attributes that would otherwise be attended to. For example, in a study by Strasser and Sievert (1969) of babies born with limb deformities, the mothers reported an initial preoccupation with the limb deformity, in some cases to such a degree that they were unable to respond to the other characteristics and behavior of their babies.

2. The person who perceives a violation of expectation feels ambivalence toward the violator. For fear of revealing the negative aspects of the ambivalence, the person who perceives the violation becomes formal and controlled and is afraid of being spontaneous.

3. The person whose expectations are violated inhibits nonverbal behavior and tends to maintain a greater physical distance from the other person than would normally occur.

4. Persons are more likely to avoid social encounters with someone who violates their expectations, and if an encounter does occur they will terminate it more quickly than in social relations where a violation of expectation is not present.

5. Our society values being nice to those who are less fortunate than ourselves. This can lead to distortion of opinions expressed toward those who violate expectations in the direction of what is perceived as more easily accepted. It can also lead to distorted feedback, which prevents the violator of expectation from learning what is inappropriate behavior.

The general thesis underlying the points so far made is summarized in a Declaration of Rehabilitation International in their *Charter for the 80s* (1981):

Throughout history, humanity has erected barriers both physical and social which exclude from full participation in its communities those judged to be different because of physical or mental variation.

Having focused on the social barriers that are a consequence of illness or disability, we now want to examine the kinds of social experiences that are missed because of the barriers and the ways in which the socialization of individuals with chronic conditions can be enhanced.

NORMAL DEVELOPMENTAL EXPERIENCES

What are the social experiences that are valuable in preparation for functioning as an adult and that occur in the transition from childhood to adulthood? The following are illustrative.

1. *Shifts in social relations.* In the early years the child's social relationships are largely controlled by the parents. As the child gets older, the initiative is gradually shifted to the child. For teenagers, opposite-sex peer relations increase in importance, and the times, place, and content of peer relationships increasingly become the responsibility of the young person.

2. *Functioning in the peer culture.* The social skills needed to function effectively in the peer culture require extensive time to develop with peers of the same and opposite sex. Participation in the peer culture is one way of gaining some emancipation from parents. Participation includes the acquisition of large amounts of information on topics currently of interest to the youth culture and of skills thought to be important in the peer culture.

3. *Taking responsibility for one's own affairs.* The focus of control during the transition from childhood to adulthood shifts from the parents to their children, although responsibility for financial affairs may be delayed if the parents provide support for higher education. Young adults become responsible for both obtaining income and controlling how it is spent. Some of the steps in this shift of responsibility include parents giving pocket money to or paying their children to do household chores. Young persons may take part- or full-time jobs during the school years, leave home for various purposes, and assume positions in which they have to help and be responsible for others (e.g., as camp counselors or looking after younger siblings).

4. *Learning adult behavior.* These behaviors include those required by and appropriate for job settings, sexual relationships, the establishment and running of a household, roles of spouse and parent, appropriate use of alcohol, and so forth. Some of this is learned through watching adult role models and knowing a variety of adults besides parents.

5. *Developing skills in social relations.* With increasing age the roles the young person has to play increase in complexity and diversity. Basic to many of these roles are language skills in one-on-one and group settings. Participation skills are needed in making group decisions, settling differences with another person, and mediating disputes. In any social relations and friendships, the initial encounters are critical.

6. *Self-regulation.* Most adults have to develop a sense of time and the ability to fit into time schedules established by job, household, recreational, and travel demands.

7. *Departures from autonomous adult behavior.* Contrary to all the illustrations thus far, adolescents in transition to adulthood will be faced with situations in which others wish them to accept more childlike and dependent roles. Some adults in authority positions, such as work supervisors, expect more childlike behavior of adolescents. The adolescent will have to tolerate and accept a more childlike role as a condition of continuing in the particular position or job.

8. *Appaearance, dress, and manner.* In adolescence personal appearance is of great importance. Adolescents generally conform to expected norms of physical appearance, dress, and manner in order to receive acceptance from peers. The child with a chronic condition who deviates from these expected norms may experience special difficulties in this area.

EFFECTS OF DISABILITY ON DEVELOPMENTAL EXPERIENCES

In all these development spheres, the natural preoccupation with the child's illness may interfere with opportunities to enhance the whole development of the child. For children with various types of chronic disease and disability, the full range of social experiences is less likely to occur. It is at the same time very easy for parents, physicians, and others in the social environment to forget that these are extremely important experiences, in and of themselves worth significant attempts to attain.

An important goal in this regard is to avoid some of the barriers to effective socialization. Achieving this goal would prevent unnecessary secondary handicapping of young people with disabilities. Here again, illustrations will be given of possible ways to aid the socialization of adolescents who have chronic impairments.

Disability in and of itself can impose restrictions on a person's socialization. To the extent that treatment through medication, prostheses, rehabilitation, or other means alleviates disabling consequences of impairments, this can in turn reduce the direct barriers to socialization imposed by the disability. However, an important first step is recognition of the unintended consequences of treatment of young people with chronic impairment, treatment that limits the experiences young people need in the socialization process. These unintended consequences stem not only from medical practice, but also from more general ways in which the behavior of people alters subtly in interpersonal relations with those perceived as different from normal and violating expectations. A change in these unintended behaviors must precede any other change.

As the child grows older, health care professionals working with parents can increasingly involve the child in discussions about treatment decisions. Further, the responsibility for carrying out treatment should be shifted in the direction of the young person. This makes for a gradual transition in the responsibility for health care from the parent to their child.

In all cases in which treatment or management programs involve segregation of young people with disorders, the reasons for segregation should be carefully examined to determine whether they are substantial. If they are not, changes should be considered. If segregation is deemed important, then there should be opportunities for training and exercise of social skills during these segregated periods. If there is a shift away from segregated programs, there should be careful social preparation before the shift and help during and after.

Adolescent peer relationships are one way of learning about body changes and developing sexual and social behavior. For adolescents with chronic illness and disorders who are isolated from the peer culture, this important sense of learning is shut off. For these young people, education about the nature of sexual relations, intercourse, pregnancy, and contraception is important. There is a stereotype held by some adults that disabled people should be asexual, and as a consequence the topic of sexuality is avoided.

One of the consequences of negative societal values toward chronic illness and disorders is that those who have these conditions incorporate societal values, and this results in self-denigration and low self-esteem. The negative societal values stem in part from the violation of expectations that occurs in initial social encounters. The strangeness of the initial encounter and the violation that occurs are likely to diminish in salience if a continuing relationship can be established, providing the opportunity to become accustomed to what is atypical. People with disabilities have described the process of "breaking through," whereby the other person stops focusing on the disability and begins to take into account those unique personal attributes that would normally be considered in interpersonal evaluation. Persons with disabilities who understand this will be less easily discouraged in social relations and can assist the other person by providing information about their nonhandicapped-related attributes. Parents can make an important contribution to their child's self-esteem by attending to and encouraging the child's gifts and talents and by helping to develop skills that are esteemed among the child's peers. Those responsible for treatment of the disorder often focus only on what is wrong with their patient, but they also have a responsibility to look for and encourage the development of any skills that help self-confidence.

Although there is a growing awareness of the need for a transition from childhood to adulthood, many of our societal institutions ignore the transition, and as a result the shifts are often abrupt, for example, from the world of school to the world of work, or from pediatric care to adult medical care. In their training and practice pediatricians gain some understanding of child development, of the interrelationships between a child at different stages of development and his or her family, and of the social conditions of the family's life. Physicians who care for adults are more frequently trained in internal medicine and gain most of their clinical experience with mature adults; they are not taught about child development and the social transition from childhood to adulthood. In addition, until recently little attention has been given to adolescents' emergence into adulthood and the special sensitivities that are needed in dealing with this transition, and far less attention has been given to adolescents with special vulnerabilities.

The institutional arrangements of our society demand several radical changes in daily lifestyle and behavior in a short period of time during the teens and early twenties. The number and magnitude of these changes can place severe stress on young people, especially those with chronic conditions. The needs of young people should be given more priority, and the needs of organizations less priority.

SUMMARY

If some of the issues that have been raised in this chapter had been taken into account, the young people described at the beginning of the chapter might well have been less immature, isolated, and unhappy as young adults. There is an important need to carry out research about the natural histories of young people with various forms of chronic disorders and to examine the issues related to the transition from childhood to adulthood. These histories should include "the progressive accommodation between an active, growing human being and the changing properties of the immediate settings in which the developing person lives as this process is affected by relations between these settings and by the large contexts in which the settings are embedded" (Bronfenbrenner, 1979, p. 21). We need to know whether, as a result of changes in society since the earlier studies were carried out, young people now entering adulthood are still experiencing the difficulties that were experienced by young people in the earlier studies.

REFERENCES

Bronfenbrenner, U. (1979). *The ecology of human development: Experiments by nature and design.* Cambridge, MA: Harvard University Press.

Charter for the 80s. (1981). New York: Rehabilitation International.

Hewett, S., Newson, J., & Newson, W. (1970). *The family and the handicapped child: A study of cerebral palsied children in their homes.* London: George Allen & Unwin.

Ingram, J. E. (1964). *Living with cerebral palsy* (Studies in Medicine No. 14). London: The Spastics Society in Association with William Heinemann (Medical) Books, Ltd.

Klapper, Z. S., & Birch, H. G. (1966). The relation of childhood characteristics to outcome in young adults with cerebral palsy. *Developmental Medicine and Child Neurology, 18,* 645.

Parsons, T. (1958). Definitions of health and illness in the light of American values and social structure. In E. G. Jaco (Ed.), *Patients, physicians and illness: Sourcebook in behavioral science and medicine.* (pp. 234–245). Glencoe, IL: Free Press.

Richardson, S. A. (1972). People with cerebral palsy talk for themselves. *Developmental Medicine & Child Neurology, 14,* 524–535.

Richardson, S. A. (1976). Attitudes and behavior toward the physically handicapped. *The National Foundation,* Birth Defects: Original Article Series, Vol. 12, (4) 15–34.

Richardson, S. A. (1983). Children's values in regard to disabilities: A reply to Yuker. *Rehabilitation Psychology, 28* (3), 131–140.

Strasser, H., & Sievert, G. (1969). Some psycho-social aspects of ectromelia: A preliminary report of a research study (pp. 422–427). In C. A. Swinyard (Ed.), *Limb Development and Deformity: Problems of Evaluation and Rehabilitation.* Springfield, IL: Charles C. Thomas.

Wood, P. H. N., & Badley, E. M. (1978). An epidemiological appraisal of disablement. In A. E. Bennett (Ed.), *Recent advances in community medicine.* Edinburgh: Churchill Livingstone.

World Health Organization. (1980) *International classification of disease.* Geneva: Author.

12

Long-Term Effects of Chronic Illness on Young Adults*

I. Barry Pless, M.D.,
Michael E. J. Wadsworth, M. Phil., Ph.D.

Over the last quarter-century research related to chronic illness in childhood has grown almost exponentially. Although many of the results are still far from definitive, for the most part they represent a major advance beyond what was known 25 years ago. At the conceptual level the most important is the firm establishment of the validity of the noncategorical, generic approach (Stein & Jessop, 1982; Pless & Perin, 1985). Whereas in the past it was customary to question whether findings related to one specific disorder could be applied to others, it is now clear that, with some important caveats, this approach is acceptable and reasonable. At a more substantive level, evidence that the risk associated with these illnesses is related causally to adverse psychosocial consequences has also been strengthened (Nolan & Pless, 1986). Finally, there are more and more intervention studies of an experimental and quasi-experimental nature that point the way to improvements in clinical care. Taken together, these recent findings have provided strong support for a variety of policy recommendations applicable at the local and national levels (Hobbs, Perrin, & Ireys, 1985).

One critically important issue, however, remains largely unresolved: whether the psychosocial problems of children with chronic illness—which

*This chapter is adapted from Publication No. 88023 of the McGill University–Montreal Children's Hospital Research Institute.

are clearly more prevalent among these children than among their healthy peers—are likely to persist into adulthood. One reason this question has not been pursued intensively is largely a practical one: to do so requires longitudinal studies of considerable size, and few investigators are willing or able to commit themselves to such an undertaking, even if adequate funding were available. In addition, because of the changing survival rates for specific diseases as a result of technological advances, the distribution of children with chronic illness who survive into adulthood will always be evolving.

This chapter summarizes preliminary findings pertinent to this issue drawn from secondary analyses of existing longitudinal or cohort data. In Britain, beginning in 1946, birth cohorts representative of all children in England, Scotland, and Wales were assembled and studied at regular intervals throughout childhood (Wadsworth, Peckham, & Taylor, 1984). In the case of the first, the 1946 cohort, and a more recent one commencing in 1958, the subjects have been followed into adult life. In each, sufficient medical information was included in the routine data collection to identify with reasonable accuracy all those who had a chronic physical or sensory disorder during childhood. These children are the principal focus of this chapter, based on analyses that seek to determine the extent to which those with chronic disorders, who may or may not have had significant emotional, behavioral, or social problems in childhood, are affected by such problems in later life.

NATIONAL SURVEY OF HEALTH AND DEVELOPMENT (1946 COHORT)

This cohort consists of a sample of all births in England, Wales, and Scotland in one week in March 1946. The sample includes all single, legitimate births to wives of nonmanual and agricultural workers, and one in four of single, legitimate births to wives of manual workers (Douglas & Blomfield, 1958). The total in the original sample was 5,362 children. Over subsequent years a wide range of medical, social, psychological, and educational data were collected at intervals of two years or less up to age 15 and at 5-year intervals thereafter. The data reported here were obtained at ages 16, 26, and 36.

As cited in Chapter 1 and used throughout the book, Pless and Douglas's commonly accepted definition was used to identify a chronic illness: "a physical, usually nonfatal condition which lasted longer than 3 months in a given year or necessitated a period of continuous hospitalization of more than one month (Pless & Douglas, 1971). In addition, conditions were included only if they were of sufficient severity to interfere with a child's ordinary activities to some degree.

PREVALENCE AND CLINICAL CHARACTERISTICS

Using this definition, the prevalence of chronic conditions arising in this cohort prior to age 16 was 112 per 1,000 children alive at age 15. At age 26 the prevalence rate was 108 per 1,000 (see Table 12.1).

For purposes of analysis, the type of disability caused by each condition was categorized as motor (61%), cosmetic (16%), or sensory (22%). The recorded age of onset for most (44%) was between 6 and 10 years. About half (53%) were classified as mild disabilities, but 35% were conditions that interfered with normal daily activity (moderate severity). The remaining conditions, 11%, were judged to be severe (requiring prolonged periods of immobilization, bedrest, or school absence). A majority of children with these disorders still suffered from the same illnesses at age 26 as at age 15, and 42% were judged to be permanent (see Table 12.2).

TABLE 12.1 Distribution of Chronic Physical Disorders

Category of disorder	N	Rate per 1,000
Respiratory	93	21
Neurological	75	17
Musculoskeletal	58	13
Vision	57	12
Hearing	10	2
Speech	15	3
Skin	38	1
Urogenital	—	—
Heart	22	5
Endometabolic	5	1
Blood	2	—
Gastrointestinal	4	1
Strabismus	57	13
Other	44	10
	480	10.6
Subclassification		
Cardiorespiratory	115	24
Neuromuscular	133	28
Sensory	67	15
Cosmetic	95	23
Systemic	11	3
Other	44	13

TABLE 12.2 Clinical Characteristics of Chronic Physical Disorders

Type of disability	N	%
Motor	307	61.4
Sensory	81	16.2
Cosmetic	112	22.4
Severity		
Mild	266	53.2
Moderate	180	36.0
Severe	54	10.8
Duration		
Indeterminate	103	20.6
Temporary	186	37.2
Permanent	211	42.2
Age of onset		
Birth	29	5.8
1—5	151	30.2
6—10	220	44.0
11—15	99	19.8

These categories are based on a clinical judgment about the functional domain most severely affected by the underlying biological disorder. Thus, for example, conditions involving hearing and vision were categorized as "sensory."* The "cosmetic" group includes children with strabismus not corrected by surgery, visible scars or birthmarks, and those with other skin disorders visible when fully clothed. All remaining conditions were categorized as "motor." It was reasoned that these disorders primarily affect locomotor functioning, either as a consequence of neuromuscular dysfunction or because of cardiorespiratory or systemic conditions limiting exercise tolerance. Also known is the distribution by age of onset.

Although there were more boys than girls in the group with chronic disorders ($p < .01$), there were no other statistically significant sociodemographic differences between the healthy subjects and those with chronic physical disorders (CPD) of either sex.

ADOLESCENT DYSFUNCTION

In middle and late adolescence, reports of habit behavior, teachers' assessments of behavior in school (Douglas, 1964), scores on the Eysenck

---

*In the original analyses, this category also included children with speech disorders. It is not clear, however, whether this was correct, and it was later decided that it was more appropriate to include speech disorders with conditions affecting social interactions—loosely referred to as "cosmetic."

Personality Inventory (EPI) (Eysenck, 1958), and official reports of delinquency were obtained. When boys with CPD were compared with those who were healthy with respect to the presence of two or more abnormal habit behaviors, there was a statistically significant difference ($p < .05$). This was not found in a similar comparison for girls.

The reverse applied when the assessments made at ages 13 and 15 by teachers were combined and divided into three clinical categories: (1) very nervous, (2) aggressive, and (3) inattentive and troublesome. The differences here were significant for girls but not for boys when the CPD were compared with the healthy ($p < .01$).

The Eysenck Personality Inventory (EPI) is a revision of the Maudsley Personality Inventory devised by Eysenck and intended for children aged 9 to 16. It yields three scores: extroversion (E), neuroticism (N), and lie (L). The short EPI completed at age 13 showed significant differences between the CPD and the healthy on the extraversion subscale for women only. No differences of note are found in the neurotic subscale when compared with the rates seen among the healthy. Similarly, chronically ill boys were neither more nor less likely to be delinquent than were healthy boys, and there were two few delinquent girls for analysis.

With respect to education, at age 15, survey children took three tests of educational achievement. (The details of these tests are given in Douglas, Ross, & Simpson, 1968.) The scores of the tests were combined and standardized, and it was found that those for the CPD group were significantly lower in both boys and girls.

Further, at age 26, when final educational achievements were compared, 5% more of the men with CPD had failed to complete high school. The differences for women were not as great, with only 1% more of those with CPD being similarly disadvantaged. Those with severe disability appeared to be at greatest risk for this measure of dysfunction. No such difference was found for the women when the two groups were compared, and there was no evidence that the results reflect differential losses between the principal study groups.

ADULT DYSFUNCTION

When the same cohort was assessed in greater depth at age 26, further details regarding psychosocial dysfunction were obtained. One key indicator of such problems is the number of hospital reports of consultations for varying types of emotional disturbances since age 15. A classification developed by Wadsworth in 1983 divides these subjects into three levels: those with no contacts reported; those with some minor disturbances or illnesses of one or more years' duration but with three or fewer episodes in all; and those having four or more episodes lasting more than one year. At the most serious level are all those with inpatient or outpatient psychiatric care and all with a diagnosis of schizophrenia.

With this classification, nearly 2% of CPD men had disturbances of moderate severity compared with about 1.5% in the general population. At the severe level, the comparable figures for men were 4.6% among the CPD and 2.6% for the healthy. For women there was a greater difference at the moderate level (10% vs. 6%), whereas at the severe level the rates were 4.5% and 4.1%, respectively. The other results suggest the importance among CPD women of cosmetic disorders and clinically severe conditions as possible risk factors for moderate levels of dysfunction. Women with severe disabilities and men with disorders of indeterminate duration also appear to be at greater risk for severe psychiatric disorders.

At age 36, the Present State Examination (PSE) (Wing, Cooper, & Sartorius, 1974) was conducted by trained interviewers. The PSE consists of a very detailed, highly structured interview schedule. Symptoms elicited are grouped into syndromes that yield a profile of the mental state of the subject.

A total of about 3,500 members of the birth cohort were assessed in this manner. Unfortunately, definitive results are not available. Preliminary findings suggest that scores judged to be clinically significant will be found for about 6% of the general population. Whether those with CPD will have an excessive rate of disturbance based on this measure remains to be seen.

Other measures of social or emotional dysfunction in adulthood include a further assessment of educational qualifications (or lack thereof), unemployment, and marital status.

When levels of unemployment are compared, the educational problems of the CPD are seen in a different perspective. Overall, only about 1% more of the CPD were unemployed. This figure is greater for women with sensory disorders and for men with severe disabilities. It is also highest among both men and women with disorders that begin after age 10, but there were no significant differences for women or for men from nonmanual social class families. However, men who had a CPD from families in which the head of the household was a manual worker were much more likely to be unemployed or employed only part time than men from similar social class backgrounds who had been healthy as children ($p < .001$). This finding is accounted for by the fact that, compared with men from nonmanual backgrounds, those of manual social class of origin were significantly less often able to work full time or at all between the ages of 21 and 25 because of serious illness.

Other findings suggest that marriage rates, separations, and divorces were significantly different between the two main groups. Notably, more CPD women than healthy women were single at age 26. The proportion of single women is highest among those with sensory disorders, with conditions that are severe, with disorders that are permanent, and with onset before age 5 or after age 10. However, none of these relationships is statistically significant for men, nor are they present for those of either sex with respect to the rates of marital breakdown. It should also be noted that for many of the previous analyses there are too few in the subgroups to detect differences of statistical significance.

Some of the unexpected findings described in the preceding sections may reflect the fact that from ages 21 to 25 many of those judged to be ill during childhood described themselves as essentially free of illness. Conversely, about 17% of men and 12% of women who were apparently free of chronic disorders during childhood were reported to have a health problem during their early twenties. It is not possible to confirm the accuracy of either of these classifications (i.e., those for the period 21 to 25 years) or to determine whether the illnesses described are the same as those reported during childhood.

FURTHER HYPOTHESIS CONCERNING THE RISK OF PSYCHOSOCIAL DISORDERS

The analyses described in the previous section attempt to test general hypotheses regarding the relationship between the presence of a chronic physical disorder during childhood and negative mental health consequences during adolescence or early adult life. The broad form of the question being examined is the extent to which any chronic disorder increases the risk of later maladjustment. More specifically, the question becomes one of determining the extent to which characteristics of the disorder, the child, or the family further influence the likelihood of adverse socioemotional functioning in later life.

Among clinical characteristics, the type of disability, the severity of the condition, its actual and expected duration, and the age of onset appear to be most salient. Although each of these has been examined to some extent, it is important to stress that none of these hypotheses has been tested fully. The classification by type of disability is arbitrary and based entirely on the clinical diagnosis recorded, which, although it may reflect the main domains of dysfunction with reasonable accuracy, is a much less satisfactory means for estimating the severity of the condition. Although an alternative classification based on a hierarchical arrangement of the diagnostic categories was shown, it is not likely to be sufficiently rigorous to warrant further testing. Unfortunately, there is no other generally agreed-upon measure of severity that can be used across diagnostic groups. Although hospitalization days and days of school absence have been used often as proxy measures of severity and were included among these data, they were not related specifically to the illness under consideration, and hence, any analyses based on these measures of severity could be misleading. Much the same concerns apply to the age of onset and the indicators of actual and expected duration, all of which are limited by the intervals between data collection and parents' recall.

Of the personal characteristics, the most important are likely to be the age at which the maladjustment was assessed (which in the case of cohort data is identical throughout the sample), sex, and attributes such as intelligence or certain personality characteristics. Unfortunately, no specific assessments of intelligence per se are included among the variables abstracted.

Finally, some social factors warrant further exploration, including social class, marital status of parents, family size, maternal and paternal education, and possibly features pertinent to the birth rank of the children or the number of siblings. This list of measures needed to further test hypotheses about the effects of CPD on maladjustment may be modified is far from exhaustive, and unfortunately many of these were not included as variables in the data set.

A further issue concerns how the presumed risk factors operate. Are the effects, if any, independent? Are they additive or multiplicative? Are there important interactions? Ultimately, the question becomes: Does any combination of these factors play a more significant and useful role in the prediction of adult psychiatric dysfunction?

The use of the term *prediction* in this context is the same as in the preceding section—to determine, in a statistical sense, the extent to which the factors explain the variance in the model used. However, survey data of this kind are difficult to analyze using conventional linear models because the numbers of subjects in the subgroups are usually unequal. Although better procedures are now available to help minimize these problems, it still remains necessary to determine, when more than one predictor is used, whether interaction effects contribute significantly. If they do, these effects must be examined closely to establish their meaning. If the answer is "yes," then there exists a realistic opportunity to reorganize mental health services, both preventive services and those aimed at reducing the prevalence or severity of existing mental health problems, in the hope of obtaining better results.

DISCUSSION

In the previous sections the results of many of the analyses pertinent to these hypotheses were presented. It must be understood, however, that for a variety of reasons these findings should not be interpreted as the final word on this subject. It is clear that many further analyses can and should be done to ensure that the full value of all the data is obtained. For example, it may be that the manner in which the present work was done failed to use the best statistical or conceptual models. Several points of strategy and limitations in both the raw data and in the available statistics should be borne in mind. First, the general analytic model was one that relied on the availability of a comparison ("control") group, that is, subjects who, as far as could be determined, were free of any chronic disorders during childhood. It is possible (but unlikely) that some of the latter did, in fact, have a chronic condition that was not recorded or not recorded adequately for purposes of identification, just as it is possible that some of the CPD group were wrongly identified as such.

It is also possible that it was not necessary to have used all the health controls in the analyses. A random sample, with or without stratification, equivalent in size to the CPD group, could have been selected. This would have had the added practical advantages of reducing costs and minimizing the possibility of reporting misleading statistical relationships.

Whatever future decisions may be made in this regard, the strength of the comparison approach seems apparent, although it should be emphasized that this is not a case-control study in the conventional sense. It would be pointless to have cohort data and not make full use of the prospective design. Accordingly, the comparison group was used to allow the calculation of odds ratios (or relative risks) after ensuring comparability on a majority of potentially confounding variables. It is also important to note that these analyses followed a series of careful comparisons between the two groups (CPD and healthy) on a large number of sociodemographic measures. As has been stated repeatedly, the only consistently significant factor was sex. Nonetheless, most of the detailed analyses take account of both sex and social class and assume from that point on that in all other relevant respects the groups are truly comparable. Obviously there is no way to prove that this is true, and because the groups were not created by simple randomization, it is possible that other important, undetected differences may exist.

The analyses that have been done are further limited by several additional considerations. The first is the fact that most of the outcome, or dependent, variables are best viewed as dichotomous, for example, present or absent, normal or abnormal. Few have any continuous properties that would lend themselves to classical linear regression techniques. Accordingly, it has been necessary to use logistic regression, an approach that is less well understood than linear regression. A second limitation is the number of potential predictor and confounding variables that could be taken into consideration. Notwithstanding these problems, it has been possible to analyze these data using this statistical model, albeit only after making some arbitrary decisions regarding the assumptions about the model used.

It should also be noted that ideally it is necessary to ensure that children with emotional disturbances that may have antedated the onset of the CPD are not included in the analysis. With the measures available in this cohort, this was not possible. Further, it is not possible to pinpoint the exact age of onset of the disorder for most children. Thus it is likely that some children are included who were disturbed before the illness began. This should not, however, lead to the conclusion that these disorders are "psychosomatic." For these reasons, as well as other considerations regarding how the data were collected, the results do not permit analyses that allow the sequence of events in time to be unraveled. This may require the use of path-analytic statistical techniques.

Regardless of the techniques chosen, however, it must be clear that to be certain of the sequence of events it is essential that the files contain reasonably precise information about when a problem or risk factor was first identified. When the intervals between data collection points are long, only rough estimates can be made about the order of occurrence. Compounding the difficulty is the absence of certain key measures, for example, measures to assess changes in self-concept, which might reasonably be hypothesized as links between a set of risk factors and more overt, pathological measures. Moreover, the structure of longitudinal files is such that the analysis is constantly plagued by difficulties arising from both random and nonrandom missing values. These problems can be largely overcome or greatly minimized in purpose-built cohort studies, but they inevitably impose severe limitations on secondary analyses of the kind described in this report.

Other testable hypotheses that could be explored with these data pertain primarily to relationships that may emerge when the sexes are examined separately and secondarily to the relationship between childhood measures of socioemotional disturbance and similar measures in later life. Although the CPD and healthy comparison groups are remarkably similar in most other sociodemographic respects, making it unlikely that further associations between such measures as family composition will be uncovered, it may be worth pursuing this further. For example, although the primary value of the cohort design would be wasted, it may be of interest to conduct a case-control study of those with disturbances in adult life to determine the extent to which CPD, along with other factors, serves to distinguish between the two groups. It would also be of interest (but is not possible using the measures included in these cohorts) to examine the effect of various forms of medical interventions and social support systems on the outcomes of interest. For example, some of the children with

CPD may have received psychosocial counseling (e.g., from social workers, psychologists, or psychiatrists) that served to ameliorate the impact of the disease on later functioning. Likewise, the supports available to the family through neighbors, community agencies, and other family members may have had the same protective effect.

In conclusion, the data described, although far from perfect, provide what is perhaps the best currently available estimate of the extent of psychosocial problems among adults who have a chronic physical disorder that began during childhood. The results suggest that a distinct risk for adverse outcomes does exist. The level of risk, for most of the measures, averages 30–50%. Although not large, this figure represents what many believe to be preventable secondary burdens or handicaps. Clearly, these children deserve the benefit of whatever intervention programs are available. Although the need for further research in this area cannot be minimized, it should not be used as an excuse for failing to provide needed services to these children and their families.

Acknowledgments: Supported by grants from the National Health Research and Development Program (NHRDP), Health and Welfare Canada, and the William T. Grant Foundation.

REFERENCES

Douglas, J. W. B. (1964). *The home and the school. A study of ability and attainment in the primary school.* London: MacGibbon & Kee.

Douglas, J. W. B., & Blomfield, J. M. (1958). *Children under five.* London: George Allen & Unwin.

Douglas, J. W. B., Ross, J. M., & Simpson, H. R. (1968). *All our future.* London: Morrison & Gibb.

Eysenck, H. J. (1958). A short questionnaire for the measurement of two dimensions of personality. *Journal of Applied Psychology, 42,* 14.

Hobbs, N., Perrin, J. M., & Ireys, H. T. (1985). *Chronically ill children and their families.* San Francisco: Jossey-Bass.

Nolan, T., & Pless, I. B. (1986). Emotional correlates and consequences of birth defects. *Journal of Pediatrics, 109,* 201.

Pless, I. B., & Douglas, J. W. B. (1971). Chronic illness in childhood. I. Epidemiological and clinical characteristics. *Pediatrics, 47,* 405–414.

Pless, I. B., & Perrin, J. M. (1985). Issues common to a variety of illness. In N. Hobbs, & H. Perrin (Eds.), *Issues in the care of children with chronic illness* (pp. 41–60). San Francisco: Jossey-Bass.

Stein, R. E. K., & Jessop, D. J. (1982). A non-categorical approach to chronic childhood illness. *Public Health Records, 97,* 354–362.

Wadsworth, M. E. J., Peckham, C. S., Taylor, B. (1984). The role of national longitudinal studies in the prediction of health, development and behavior.

In D. Klein Walker & J. B. Richmond (Eds.), *Monitoring child health in the United States: selected issues and policies* (pp. 63–83). Cambridge, MA: Harvard University Press.

Wing, J. K., Cooper, J. E., & Sartorius, N. (1974). *The measurement and classification of psychiatric symptoms.* Cambridge, England: Cambridge University Press.

IV

Promising Approaches to Service Delivery

13

Pediatric Home Care: An Institutionally Based Outreach Program*

Henry M. Adam, M.D.

The Pediatric Home Care program at the Albert Einstein College of Medicine and the Bronx Municipal Hospital Center was developed in 1970 as a special ambulatory care unit for children with chronic illnesses. An understanding of the program as a model for the delivery of services to these children has to begin with an appreciation of the children themselves.

THE CHILDREN

Case 1. V. is now 9 years old. She was born with a disease, biliary atresia, that left her with almost no functioning liver. For the first 5 years of her life V. invested nearly all her energy while awake in scratching, never able really to escape the intense itching from her extremely high level of jaundice. She did not speak; she certainly did not play. She scratched. Her body was so densely covered with xanthomas (abnormal deposits of fat in her skin from a liver that would not work) that finding a vein when she needed blood drawn became almost a search for the lost ark. V. was lucky; 3 years ago she received a liver

---

* For administrative reasons, the name Pediatric Home Care was recently changed to Pediatric Outreach. I have chosen to use here the older name by which the program has become widely known.

and she no longer scratches. The fight is not over. She must take medicine for the rest of her life, medicine that compromises her ability to fight infection and that one day may giver her cancer. V. is small, looking years younger than her sister, who in fact is 2 years younger than she is—something V. may like if she gets to be 40, but that is not easy for a 9-year-old to take.

Case 2. R. likes to talk about sex. He is 15 now, so that is perfectly normal. But to talk at all, R. has to cover the opening of his tracheostomy tube with his chin. He needs that tube because he has a progressive neuromuscular disease, spinal muscular atrophy, that has left him without strength enough to cough up his lungs' secretions; he must be suctioned through the tube every few minutes, or he will drown in his own mucus. R.'s mind is sharp, and so is his tongue; the disease has taken tone and vigor only from his muscles. To talk with him is a delight and an education. He has told me how, when he was 8 or 9, he used to worry that as he grew older his mother would no longer be able to lift him, turn him in bed, or put him in his wheelchair—not the kind of fear my 9-year-old son has to live with. But at 15, R. weighs only 45 pounds. At 15, R. has also thought a lot about death, and he knows, too, that for him sex will never be more than talk through his trach tube.

Case 3. B. has a disease that we do not even have a name for. It has destroyed her hormone system, so that she must take each day, by mouth and by needle, nearly a dozen chemicals that her body ought to make but does not. At age 17, she also has chronic hepatitis and a fungus infection that invades her mouth, her gut, and her genitals. B. is a child of extremes; her blood levels of salts, minerals, and sugar swing from too high to dangerously low as we grossly try to mimic her body's lost internal controls. When she is not at home or school, she lives in the intensive care unit; there is no in-between. We know, and B. knows, that even without a name her disease has already killed her older sister, and that her father, surely in part to assuage his guilt, hanged himself.

These children have very special needs (Hobbs, Perrin, & Ireys, 1985; Mattson, 1972; Pless & Pinkerton, 1975). The traditional medical model has taught pediatricians how to diagnose and treat disease, and in the acute situation this model is generally effective; the child with a sore throat or an ear infection, with a laceration or even a broken bone, usually will suffer no more than transient physical dysfunction if we can make an accurate diagnosis and prescribe an appropriate treatment. But when an illness persists over time its impact is much more pervasive, and the risk it poses to function is not physical alone. A chronic disease becomes enmeshed in the developing child's experience, a reality that day after day, by its inescapable presence, contributes to the shape of how the child grows—biologically, psychologically, and socially. To treat the illness without nurturing the child is to do only one part of the job at hand; our job is to care for children, not just for their illnesses. Furthermore, because the child lives within a family, a school, and a community of both elders and peers, the child's illness extends outward, influencing all the relationships any child must form.

THE PEDIATRIC HOME CARE PROGRAM

The Target Population

Our goal in caring for children with chronic illness must be to normalize as much as we can the life of each child in a family and community setting and to minimize the disruptive impact of the child's condition, thus fostering for the child the best chance for growth and development. The Pediatric Home Care program, now 18 years old, has tried to create a model through which this goal can be approached (Stein, 1978). We aim not only to provide direct medical services—treatment for the illness— but also to work with the child as an individual, to build on personal strengths through education and counseling, by listening and encouraging. Our work involves us closely with the children's families, in both our office and their homes, trying to help them respond to illness in a way that supports their child and maintains their function as a family. We visit schools and service agencies in the community, advocating for the children and their families, helping them to organize a social structure responsive to their needs. Ultimately, the goal of our intervention is to return the care of a child to his or her family by providing the family with the information, skills, and supports needed for safe and appropriate care.

With a capacity to serve about 90 children and families at any one time, we have clearly had to be selective in accepting referrals to our program; in our community, the Bronx, there are many more children with significant chronic illnesses than Pediatric Home Care can hope to serve. We have come to recognize several types of situations in which our program is particularly needed and in which it can be effective (Stein, 1988):

1. Children for whom the presence of outreach services, especially work with the family in the home, makes possible a significant reduction in hospitalization or, in the extreme case, makes possible a return to the family rather than placement in a chronic care facility.
2. Children whose families have experienced difficulties in coping within the traditional ambulatory setting, either because of the intensity or diversity of the medical services required, or because the burden of a child's medical needs has stressed the family beyond its abilities (emotional, economic, or social) to keep appointments and manage a treatment plan.

3. Children whose medical problems are so complex that they require care from a multitude of specialists, without adequate coordination provided within a traditional outpatient setting.
4. Children who have significantly debilitating emotional and social problems related to a chronic illness.

The children enrolled in Pediatric Home Care range in age from infancy to adolescence, with a wide variety of illnesses, including congenital anomalies, end-stage renal disease, neuromuscular disorders, insulin-dependent diabetes, inborn errors of metabolism, sickle cell anemia, airway disease requiring a tracheostomy, disease of the endocrine system, rheumatologic diseases, and liver failure. Many of the children, in fact, have more than one illness; we care for a 6-year-old boy with panhypo-pituitarism, an atrial septal defect, upper airway obstruction with a tracheostomy, and asthma; a 2-year-old girl in our program has a high myelomeningocele with hydrocephalus as well as sickle cell anemia.

Referrals

Referrals to Pediatric Home Care come principally from within the medical center, although we occasionally have had a child sent to us from a practicing pediatrician in the community. Although many of the children are enrolled at the time their illness is first diagnosed, a substantial number of our patients come to us from the hospital's clinic system, having failed over time to respond to management within the traditional ambulatory setting. Still another group of children is referred to us from the inpatient wards, when hospitalization has not led to significant improvement, and a family is thus faced with taking home a seriously ill child.

Most of the families in our program live with multiple stresses, both medical and psychosocial, that threaten to overwhelm them, often compromising their ability to function in even a minimally adequate way. The majority are medically indigent as defined by Medicaid standards, and well over half are dependent on public assistance for their incomes. Two-thirds of our children live in single-parent families, and a significant number are in foster homes. We have several families with more than · one child enrolled in Pediatric Home Care. As many as a third of our families are known to Special Services for Children, the child protective agency in New York State.

The Home Care Team

The Pediatric Home Care staff works together as a team, consisting of three general pediatricians, three pediatric nurse practitioners, and a social worker. The pediatricians are all on the faculty of the Department of Pediatrics of the Albert Einstein College of Medicine, and in addition to their responsibilities within Pediatric Home Care they also work as teachers and physicians in the hospital's clinic and emergency room and on the wards. We are based in a hospital office that is open five days a week for both scheduled visits and emergencies, so that our children come directly to us for health care maintenance as well as for acute illnesses. During the week, either a nurse practitioner or a pediatrician is always in the office, available for any visit. When a nurse practitioner covers the office, one of the doctors is on back-up call in case a consultation is needed or an emergency arises. Over nights and on weekends, we leave a summary file of all our patients in the pediatric emergency room, so that pertinent information is immediately available to whoever may see one of our patients, and one of our pediatricians is always on call by beeper to discuss or come in to see any child who arrives at the hospital when our office is closed. To maintain continuity for the child and family, when any of our patients is admitted to the hospital, his or her pediatrician on our staff serves as the attending physician, coordinating and directing care on the wards.

But children do not belong in hospitals; they belong at home and in school. Our nurse practitioners visit the children outside the hospital on a regular basis, depending on individual needs. Our pediatricians also visit their patients at home—always when a child is first admitted to our program, and then as special needs arise. The team social worker is also available to provide services both in our office and in the field.

These visits outside the hospital provide the core of what is special about our program. First, and obviously, they help keep our children where they belong, with other healthy children. They help the children themselves integrate their medical care into the routine of their daily lives. Drawing a needed blood sample or performing a follow-up examination in the home or at school can save the child from missing a day of normal activity. For our families, the hospital office is foreign territory; in their homes we are their guests, and our relationship becomes entirely different. Their ease with us and our understanding of them take on a perspective that is rarely offered by hospital visits alone. Home visits allow us to teach and monitor special caretaking skills within the household setting—for most people, learning how to suction a tracheostomy tube or inject insulin under supervision on a hospital ward or in a clinic is vastly different from performing that same procedure alone at home. Seeing families on a regular basis within their own homes also provides us with the opportunity to assess the individual styles different people develop for coping with the psychological and social stresses created by the presence of a seriously ill child (Mattson, 1972). Such insights into how a family functions are not afforded in the course of an office visit in the hospital.

When a child enters our program, he or she is assigned primarily to the care of one nurse practitioner and one pediatrician, but the whole team participates in the care of all our patients. This system allows our families to identify two main providers, while assuring continuity and coverage when the primary nurse or doctor is not available. As a team we meet together once each week to discuss our patients, thus keeping each other informed as well as benefiting from each other's advice. In addition, each nurse practitioner and each doctor regularly meet as pairs to discuss in more depth the patients they share as primary providers. At our weekly team meetings we have the help of a child psychiatrist, who is able to guide us in our approach to some of the special problems our children and families face, as well as to provide direct consultations or referrals when needed.

Patient Acceptance

When a child is referred to Pediatric Home Care, our staff meets together to assess whether or not our program seems appropriate. If not, a member of our team meets with the referring physician to discuss our assessment and offer advice about possible alternative services. When it seems to us that a child will benefit from Pediatric Home Care, before formal enrollment we arrange to meet with the family, including the father, whom we make a special effort to involve both as a support for the child and the mother and as a key person in the child's care. For a child who is hospitalized, this meeting takes place before discharge so that we can involve ourselves in planning for the child's return home. Our first contact with the family, usually involving the pediatrician and nurse practitioner who will be the child's primary providers, as well as the team's social worker, is designed to introduce ourselves and the program; only if the family chooses to accept our services do we then enroll the child.

Early in our work with a family we focus on hearing their story, giving attention to their understanding of their child's illness, and, very particularly, to what their concerns may be. We try first to address the family's own concerns, to provide them not only with information but also with a sense that we hear them. Whenever a hospitalized child will need special nursing procedures at home, we begin to teach the family on the ward the skills necessary to provide appropriate care after discharge. As much as possible, in such a case, we encourage the family to assume the day-to-day care of their child in the hospital. If special equipment is required at home—for example, a suction machine for a child with a tracheostomy or a pump for a child who is fed through a tube—our nurse practitioner makes a visit before discharge to ensure that the equipment works properly and that the family can use it competently and will know what to do in case of breakdown.

As our relationship with a family evolves, we develop an "informal contract" with them. This is a plan for care that incorporates the family's priorities within what we judge to be a medically safe management scheme. Services for the child are provided through the Pediatric Home Care team; in many cases the pediatrician, nurse practitioner, or social worker is able to provide care directly, but when, for example, a sub-specialist is involved with the child, this "outside" service is channeled through our office. In this way, our staff is able to screen, coordinate, and advocate for the child and family (American Academy of Pediatrics, 1984; Pless, Satterwhite, & Van Vechten, 1978).

Nature of Home Care

Much of the routine care for a child, particularly through home visits, is performed by the nurse practitioner, who becomes the most thoroughly familiar of all the team members with the child and works most closely with the family. The child's pediatrician is always involved in supervising the medical plan of care and, especially when the illness is complex, will have substantial direct contact with the child and family. But it is the nurse practitioner who in the home setting encourages and assists the family to assume the daily care of the child. This availability to work with the family, to help them reestablish a sense of competence and thus control, has added immeasurably to the success of the Pediatric Home Care program. We are likewise convinced that our use of nurse practitioners making visits to the home not only is medically safe, given the consistent availability of back-up from our pediatricians, but is in fact crucial to our effectiveness. The nurse practitioner's orientation toward health rather than disease, her focus on care rather than cure, her attention to details often overlooked by physicians (for instance, actually taking the family of a diabetic child on a marketing trip to make concrete the lessons of diet planning), her skills in psychosocial as well as physical assessment—all these characteristics make the nurse practitioner an ideal ally of the family with a chronically ill child.

Because our program aims to involve the family actively in the care of their child, not only at home but also in the process of significant therapeutic decisions, we have worked hard to establish a good rapport with many subspecialists within our institution. Understandably, it has been difficult for many physicians trained within an acute care setting, where the patient is in effect "captive," to come to terms with the loss of control that follows from managing an ill child at home. The frustration of dealing with a disease that cannot be cured, of not being able to make a child "all better," is often compounded by a family's inability to follow a treatment plan strictly or even to keep all appointments. By being available to mediate—on the one hand, willing to advocate for the family and, on the other, to monitor and coordinate for the subspecialist—we have often been able to defuse potentially adversarial relationships (Pless et al., 1978). This is not to suggest that we always avoid conflict, even among ourselves, when we must come to terms with a family's "noncompliance" for example, an inability to give a needed medication consistently or, on rare occasions, when we have had to face removing the child from the home. The fact is that many of our patients are referred to us as a last resort, when a child is perceived to be in jeopardy because of a family's failure to follow a prescribed treatment.

We have often had to argue for patience, for accepting, at least initially, an "adequate" if not "optimal" level of care. Several years ago, a 3-year-old girl with recently diagnosed diabetes was enrolled in our program when, during the child's "honeymoon" period, her mother stopped giving her insulin. The mother was convinced that the girl was cured, that in fact the doctors in the hospital had actually given her child diabetes. Our nurse practitioner visited the home frequently, monitoring the child's blood sugar but also working empathetically with the mother, accepting the only compromise the woman was at first willing to offer—she would not do blood testing but would check her daughter's urine for sugar, and she would tell us whether or not she was giving insulin. In one 4-month period the child was admitted to the hospital three times in diabetic ketoacidosis. With time, and a sense that we respected her concern for her daughter as genuine, the mother has begun to come to real terms with her child's diabetes. She now injects the girl with insulin twice a day and, if not with perfect consistency, monitors blood sugars well enough that the child has not needed hospitalization for the past 3 years. Although the child's diabetes could be kept in even better control, we nonetheless think this is a success story.

Services Offered by the Home Care Team

Given the diversity of the children with whom we work, and the variety of stresses they, their siblings, and their parents must face, the Pediatric Home Care staff has learned the necessity of being flexible, willing to individualize the services we deliver for each of our families. In general, these services can be categorized into four major areas (American Academy of Pediatrics, 1984; Hobbs et al., 1985; Stein, 1978).

1. *Monitoring the patient.* This includes both medical and psychosocial follow-up over time. We may need to do serial physical examinations (watching for development of congestive failure in a child with heart disease or following the response to treatment of a decubitus ulcer in a child with a myelomeningocele); the child may need to have regular checks on some laboratory parameter (blood sugars for a diabetic, tests of kidney function for a child with renal disease). We may be called on to monitor the administration of medication or to watch for the side effects that may develop from a treatment regimen. Along with these more concrete functions, part of our work is always to assess how well the family is providing needed medical and nursing care, and how well the family and child are coping with the stresses placed upon them.

2. *Direct delivery of services.* Again, this involves us in both medical and psychosocial activities. Medically we provide the child with routine health care maintenance as well as with treatment for the intercurrent illnesses that may arise in any child. In cases where we are comfortable managing a child's underlying chronic illness, we directly supervise whatever diagnostic and treatment services may be needed; when we share the care of a child with a subspecialist, we are available when the child becomes . ill—at least to screen and then to facilitate whatever consultations are necessary. We are also able to provide such direct nursing services as dressing changes, stoma care, tracheostomy tube changes, and bladder catheterizations in both our office and the child's home. Likewise, we are able to arrange for our children a wide range of ancillary services, including developmental evaluation and physical, occupational, and play therapy. The social worker on our team offers our families counseling and therapeutic interventions, as well as assistance in obtaining needed services from outside our institution: specialized nursery school placements, homemaker services, transportation, public assistance, and medical insurance.

3. *Coordination of services.* This involves us with both other services within our medical center and agencies outside the hospital. Many of our children require attention from several subspecialists, each of whom may make therapeutic decisions in relative isolation from the others, often without a full awareness of what the family's priorities, abilities, and limitations may be. By channeling visits to subspecialists through our program and, when necessary, by arranging case conferences that bring together all the physicians involved in a child's care, we are able to organize a treatment plan that makes sense for the child and the family, and reduce noncompliance that comes from contradictory or incompatible prescriptions. Similarly, many of our children receive services from a wide variety of social agencies and schools in the community. By maintaining contact with these, often directly through field visits, we can function

as a focal point, helping to keep in perspective both for the family and for the various professionals how the needs of the child can best be met.

4. *Health education.* This is a process that evolves over time as our relationship with a child and family develops. Our early efforts at education are directed first at hearing the concerns of the family, at answering their questions, and at providing them with an essential understanding of the disease process affecting their child and the necessary treatments. A priority, of course, is to be sure the family understands what signs and symptoms to watch for at home as evidence that the child may be developing a problem requiring attention, and to be sure the family will know how to respond in case of an emergency. As the family becomes more comfortable with the child at home, we concentrate on encouraging them to participate more actively in the child's management, to express their preferences and help make choices among possible therapies, to feel themselves part of the team setting the priorities for the plan of care. We meet with our families frequently to discuss their inevitable feelings of anxiety and guilt, and to make ourselves aware of the particular burdens each is feeling as a result of the child's illness (Hobbs et al., 1985; Pless & Pinkerton, 1975). Ultimately, we work toward making ourselves vestigial; we have to deal in the long run with the potential dependence many families develop by building their own sense of confidence and mastery. Our aim, in the end, is to help the family become independent of the Pediatric Home Care team, able to provide and advocate for their child on their own.

Although these four areas of service provided by the Pediatric Home Care team are all related to the special needs that follow from a chronic illness, the focus of the program is on the child as a person rather than on his or her disease, on function rather than on disability, on the strengths rather than on the deficits of the child and family. Our approach to our patients and their families is noncategorical; it is not the particular medical diagnosis, we believe, but the reality of illness itself that has most impact on the children's lives (Hobbs et al., 1985; Pless & Pinkerton, 1975; Stein & Jessop, 1982). Not all diabetics are the same, either in their disease or in their health. Being sick is terrifying, whether the sickness is asthma or kidneys that no longer work. What is really important is how the fact of chronic illness can either overwhelm or make an accommodation with life, so that growth and development as much as possible are ongoing.

Before anything else, we as providers of care must be able to listen to the children and their families; only when we have really heard them can we provide the information and education they need. When we counsel, it must be honestly and patiently if there is to be trust. Particularly for the children we see, whose medical problems often are complex, somebody must coordinate and advocate for the child as a person and for the parents as the ultimate givers of care. A child with spina bifida may need the services of a neurosurgeon and a neurologist, of an orthopedist and a urologist, of a physical therapist and an occupational therapist, each of whom has different priorities and different advice, each of whom speaks a different language. If the hospital, the medical care system, is not to be a tower of Babel, someone has to be at the center to translate all the words and tests into a concern for helping the child cope, for finding and supporting the strengths that make coping possible. A chronic illness, unfortunately, is chronic; the child and the family need from us a sense of continuity and relationship. And, as the bottom line, they need from us the best quality of service we can provide, with the understanding that we care about the people for whom we are providing these services.

EVALUATION OF THE SERVICE

The Pediatric Home Care program has been evaluated in a prospective, randomized, controlled study (the Pediatric Ambulatory Care Treatment Study), which has demonstrated a significant benefit to the mental health of our families, to their satisfaction with the services they receive, and to identifying and meeting previously unfilled health needs (Stein & Jessop, 1984). For us the goal has been to help our children make their lives as normal as possible, to get them out of their beds and into schools and playgrounds.

Our program is based in a municipal hospital, serving a population of inner-city children, the vast majority of whom are poor and are insured by Medicaid. Government regulations for reimbursement of home care services have been based on a model designed for the needs of geriatric patients who are bed-bound, unable to leave their homes for care. Many of the services we provide, such as meeting with teachers and school nurses to make it safe for a child to be with friends in a classroom instead of isolated at home, are not reimbursable under current regulations. We desperately need new legislation that recognizes the special needs of our children (Hobbs et al., 1985).

Other Target Populations

In our program we have had little experience working with middle-class families, who more often receive care at voluntary hospitals. It would be important to know if an outreach intervention similar to ours could afford these families the same kinds of measurable benefits that our program has been shown to offer the impoverished families we serve (Stein &

Jessop, 1984). No doubt the different setting would call for a program different at least in its details, but there is nothing, we believe, in the spirit of our model that would keep it from working in communities other than our own. Nevertheless, we are the first to insist that Pediatric Home Care, as a model, is not easy, not for everyone, not cheap, and not by any means a total solution to the problems of children with chronic illness.

Our program has been designed to deal with the needs of children. A happy consequence of the dramatic improvement over the last decades in the quality of medical treatments is that many of the children we care for now in their families' homes will live to make homes of their own. Our last challenge, still unmet, is to find for them when they leave us other programs devoted to what will be another set of special needs.

REFERENCES

American Academy of Pediatrics. (1984). Ad hoc task force on home care of chronically ill infants and children. *Pediatrics, 74,* 434–436.

Hobbs, N., Perrin, J. M., & Ireys, H. T. (1985). *Chronically ill children and their families.* San Francisco: Jossey-Bass.

Mattson, A. (1972). Long-term physical illness in childhood: A challenge to psychological adaptation. *Pediatrics, 50,* 801–811.

Pless, I. B., & Pinkerton, P. (1975). *Chronic childhood disorder: Promoting patterns of adjustment.* Chicago: Year Book Medical Publishers.

Pless, I. B., Satterwhite, B., & Van Vechten, D. (1978). Division, duplication and neglect: Patterns of care for children with chronic disorders. *Child: Care, Health, and Development, 4,* 9–19.

Stein, R. E. K. (1978). Pediatric home care: An ambulatory special care unit. *Journal of Pediatrics, 92,* 495–499.

Stein, R. E. K., & Jessop, D. J. (1982). A noncategorical approach to chronic childhood illness. *Public Health Reports, 7,* 354–362.

Stein, R. E. K., & Jessop, D. J. (1984). Does pediatric home care make a difference for children with chronic illness? Findings from the pediatric ambulatory care treatment study. *Pediatrics, 73,* 845–853.

14

REACH: A Rural Case-Management Project

Steve A. Freedman, Ph.D., Patricia M. Pierce, R.N., Ph.D.

Most children in the United States are healthy, afflicted only by minor, self-limiting illnesses. But for those children who suffer from severe chronic conditions, the situation is very different. Because the range of these chronic conditions is so broad, their management at the community level is particularly complex. Few diseases occur frequently enough for local physicians to feel competent to treat these children, and families often must take their children to regional hospitals even for relatively minor treatment. This situation, prevalent everywhere, is more acute for the children of poor rural families. Further, these children with chronic disease are the cause of enormous financial burden, not only on the families involved (see Rowland, Chapter 2), but on the health care system itself (Freedman, 1981).

On April 1, 1981, a program called REACH—Rural Efforts to Assist Children at Home—was launched in 16 counties of north Florida to address this problem. This demonstration project sought to improve the functional ability of approximately 1,000 children with chronic illnesses from poor families who resided in the largely isolated area, which is equal in geographic size to the state of Maryland. A fundamental assumption of the REACH program was that services could be provided that would result in an overall reduction in costs to the health care system.

THE NEED

As a rule, developments in human services delivery evolve in response to observations of unmet needs or from the requirements imposed on an agency by a legislative body. REACH originated from both sources, from the patient-related experiences of health care professionals at the University of Florida Health Science Center in Gainesville and the administrative experience of government professionals at Children's Medical Services, a division of Florida's Department of Health and Rehabilitative Services. The dual goal was to diminish the hardships and despair associated with access to tertiary care for a rural population of chronically ill children and to avoid unnecessary costs of misutilization. Implicit in the challenge was the possibility of modifying an established system of care to better meet the human needs which that system had already attempted to address. According to Pierce and Freedman (1983), "diagnosing and treating the child's chronic medical conditions without also responding to other needs will only produce a limited improvement in functional status" (p. 86).

Vignette

The health care delivery problem is clearly demonstrated by a child named Joey. Joey was born with a myelomeningocele and developed hydrocephalus shortly after birth. While he was still in the hospital all of the routine surgeries and other medical procedures for the initial corrections of his congenital anomalies were accomplished. Because Joey and his mother lived 150 miles south of Gainesville, the pediatric multidisciplinary team devoted much time and effort to ensuring that, when discharged, Joey's condition was as stable as possible and that his mother was provided all the information she needed to manage her son's condition. Within a month after discharge, Joey was admitted to the small community hospital near his home. He was transferred back to the tertiary care center and treated for sepsis; his mother was again given the information the staff thought she needed in order to care for Joey. Joey was discharged after a week in the intensive care unit and 16 days on the pediatric ward. Over the next 18 months, Joey was admitted several times for similar problems. His mother was given home care instructions during each hospital stay. Several corrective surgeries had to be postponed because of Joey's recurrent infections and precarious condition.

Joey's situation was not atypical. Joey's problems encompassed more than his medical condition; he and his mother were both geographically and conceptually at a great distance from the professionals providing his care. Joey's case illustrates that often professionals and parents engage in an unwitting conspiracy leading to the benign neglect of the child for whom both parties care.

HISTORY

In 1975, the Florida legislature created a major state agency called Children's Medical Services (CMS), which was charged with organizing and financing health care for chronically ill children. The new agency grew out of the old Crippled Children's Bureau and was established at a bureaucratic level equal to that of such other major agencies as health, mental health, and public assistance. Because the CMS was new, it also had a new level of accountability. As the CMS staff began to sort out the programmatic issues associated with providing sophisticated tertiary care, they also analyzed the differences between expected costs and actual expenditures. Careful examination revealed unexpectedly high costs for some children served by the state's tertiary care centers. By 1979 the covert costs of inadequate follow-up became apparent.

Professionals from the tertiary care center at the University of Florida (Drs. Gerold L. Schiebler and Martin L. Schulkind) and Children's Medical Services (Steve A. Freedman) identified groups of children who exhibited what came to be known as the "revolving door syndrome." These children, like Joey, were involved in a cycle of health care resource utilization that far exceeded their medical need; they were experiencing unnecessary and, for the most part, preventable exacerbations of their chronic illnesses. Some of the children who received inadequate follow-up died. The university-CMS group approached David H. Pingree, Secretary of Health and Rehabilitative Services, to solicit support for a state appropriation to develop a demonstration project designed to address the multifaceted problems of this population, which were so costly in both human and economic terms. Because state revenues were not available, the Secretary joined in the effort to find extramural support for the proposed project.

FUNDING THE REACH PROJECT

The Robert Wood Johnson Foundation was identified as the most appropriate and involved philanthropic organization in such health issues. When approached, the Foundation expressed interest in assisting with the development of the model and helped refine the project design. A source of state-controlled revenue was also sought to match the private foundation support. With the assistance of the state's Medicaid Director, Charles M. Daly, the Early and Periodic Screening, Diagnosis, and Treatment (EPSDT) program was identified as the source for providing matching support.

The federal Medicaid bureaucracy was reluctant to allow Florida to expand the prevailing EPSDT case-management model from one designed as a clerical function into one based on professional services, even though the group of children to be served was demonstrably different from the normal EPSDT population. After extensive but inconclusive negotiations with the regional Health Care Financing Administration (HCFA), two Florida legislators, Senator Lawton Chiles and Representative Don Fuqua, assisted in obtaining proposal review by the HCFA central office. Following that review, the state was permitted to proceed with the project as planned. The terms of the project called for a 75% share of federal EPSDT Medicaid funds for the salaries and training of the nurse case managers. Additionally, the state was permitted to use private funds as its share (25%) of the project funding. This was a unique combination of Medicaid and private resources to support a unique effort on behalf of a special group of children while avoiding the necessity of a federal waiver.

THE MODEL

The proposed model had a simple elegance: (1) Find nurses indigenous to the rural communities to be served. (2) Train the nurses to recognize and manage the problems of chronically ill children and their families. (3) Integrate the nurses into the health care team at the tertiary care center so that they might serve as a communication bridge between the family and local health providers. (4) Charge the nurses with serving as on-call consultants and liaisons with the tertiary care professionals, helping the families understand and provide the interventions necessary to manage the child's chronic health problem. Thus REACH evolved as a community-based, family-centered, cost-avoidance health care case-management model.

THE DESIGN

Recognizing the inherent limitations of human services, which are planned from an administrative point of view, the project staff committed themselves to designing a service structure that made the child and family the focus and, at the same time, gave consideration to assuring satisfaction on the part of the nurse case managers. In their efforts to meet all the priorities, the project staff employed a flow chart to plan the process and integration of the case-management system.

Training

After the service delivery system had been structured, it became apparent that a specialized curriculum was needed to augment traditional nursing education, which focuses on acute care and service to normal populations, in order to prepare the nurses for their role as case managers. The REACH curriculum that was developed consisted of four courses. The first course, Case Management of Chronically Ill Children, was based on a general systems approach to illness and provided information about the pathophysiology and treatment of childhood chronic illness. The second course, Facilitating Growth and Development of Chronically Ill Children, provided information regarding family issues, cultural considerations, and methods for encouraging parents to stimulate the growth and development of their chronically ill or handicapped child. The third course, Communication Skills for Nurse Case Managers, provided instruction in negotiating and integrating various communication styles to achieve the goals of the case-management plan. The fourth course, Practicum in Case Management of Chronically Ill Children, taught the nurses to integrate information from the previous courses so that a comprehensive case-management plan could be developed and successfully implemented.

All of the courses were approved for academic credit by the University of Florida College of Nursing. After the demonstration phase of REACH was completed, the courses were converted into independent study for academic registered credit and were made available to employees of CMS throughout Florida, as both continuing education credit and a block of courses for nursing students.

To augment the basic curriculum and provide a broad perspective, individuals from diverse fields participated in the case managers' ongoing training program. A former school teacher who had established a day care center for indigent families provided instruction on cultural aspects of communicating with the rural poor. Subspecialist physicians lectured on the medical management of childhood chronic illness. Methods for managing on-call encounters were taught. Nutritionists, occupational therapists, physical therapists, and other professionals also participated in the ongoing training of field staff.

ASSEMBLING THE ELEMENTS

To recruit nurse case managers indigenous to the rural communities to be served, the project staff advertised in community newspapers in the target areas. The 20 nurses needed for the project were selected from more than 80 applicants, who were screened according to the specifications for the positions: licensure as a registered nurse; a minimum of 2 years experience in public health, pediatrics or orthopedics; and a willingness to be on call 24 hours a day, 7 days a week. In addition, the nurses had to be willing to establish a home-based office, furnish their own transportation, and work independently within a decentralized service system. Recruitment proceeded smoothly because this unusual type of professional practice was attractive to the majority of applicants.

As an expression of the project's commitment to child-centered service, an adaptation of the "problem-oriented record" was developed and referred to as the "Progress-Oriented Record" (POR). The taxonomy for the POR was directly related to outcomes paralleling the goals of the project, that is, school adaptation elements, self-help skills elements, and disease-specific elements were included. This permitted the project's administrative staff not only to track the child's progress but also to compare the nurses' case-management strategies within the service delivery system.

Because the nurse case managers were decentralized geographically and practiced independently, a system was developed to monitor services and to provide comparisons of efficiency and effectiveness among the field staff. The "Time and Effort Reporting Systems" (TERS), as it came to be known, was designed to permit encoding of relevant information about each case-management encounter. All coding was done in digital form, which permitted the encounters to be coded in less than 10 seconds each. Computerization of the coded data provided each case manager with a numerical picture of her/his practice and provided project management with the information necessary to assure the appropriateness of the nurses' efforts. In addition, the data were useful in comparing the relative intensity of services needed from the perspective of both diagnosis and duration of service.

A quality-assurance program, using a chart audit procedure, was initiated. Randomly selected cases were reviewed by the clinical supervisors to determine whether the POR was properly maintained and whether the interventions it reflected were appropriate to the needs of the child and family. Information derived from the chart audits was used to help the individual case manager improve practices. In addition, the information was aggregated to identify best practices to be shared among field staff. The quality-assurance program and the chart audit were verified by clinical supervision in the field.

Because the population of children needing services was greater than the staffing level the project would permit, a triage system was developed. The clinical supervisors reviewed each referral against a set of criteria to assure that the caseloads included those children and families with the most complex and potentially costly conditions. The inclusion criteria for the project caseload gave highest priority to those children whose conditions required multiple service providers and directly impaired activities of daily living. The second priority was defined as those conditions which, if inadequately managed, had great potential for interfering with activities of daily living and required coordination of several agencies involved in the child's care. The third and final priority was given to those children whose condition interfered little with activities of daily living and could be managed adequately by the family. For example, a first-priority case was a child with myelomeningocele, a second-priority child was one with a seizure disorder that could be controlled if prescribed treatment was correctly and regularly provided, and a third-priority child was one with mild cerebral palsy requiring home-based exercises.

METHODOLOGY

One significant concern in the introduction of a new service is the political action necessary to avoid initial rejection. Consequently, contacts were made with, and endorsements sought from, the state medical association, the pediatric society, the faculty of the regional nursing and medical schools, and related institutions. An advisory board was established to assure broad support and a vehicle for coordination within the academic health center.

Within the project, the leadership performed a supportive function in addition to its more formal management responsibilities. Even though the nurses were experienced, they had not experienced role rejection and work isolation, which were inherent to this practice model. Similarly, because the transdisciplinary and integrating nature of the service interfaced with a variety of other professionals, the possibility that other providers might misunderstand the nurses' activities was an initial concern. As a result the project administration made special efforts to create an atmosphere of collegiality and cohesiveness. Among other strategies employed by project management, the field staff were invited to participate in the continuing reevaluation and redesign of all elements of the service delivery activity.

Structured into the normal routine of the project were weekly administrative meetings to provide a forum for the field staff to share their concerns and accomplishments with each other. This peer interaction served to improve the morale and enhance the quality of practice among the staff, who spent most of their time in solo activities. In addition, the management staff of the project were on call to the field staff to assist them in problem solving and to provide counsel as needed.

The service environments and lifestyles of the children and their families were a continuing source of learning and surprise to the project staff. For example, when one of the nurses was making a home visit, she encountered six fly-infested hogs' heads arrayed on a table in the front yard; the family was preparing to make head cheese. In another case, a local clergyman undertook to perform an exorcism to rid a neurologically impaired child of his deviant behaviors. In coastal areas, the nurses were specifically counseled to avoid observation of illicit importation activities. The variety of homes seemed to be infinite—from a working shrimp boat to a shack made out of cardboard. Some families were so poor that they resorted to using a toaster-oven as the household source of heat. Extremes in parenting styles were also observed. In spite of poverty and lack of education, many parents were extraordinarily conscientious and competent at managing severely impaired children. Some parents, however, could not manage the chaos of their own lives, much less handle the presence of a chronically ill child. In some cases, project staff had to involve the state's child abuse and neglect system in order to encourage neglectful families to assume an appropriate level of responsibility for their sick children.

During the course of the project, it became apparent that not all families wanted the assistance of the project's field staff. Inasmuch as there were more children who could benefit from project services than there were staff to meet the need, the nurses were advised to employ an approach that gave the family an opportunity either to participate or to lose access to REACH services. Such ultimatums were rare but were sometimes effective in renewing parental involvement.

FORMAL EVALUATION

An extensive formal evaluation of REACH was designed and conducted by an external agency. The evaluation, formalized prior to the inception of the project, was designed to respond to the following five questions:

1. Were the children functioning better in terms of school attendance and participation in school activities?
2. Were medical expenditures reduced in comparison with those documented prior to the demonstration?
3. Was the financial and psychological stress on families reduced?
4. Was the program acceptable to other professionals involved with the children served?

5. Did the program work significantly better for children with some specific conditions than for those with others?

Because of the pre–post design of the project evaluation, the triage system used to determine the REACH caseload, which was established after the onset of the project, could not, empirically, be taken into consideration. Consequently, many of the findings of the formal evaluation need to be reinterpreted in light of the differences between the level of impairment of the population served and that of the population with which it was compared.

No differences in school attendance were reported in the formal evaluation. However, it may be reasonable to assume that children with more severe impairments would have poorer school attendance. One interpretation of the findings might be that, since severely impaired children had no greater attendance deficit than less severely impaired children, attendance for the children served by the project was positively affected.

The average total pre–post increase in health care expenditures for the demonstration population was only 37.5% of the increase documented for the comparison population. For example, the rate of increase of emergency room use in the demonstration population was 35.6% of that experienced in the comparison population. This was achieved through the triage of high-risk/cost families from the demonstration population into the case-managment service system while systematically excluding, whenever possible, low-risk/cost families.

Although the formal evaluation data seem to reflect no significant reduction in family stress, a survey measuring family satisfaction found that 92.5% of the families served were satisfied with REACH services. A finding of equal importance was that 88.3% of health care and allied health providers surveyed were satisfied with the overall performance of the case managers.

It was found that there were no significant differences among relevant variables as related to diagnostic categories. This confirms Perrin's (1985) conclusion that approximately 85% of problems expressed by families of chronically ill children are generic and not related to a specific disease process.

The EPSDT appointment compliance rate for the families served by the project was twice that experienced in the unserved EPSDT program population. The performance assessment system of the nurse case managers emphasized compliance rates of their caseloads. The reduction of so-called no-shows was an explicit objective of the project.

POLICY IMPACT

At the request of the Secretary of the Florida Department of Health and Rehabilitative Services (HRS), the Governor, and, through an Act of the Florida legislature, the service system developed within the REACH project has been incorporated into the statewide service system of Children's Medical Services and is now available in each of the state's eleven service districts. A study conducted by the project staff (Pierce, Freedman, Frauman, & DeBusk, 1985) suggested that substantial cost savings could be achieved through the provision of project services. In addition, close monitoring of project staff activities indicated broad satisfaction on the part of both the professional community and the project clients. Implicit to the objectives of the project was the commitment to the dissemination and statewide adoption of the demonstration services.

In addition to the adoption of the REACH service model, a new state personnel classification has been established for nurses who are employed to provide health care case-management services for chronically ill children. The training and experience requirement for this new classification includes completion of the curriculum developed by the project. Also an adaptation of the REACH project, designed to delay the onset of institutionalization of the frail elderly, is currently being developed by the state of Florida.

POLICY IMPLICATIONS

The two major implications of the project are in the areas of service design and financing. In terms of service design, REACH focused on structuring a family support case-management system that could empower the family to assume an appropriate level of responsibility for interventions that might otherwise have been provided in a fee-for-service mode. More importantly, the case-management service was sufficiently flexible to mold itself continually around both the fixed and emerging needs of the families it served. The REACH approach differed from many existing human service models in that most models have an established service design that exists independent of changes in client needs. In addition, the experience with the project pointed out that, with additional specialized training, an existing cadre of health professionals could take on an adjunct role in support of a variety of health, social, educational, and economic services.

One of the more important lessons learned through the REACH project was that providing family members opportunities for competence and caring are critical factors in containing the chaos that breeds excessive cost. Parents were shown how to meet the special needs of their children as part of their parenting, instead of merely performing those special interventions required by the child's medical condition. The less the child is an object, the less will be the potential for parental rejection and abuse. Similarly, the more competent the parents become at managing the child's care, the less frequently they dash unnecessarily to the emergency room or the tertiary care center. The REACH case managers helped them distinguish between problems and crises and taught them to act accordingly.

The financial implications of the project were twofold. First, cost savings emerged as a significant area of potential impact. As outlined above, the service population characteristically required extensive and expensive health care; without the assistance of a case manager, they tended to misutilize health care resources. The project made no effort to suppress the appropriate use of health care resources. However, by increasing parents' competence, unnecessary emergency room visits, clinic visits, and admissions, with their attendant costs, could be avoided. Second, the formula for utilizing Medicaid participation to support the professional case managers was agreed to be, in the main, an appropriate use of those resources. However, controversy still exists about the appropriateness of federal financial participation in certain elements of the REACH case-management service. That controversy is being addressed in appropriate legal forums.

SUMMARY

The successes of the REACH project and similar efforts by Stein (1983) and her colleagues point to the broad utility and applicability of case-management services for both rural and urban populations. Several important observations seem appropriate. First and foremost, this specialized service, which is clearly effective in human terms, is justifiable for only a small proportion of chronically ill children from a cost perspective. Second, it is possible to decentalize the management of outpatient services for tertiary care patients to the satisfaction of the attending physicians. Third, families and children enjoy the security of having a community-based professional who has an understanding of their specific needs and who is committed to helping them become as self-sufficient as possible. Fourth, a proportion of costly health care encounters can be avoided through the provision of a structured, coordinated case-management service.

As with any other endeavor, external recognition is desirable to validate both the effort and the outcomes. In this regard the REACH project has been especially privileged. Not only was the project model adopted by the state within which the demonstration took place, but the service model has also been recognized and sought out by a number of other agencies and institutions. For example, the REACH project was selected as one of the five exemplary child health initiatives in the nation to be included in the social marketing project entitled "Healthy Children," based at Harvard University's Division of Health Research and Education. Similarly, the REACH model was highlighted by the Vanderbilt University Institute for Public Policy Studies (1985) in their definitive work, *Chronically Ill Children and Their Families*. (Another project cited by the Vanderbilt study, the Pediatric Home Care program of the Albert Einstein College of Medicine/Bronx Municipal Hospital Center, New York City, is discussed in Chapter 13.)

In sum, the REACH project is an example of a simple solution to a complex problem. The solution had historic precedent in early public health nursing and seemed to be a good fit with the various elements of the problem. That solution trained nurses to understand the problems of chronically ill children and their families, to understand the problems of tertiary care physicians, to understand the factors that link and separate those groups, and, at the same time, to provide the interventions necessary to ensure that the children received all the appropriate care while discouraging inappropriate utilization of health care resources. Although REACH served a client population associated with a public agency, the implications for professional case management extend beyond the public sector to the many emerging forms of service delivery on the health care horizon.

REFERENCES

Freedman, S. A. (1981). Rural efforts to assist children at home: Project plan [Florida Dept. of Health and Rehabilitative Services, Tallahassee, FL]. Princeton, NJ: Robert Wood Johnson Foundation.

Perrin, J. M. (1985, April) *Policies affecting children with chronic illnesses*. Speech given at Arizona Conference on Children with Chronic Illness, Phoenix, AZ.

Pierce, P. M., & Freedman, S. A. (1983). The REACH project: An innovative health delivery model for medically dependent childen. *Children's Health Care, 12*(2), 86–89.

Pierce, P. M., Freedman, S. A., Frauman, A. C., & DeBusk, F. L. (1985). Reducing costs with a community outreach program. *Pediatric Nursing, 11*, 361–364.

Porter, P. J. (1984). Healthy children: A program to encourage the development of children's health services. Cambridge, MA: Harvard University, Division of Health Research and Education.

Stein, R. E. K. (1983). A home care program for children with chronic illness. *Children's Health Care, 12*(2), 90–92.

15

The Illinois Model:
A Statewide Initiative

Gene E. Bilotti, M.S.W.

Everett Dirksen, the late Senator from Illinois, once began an address to Congress by saying, "A billion dollars here, a billion dollars there, if we keep it up pretty soon we'll be talking about real money." Our Illinois experience indicates that although we are not touching the billions, we are involved in the millions in regard to home health care for chronically ill and disabled children who can be better cared for in their homes or home-like settings than institutions.

Our entry into this activity was brought about by serendipity rather than deliberate planning. Our first case occurred in September 1979, when a prominent children's hospital in our state decided that a child should go home on a ventilator rather than stay in the hospital. Since that time, the Illinois Division of Services for Crippled Children (DSCC), through a program based at the University of Illinois, has been involved in planning for the discharge, monitoring, and case management of approximately 100 children. Of this number, approximately 30 children are now residing in their own homes with the regular use of a ventilator or other high-technology equipment necessary to sustain life functions.

Several years later, we still find ourselves struggling for a definition of home care for chronically ill and disabled children. Although Pless and Douglas's commonly accepted definition of chronic illness, which is cited by Hutchins and McPherson in Chapter 1 and used throughout the book, is acceptable, it is necessary that our functional definition be expanded to include the reasons why a child is placed in home care and the concomitant home care plans and arrangements that are made for that child.

A thorough definition acceptable to all involved parties has eluded us through the years. It now includes a portion of Pless and Douglas's definition and also includes a chronic physical condition with complex needs requiring frequent, ongoing intervention on the part of skilled and technical personnel to administer either nursing surveillance, medications, positioning, suctioning, or other specified life-sustaining equipment or procedures. Additionally, the definition includes ongoing assessments necessary to avoid life-threatening situations that would require the immediate technical intervention and expertise offered by nurses or other professional personnel to maintain life safety.

In addition to the physical and medical problems, other social and environmental factors must be considered in determining and/or defining a home care need. The DSCC and the Illinois Department of Public Aid, the primary funder for such home care activities, are in agreement that certain social and environmental factors may indicate the need for specialized assistance at home in order to maintain a child who otherwise could be adequately managed only in a hospital or institutional setting. These social and environmental factors should include, but are not necessarily limited to, single-parent families, inner-city situations involving low-income housing, rural situations where the family resides at least 50 miles from a major medical center, and those cases in which five or more vendors or suppliers are involved, the presence of other small children in the family who require the attention of the parents. Additional health and social factors include other family problems indicating that the available adults cannot spend much time in caring for the child, foster-family situations where the foster family agrees to take the child only if special assistance and consideration are given, the availability of extended family to assist in the care of the child, and the availability of other helping community resources such as health care groups or church groups.

Any assessment of the social and environmental factors affecting home care needs to be done through an informed consent process, wherein the family is thoroughly informed of its alternatives and formally requests assistance from the Illinois DSCC. Part of this informed consent will often include the family's agreement that they can manage the care of the child without additional assistance; the family's request and needs should be considered before care is either offered or encouraged by health care professionals. The underlying decision should be made in concert with the family and the Division case manager.

CASE-MANAGEMENT APPROACH TO HOME CARE

The Illinois Division of Services for Crippled Children is staffed by Public Health nurses, medical social workers, and speech and hearing consultants or audiologists who are supervised by locally based Program Service Managers. This unit can be defined as the DSCC multidisciplinary team. Other professional disciplines can be included on the team, depending on the child's or family's need for greater professional input than exists within the DSCC.

Central to the Illinois approach to home care is the concept of case management, which begins with the identification of a child who is a potential home-discharge candidate. Such children may be ventilator-dependent or may possess other chronic disabilities that will require special care and services at home. "Special" treatment includes those situations in which equipment is needed for sustaining life or in which a documented need for nursing service exists. When the discharging hospital identifies such a child as a possible candidate, the Illinois DSCC local office is informed of the child's condition, and an initial staffing is usually arranged with the hospital discharge-planning team. Following the first meeting, usually two months prior to discharge, the Program Service Manager (Regional Manager for DSCC) appoints a case manager to coordinate all the activities of the multidisciplinary team related to this child's subsequent discharge and home care management. The individual needs of the child and the social and environmental conditions in the home will determine the appointment of the case manager.

An initial meeting of the Division's multidisciplinary team and the hospital discharge unit is held in order to determine if the child is potentially eligible for home care and to consider the manner in which planning needs to proceed. Eligibility includes the following criteria:

1. need for technology, such as a ventilator, or special nutritional assistance;
2. chronic illness lasting at least three months;
3. need for special nursing or other home care services, such as therapy and/or regular respite care;
4. a clear definition of the social and environmental factors within the home that have brought the family sequentially through counseling and informed consent to request special home intervention.

Ideally, the case manager and the team should become involved at least two months prior to discharge in order to assure that the discharge plan developed will be one the DSCC can approve, support, and monitor. Moreover, it needs to be a plan that can be financed through either the Illinois Medicaid program, private insurance, or a combination of Medicaid and private insurance.

When the plan is completed and all parties, including the primary attending physician and the family, have indicated their agreement, an actual discharge date is agreed on. At the time of discharge, the role of the discharging hospital is reduced considerably and the case-management role of the DSCC is greatly increased. The role of the case manager and the multidisciplinary team is to see that all elements of the home care plan are indeed carried out. Other specialists, such as counselors and therapists, may be included as participants in the case at any time, should the need arise. Although the role of the hospital discharge team is diminished considerably, it is necessary for it to remain ready for consultation should problems arise with the actual implementation of the plan in the home. It is also necessary that the discharging hospital be willing to readmit the child in the event of an emergency and/or if other medical problems arise that would interfere with the child's ability to be cared for adequately in the home. It is usually preferable to have the home health agency (nursing agency) and the durable medical equipment vendors involved in case planning.

CASE DEVELOPMENT IN PREPARATION FOR HOME DISCHARGE

Following consultation with the hospital, the DSCC case manager contacts the family to obtain authorization for the release of prior medical history summaries of the child's growth and development, as well as all other medical reports. Additionally, medical reports are sought from the child's primary physician.

Following a preliminary assessment of these data, a home visit is planned by the case manager and medical social worker assigned to the case. The home visit is designed to counsel the family in regard to their rights of placement rather than home care, to ascertain their wishes regarding home placement, and to review family dynamics that may affect the home placement. Environmental factors considered are the location of the family's home and its suitability (e.g., size, location of rooms, ramps, the heating system, accessibility, electric wiring, a work area for nursing personnel and other involved professionals. An overall assessment of the family's ability to cope with the home care situation is a focal point of this process. Often additional planning sessions are needed with the parents or other legally responsible adults to explore the respective roles of the managing agency and the family, to better assess the family's understanding of the illness, to encourage the family to express their views and goals, to determine the family's perception of the child's needs, and to better clarify the roles of all involved providers, including DSCC, the home health agency, and durable medical equipment vendors.

At this point, a preliminary individual service plan is developed by the case manager, with maximum input from the other members of the team as well as the providers, to define all the steps needed for the completion of the home care plan. An overall view for case planning should identify the appropriate liaisons with the discharging institution, the home health agency, and all involved vendors. The preliminary plan will lead to the final development of an individual service plan, which should define, at a minimum:

1. suitability of the home, including a description of the home or alternative situation in which the child is to be placed;
2. the appropriateness of the medical care, including a statement from the multidisciplinary team and the child's primary care physician, signed by the legally responsible adult, attesting to the fact that the medical care the child is to receive in the home is agreed to by the legally responsible adult and is appropriate in the opinion of all involved parties;
3. the need for nursing care, including documentation of the agreement with the home health agency and a statement that the child could not live in his or her natural home or home-like setting without the special assistance of nursing care;
4. equipment needs, including a list of all prescribed equipment agreed to in the child's hospital discharge plan, defined in the child's Individual Service Plan for Home Care, and signed by the attending physician; and
5. a statement designating the home health agency and the vendors who are to provide the equipment to be used in the child's home care plan.

Once the child is actually residing at home, the role of the case manager as the primary contact person for the family and all other involved personnel is of paramount importance. It is the full intention of DSCC that this function be clearly defined to all involved people and followed accordingly to provide for good communication and solid relationships over a long time period.

FINANCIAL PLANNING FOR HOME CARE

It has been our experience that many well-planned home care cases never come to fruition because of the lack of financial planning and/or payment for the home care costs. In Illinois, there are six primary funding patterns for chronically ill children who are placed in their own home or a home-like setting with special facilities. These six primary funding approaches are:

1. Finance Plan for Home Care, Illinois Department of Public Aid,
2. the Title XIX Model Waiver for Disabled Children, Illinois Department of Public Aid,
3. private health insurance,
4. a combination of public aid and private insurance,
5. community resources, and
6. personal family resources.

Finance Plan for Home Care

Approximately 60% of the home health care cases in Illinois are funded by obtaining approval for a Finance Plan for Home Care. The Finance Plan for Home Health Care is developed by the DSCC case manager and is intended to allow the Illinois Department of Public Aid to authorize payment for special equipment, supplies, and nursing service. The Finance Plan for Home Health Care succinctly describes the suitability of the home, appropriateness of the medical care, need for nursing care, and need for equipment. A proposal indicating that it is in the patient's best interests to reside in a home setting, and explaining that DSCC will have the responsibility for case management and coordination of all activities, is also part of the home care plan (see Table 15.1).

Title XIX Model Waiver for Disabled Children

As discussed in Chapter 2, the Title XIX model waiver for severely disabled children, granted by the Health Care Finance Administration of the Department of Health and Human Services, allows 50 children to be placed in a waiver category if they meet the state requirements as defined in the waiver. The Illinois Department of Public Aid applied for and was granted such a waiver.

To be eligible for a waiver, the following criteria must be met:

TABLE 15.1 Finance Plan for Home Health Care Developed by the Illinois Division of Services for Crippled Children

Elements of the plan	Documentation required
Suitability of the home—the fashion in which the patient is to be cared for at home	Statement that it is the parents' desire for the child to be placed in the home
	Statement that the physician concurs with home care
Appropriateness of the medical care	Documentation that the patient can be cared for at home
	Indication that the patient will receive emergency care should the need arise
	Frequency of physician contacts
	Number of visits, estimated cost, and manner in which the family will pay for these services
Need for nursing care—an explanation of the family's situation and the reasons why the child requires nursing care in the home	Name, address, and telephone number of the home health agency, cost per hour, number of hours per day and number of days per month that nursing service is to be provided
	Letter from the patient's physician stating the need for the home nursing care and the number of hours recommended by the physician
	Recommendation as to the need for appropriate therapies as prescribed and signed by the attending physician
Equipment needs—a detailed list of all special equipment needed in order to actualize the home care situation	Purchase costs
	Pertinent information regarding the vendor
	Rental fees
	Physician's prescription for the equipment
	Prescribed list of medications detailing the approximate monthly cost and the provider's name, address, and telephone number
	Patient's Medicaid card number that is to be utilized for medication
Proposal	Indication that it is in the patient's best interest to reside in his or her natural home or a home-like setting
	Indication that DSCC will have the responsibility for case management
	Indication that DSCC will coordinate all activities with the home health agency and the durable medical vendor

1. The child must be under the age of 21.
2. The child would require institutionalization if the waiver were not approved.
3. The cost of the care in the home must not exceed the Illinois Department of Public Aid reimbursement schedule for either a hospital, skilled nursing facility, or intermediate care facility if the child were to return to any of those institutions for care.
4. The quality of care in the home must, in the opinion of the attending physician, be at least equal to the care that the child would receive in one of the aforementioned institutions. (This statement must be included in the waiver.)

If a patient meets the above criteria, application is made to the local Public Aid office, which in turn makes a waiver referral to the Illinois DSCC, which completes the waiver process in agreement with the Illinois Department of Public Aid.

The philosophical intent of the Title XIX waiver for chronically ill and disabled children is to waive financial eligibility by deeming the family's income as not applicable for the care of the child at home. The waiver thus applies to children who would not be eligible for financial assistance in the home but would be eligible for financial assistance in the hospital. Additionally, all eligible waiver children in Illinois must also have a Finance Plan for Home Care approved by the Department of Public Aid. Guidelines for the waiver process and Finance Plans for Home Care have been made available to all of the involved case managers.

Private Insurance

On occasion, private insurance carriers have agreed to assume the financial responsibility for home care cases. This has happened even when the child's insurance policy does not indicate a home care liability on the part of the insurance carrier. Insurance companies often recognize the cost effectiveness of home care and are willing to participate, with the appropriate case management being assumed by the Division of Services for Crippled Children.

Usually, if an interview can be arranged with an insurance carrier claim representative and a DSCC case manager, an agreement can be reached that will be in the best interests of the family and will commit the company to fully or partially fund the child's care at home. Arrangements and agreements with individual insurance companies vary.

Combination Agreements Between Insurance Companies and Public Aid

Insurance companies often interpret their liability to end at 80% of the total cost for the child's care in the home. If this arrangement does not void the cost-effectiveness section of the Title XIX waiver, then a waiver may be developed and approved for the child. (However, children who have private insurance are not generally eligible for waiver consideration because they do not normally meet the cost-effectiveness clause.) In such cases, a Finance Plan for Home Care that clearly defines the respective payments in actual amounts to be made by the insurance company and the Department of Public Aid can be developed following the procedures mentioned above. Such agreements are often of long standing and end only when the child's physical situation changes or the insurance coverage lapses.

Community Resources

Home health care development has been greatly aided in Illinois by the assistance of private voluntary health agencies. Often, when a child has a diagnosis that is covered by a voluntary health agency, some assistance may be obtained from that agency. Such agencies include, but are not limited to, United Cerebral Palsy, Muscular Dystrophy Association, the American Cancer Society, Leukemia Society, and other voluntary agencies of the health care community. Usually the assistance from such groups is supplemental in nature and valuable in helping the family to meet service gaps. Additionally, churches and other religious groups, as well as community service clubs, have been very helpful from time to time in assisting families with minor costs, with unusual one-time cost items, and respite assistance.

Personal Family Resources

The cost of home health care usually exceeds the family's income. The average cost for home care in Illinois is approximately $10,000 per month. Since this cost is greater than most families can assume, they need to turn to one of the five other areas for assistance. The family, however, is required to meet the ordinary needs of the child, such as clothing, food, and shelter. Many families have discovered that additional hidden costs of home care have placed a severe strain upon the family budget.

In almost all cases, when the hospital discharge team and the DSCC case manager have joined forces to plan carefully for the financial discharge of a child, outside resources have been uncovered to finance the child's care at home. The Medicaid level of approved payment for 57 children during the last 30 days in the hospital averaged $15,735.09. The average approved monthly level of payment for the same population in the home is $7,326,85. Thus the potential savings to the state of Illinois for home care exceeds $500,000 per month, and it is anticipated that the home care costs can be further reduced and that the caseload will continue to increase.

PROBLEMS AND CONCERNS

On the surface it appears that the Illinois home care program is successful and that all involved parties are pleased with the results. Although the cost effectiveness of the program can yield some impressive figures, there is currently no mechanism to evaluate the overall success of the program. To be sure, children are being placed in their own home or home-like settings at an increasing rate each year; a strict adherence to the home care definition offered earlier may well mean that up to 200 children will be served in their own homes in this fashion before the end of the calendar year 1988.

However gratifying the success may be, major problems and questions exist in the minds of the families and most of the team members involved in home care management. These problems center around a need to develop a better system of counseling, supporting, and assisting the family when their child returns home with the necessary support services. Many of the professionally involved personnel feel that a system needs to be put in place that would enhance the family's ability to cope with this unusual situation.

Other problems center around the need to develop standards, criteria, and protocols for home health agencies, vendors, and other involved professional personnel. Although we have draft standards and guidelines available for professional staff use at this point, our body of knowledge has not evolved to the point where we are able to write definitive procedures that would stand up under constant use.

There is also an awakening awareness on the part of team members and families that measures really do not exist to determine how well the child is actually doing in the home. Many share the opinion that the children are doing very well to exceptionally well, but no objective criteria have been put in place to assist the Illinois program in developing a solid data base. Additionally, it is impossible to know how many of the children served in the home care program would have remained institutionalized had it not been for the DSCC intervention. DSCC staff have also indicated that they need additional, different, and better training in order to serve as case managers for these children.

FUTURE DIRECTIONS

The effective provision of long-term, complex services in the home as an alternate to hospital care (with hospital cost-containment plus child care considerations) needs to be developed in an innovative fashion that is oriented to the community and creates a family-like system of care. The professional literature indicates major gaps in defining the assurance of quality home care, creating a system to help the family develop family support services that will exceed the boundaries of the past, and developing a sophisticated total funding package that would include direct and indirect costs, such as telephone and other utilities, that may be intensified because of the home care program.

There is also an indication that an effective management system should be developed within the crippled children's agencies to allow the entire team to remain involved with all parties concerned with home care. More consideration should be given to seminars, research and sharing of experiences, the development of quality-assurance mechanisms, and monitoring of case-management and nursing standards to assure the involved professionals of the viability of the plan that is carried on in the home. Health care planners, as well as providers, need to address these issues as well as develop a data base to measure expected outcomes. If the Title V or crippled children's agencies are going to provide case management for pediatric home care cases, then additional funding is going to be necessary for these agencies to retool and replan their efforts in this comprehensive fashion.

16

Project SERVE:
A Needs Assessment
and State Planning Model
for Massachusetts

*Susan Gilbert Epstein, M.S.W., Ann Boyd Taylor, Ed.D.,
Deborah Klein Walker, Ed.D., Allen C. Crocker, M.D.,
Jane Gardner, R.N., Sc.D., Alexa S. Halberg, B.A.
Serena E. H. Mailloux, M.D., Ann Murphy, M.S.W.,
Gerald A. Tuttle, Ph.D.*

As health policy makers, health care providers, and families look at services for children with chronic illness or disabling conditions today, they are asking new questions. How should community-based, family-centered services really be organized? How should eligibility for services be determined? Who will pay for home care? How will the quality of specialized care be assured? Governmental agencies, state departments of health, and especially publicly funded programs for children with chronic illnesses or disabling conditions are being challenged to assess the changing needs of these children and their families and consider a redefinition of the most appropriate public role in serving children with special health care needs.

To date most of the questioning about services for these children has occurred within the constraints of existing structural units, with little overall assessment of the logic of the patchwork of public and private agencies and jurisdictional units. As a rule, most new plans have been grafted onto existing structures. Often, they further exacerbate the fragmentation of existing services by creating complex subunits and ignoring the need to integrate and possibly reorganize services.

Recent policy studies and dissemination activities of Vanderbilt University concerning chronically ill children and their families have sparked a new concern about this group of children at all levels of government and in the private health care and social services sectors. In response to the questions listed above and in the context of a renewed national focus on this population, a group of child health professionals in Massachusetts initiated a new type of collaborative planning process, called Project SERVE. Planners from three institutions endeavored to assist the state's health department program for children with special health care needs to:

1. define a rational public role that complements and enhances the larger private health care system,
2. utilize public resources in a manner that is equitable and has the ability to reach an expanded proportion of the target population,
3. promote a comprehensive definition of quality care for the target population,
4. support families in their roles as caregivers and advocates for children with special health care needs, and
5. avoid duplication and fragmentation of services across public and private agencies.

This chapter gives an overview of the participatory planning process that was designed in Massachusetts to address the unmet needs of children with chronic health conditions and their families. It includes a statewide model for a comprehensive assessment of the public role in serving children with special health care needs and a unified plan that evolved from the collaborative experiences of all involved in the care of these children—the state agencies, the providers, and the families. The results are currently being implemented by the Department of Public Health in Massachusetts, and the model is also being adapted for similar reassessments in other states. In the discussion below, we highlight some of the principles that we believe were critical to ensuring the success of this attempt to restructure services.

More details about the data collection tools and the findings and recommendations for Massachusetts are available in other documents.* The first

---

* Two companion reports, *New Directions: Serving Children with Special Health Care Needs in Massachusetts* (1985) and *New Directions: A Needs Assessment and State Planning Model for Children with Special Health Care Needs* (1987), are available from New England SERVE, Massachusetts Health Research Institute, Inc., 101 Tremont St., Boston, MA 02108. This chapter is adapted from the 1987 report.

section of this chapter provides a general description of the project and summarizes 10 key characteristics of this planning process as well as the organizational framework that evolved. The second section briefly describes the major components of the data-collection goals and instruments. The third section documents the strategies used by the project to enhance implementation of the planning recommendations, including the development of a statewide coalition for children with special health care needs. It is hoped that the articulation of the critical elements of a systemwide planning process used in one state will help others who wish to implement a similar process for needs assessment, program planning, and organizational change on behalf of children with special needs and their families. Although this process was developed for a state, the key elements could be easily adapted for use in other clearly identifiable geographic areas—that is, counties or regions.

THE MASSACHUSETTS PROJECT: A DESCRIPTION AND SUMMARY

Three Title V agencies in Massachusetts joined forces in October 1983 with the funding support of the Division of Maternal and Child Health, U.S. Department of Health and Human Services, to address the five public policy goals outlined. These three organizations were the Division of Family Health Services (DFHS) in the Massachusetts Department of Public Health (the Maternal and Child Health leadership agency in the state), the Developmental Evaluation Clinic at The Children's Hospital (a major specialty care and developmental services provider), and the Department of Maternal and Child Health in the Harvard School of Public Health (a longstanding training center for practitioners and policy makers in maternal and child health).

This planning process was characterized by 10 design, resource, and process elements believed to be crucial to its success and therefore worthy of note by other groups that may be considering a similar planning and policy development exercise. These elements and the major reasons for their importance are outlined below.

Key Characteristics of the Planning Process

1. *Public–private collaboration.* From the beginning, the planning activity, while focusing on the public agency's role in serving children with special health care needs, took advantage of both public- and private-sector leadership. Principal investigators for the project came from a private tertiary care center and a private academic institution as well as the state

public health agency itself. It was seen as important to the plan's success that it not be viewed as being designed by or for only one segment of the health care system.

2. *Off-site administration.* The project was managed by and housed in a neutral and independent agency, the Massachusetts Health Research Institute, Inc. The presence of a longstanding public health grants management institute in Massachusetts provided an appropriate administrative vehicle. This allowed for a neutral territory where difficult issues that could be expected to have a significant impact on existing organizations and bureaucracies could be openly and honestly explored.

3. *Interdisciplinary steering committee.* Utilizing monthly full-day meetings as the primary strategy for defining project activities and conducting problem-solving sessions, the project evolved a team model that included nine members: three principal investigators, three part-time program specialists, and three staff people. This group, which shared in all data-collection and data-analysis responsibilities, was supported partly through grant funding and partly through in-kind contributions of agency time. Participants were selected based on their willingness to remain active over a 3-year period and high degree of interest and planning expertise at both the health system and individual client levels. Interdisciplinary membership in the group included social work, education, medicine, nursing, and public health. Contracts with outside consultants were developed in selected areas such as health care financing and consumer leadership.

4. *Active, participatory group process.* The decision-making processes used by the steering committee relied heavily on the active participation of all members. Strategies used by the group included preparing written statements in response to individual assignments that were circulated before group meetings, conducting open debates about areas of conflict, subteam assignments to draft position papers, and staff interviewing of individual committee members to develop consensus positions when conceptual or operational roadblocks emerged.

5. *Acknowledged professional leadership.* All three principal investigators involved in the Massachusetts project were acknowledged leaders in the public health community. This status, as well as their expertise and longevity in the professional community, provided respectability to the project and its staff.

6. *Parent/consumer participation.* A high priority was placed on securing active consumer participation in the needs assessment process. This included hiring a parent/consumer advocate as an early advisor and consultant to the project and developing effective linkages to other parent groups, advocates, and spokespersons for children with varying disabilities or chronic illnesses.

7. *Commitment to organizational and policy changes.* Critical to the project were both the active participation and in-kind donation of professional time of both a principal investigator and a program specialist from the public agency (DFHS) that was the focus of the study. The original project included a clear commitment by the state health agency to an implementation phase within the three-year funding period. Therefore, the grant was accepted with the open and public promise that the study would lead to some significant organizational changes.

8. *Belief in local availability of information and skills.* An externally contracted needs assessment or consultant service can quickly contribute to a feeling of internal organizational inadequacy and a desire to get the answers from outside the system or the state. National experts are often assumed to know more than local resources and may be pursued to provide easy answers. This project was based on a firm belief that the information necessary to make the difficult decisions regarding unmet needs and new public policy directions was available right at home. In fact, it was available *only* at home. Massachusetts providers, families, and public agency personnel had to become the key informants for this process.

9. *Avoidance of assessment of quality of care.* Throughout the needs assessment and data-collection process, the project attempted to avoid even the slightest impression of being a program evaluation. All data-collection tools and interview formats clearly defined the activity as planning in order to maximize public resources and develop the most appropriate public role in serving children with special health care needs. No attempt was made to observe or assess the quality of current programs and services, only to define their components and objectives.

10. *Encouragement of the "ideal model."* From the outset of the planning process, all participants—whether as interviewees, consultants, or steering committee members—were encouraged to think creatively to define the ideal service system without considering the limitations of existing financial or program realities. This philosophy allowed the project to define the fullest set of health service needs and to identify barriers to implementation.

Organization of the State Planning Process

The project in Massachusetts was organized into four main phases—data collection, data analysis, model development, and implementation—that stretched over a 3-year period of time. Data collection and data analysis efforts were designed to document existing services for children with special health care needs in the public sector, to explore sample model services in the private sector, to identify unmet service needs, to examine how services were being financed, and to consider alternative roles and functions for the public health agency.

In order to facilitate the development of meaningful recommendations for the state health agency, the project endorsed a set of commonly held principles and values that define quality in health care for the target populations of children (see Table 16.1). Although many, if not most, of these program and system characteristics could have been identified from other sources, the process of collectively brainstorming and debating these statements served to make explicit the values and assumptions held by the steering committee. This important process, completed early in the data collection phase, established a common vocabulary and set of assumptions that became critical in the later consensus-building discussions. The principles and values provided a framework for data analysis and guided the thinking of the group regarding the most appropriate public role in serving children with special health care needs.

A thorough analysis of the project's findings and conclusions produced consistent themes regarding the needs of children and families, patterns of resource availability and service utilization within the state, and current issues in medical care and health care financing. These themes, considered in the context of the principles of care, led the project to identify new directions and priorities for the state health agency.

Table 16.1 Principles and Values for Quality Care for Children with Special Health Care Needs

---

Comprehensive—assuring access to a broad range of health, education, and special services

Universally available—assuring access to all children regardless of age, race, economic status, or geographic location

Developmentally appropriate—based on assessment of child's functional development and chronological age

Family-oriented and community-based—in the least restrictive, most normalizing environment

Individualized—based on child and family needs as determined by relevant evaluations

Multidisciplinary—to reflect the multiple needs of the child and family

Continuous—to maintain without interruption a course of appropiate treatment and care

Coordination—through a written plan of care across public and private agencies

Managed—through a single individual who can assist the family to implement the service plan

Financially supported—to protect the fiscal integrity of the family

---

After receiving the recommendations, the state agency began an internal analysis and critique of the project's recommendations as its first step toward implementation. Project personnel served as consultants and resource persons to the internal review. Leadership responsibility was then formally transferred to the state health agency. This probably could not have been accomplished successfully with the agency's central participation from the beginning of the process, the creation of a project structure that had been designed so that it would not perpetuate itself, and an up front commitment to building a broad base of support to help implement the recommendations.

In the remaining months of the project, staff and resources were also used to address issues outside the DFHS that would be critical to full and successful implementation of the project's recommendations. Of special importance were constituency-building efforts to bring the needs of this population of children into the public and eventually legislative arena.

DATA COLLECTION STRATEGIES TO ENSURE PARTICIPATORY PLANNING

Data collection, the heart of the needs assessment process, was never viewed as an isolated event, but as the first step of the implementation process for any future changes. The goal was to conduct a systematic policy study that would provide answers to the questions outlined in the previous section from all the key stakeholders in the system of care. Although this was time consuming, it was well worth the effort, since the contacts made during this phase of the project were key to the development of the program plans and implementation of subsequent recommended changes. This study was hampered by the state's lack of a comprehensive child health monitoring system with population-based survey statistics, and the necessary planning and policy development had to be done without those data.

Data were collected in five main areas, including the state health agency, other health care services in the state, families, other states, and current patterns of health care financing (see Table 16.2). Successful participatory planning must identify and reach key groups that are not normally included in planning for state health agencies. Two such groups targeted in the Massachusetts planning process were parents and private sector health care providers. Data collection strategies were designed to include extensive outreach to ensure in-depth information from key informants in these groups. This was a labor intensive process involving multiple telephone and written contacts with over 25 parent advocacy groups across the state and necessitated outreach to neighborhood health centers in

TABLE 16.2 Data Collection Strategies Used by Project SERVE for Statewide Planning

Agency context
Focus on existing services and management structures within the state public health agency

Information obtained via:
in-depth structured interviews with staff members
in-depth face-to-face semi-structured interviews with medical consultants
a systematic review of program and budget information

Statewide context
Focus on the broad picture of public and private health care services for children with chronic illness or disability across the state

Information collected via:
a mailed questionnaire to members of the state chapter of the American Academy of Pediatrics
telephone interviews with primary care physicians in neighborhood health centers
in-depth semi-structured interviews with administrators of other state programs
in-depth semi-structured group interviews with members of specialty care teams across the state
in-depth face-to-face interviews with social service and ancillary health personnel in tertiary centers

Consumer and family context
Focus on health and needs of existing health care services for children with chronic illness or disabilities as experienced and reported by consumers, family, and advocacy groups

Information collected via:
a mailed questionnaire to parents of children with chronic illness or disabilities across the state
telephone interviews with parent advocates

National context
Focus on proposed and existing models for service delivery systems and evaluation/quality assurance practices in other states

Information obtained via:
review of information from other states
telephone reviews with national leaders in state Title V programs

Fiscal context
Focus on proposed and existing models for financing health care services for children with chronic illness and disability

Information obtained via an in-depth analysis of three major financing sources:
Blue Cross/Blue Shield
Medicaid
Health maintenance organizations

urban areas with large minority populations. Input from specialty care teams required time-consuming meetings in tertiary care settings at the convenience of providers; these meetings typically lasted 2 to 3 hours and included ten or more professional staff.

Although collecting data in each of the five areas outlined in Table 16.2 required different methodologies, an attempt was made to collect parallel information across data sources. A standard set of questions was repeated whenever possible on separate instruments. These included questions regarding unmet service needs (medical and nonmedical), the most appropriate role of the state health agency, roles for families, and barriers to providing or obtaining existing services. From the analysis of these questions, a master list of unmet needs was developed (see Table 16.3) and was used in coding and analyzing other data sets.

STRATEGIES FOR IMPLEMENTATION

A critical issue for any project that uses outside personnel to develop recommendations for organizational or programmatic changes is what will happen with those recommendations once they are developed and presented to the target agency. State agency bookshelves are filled with reports recommending changes that were only partially implemented or not implemented at all. Significant resources were allocated to Project SERVE for future planning purposes, and the project had the potential for generating major changes within the system. How did the project address the risk of becoming just another bound volume in the offices of the state Department of Public Health?

The long-range impact of such planning efforts is directly linked to both the degree of internal (i.e., within the Department of Public Health) involvement and identification with project findings, and the level of external (i.e., outside of the Department of Public Health) awareness of those same findings among providers and consumers. In addition, linkages between the two groups are required so that the external advocacy efforts are accessible to those within the bureaucracy.

Strategies to facilitate implementation began early in the project. Even the first data collection activities were designed to inform participants of project goals and to minimize potential polarization of current providers and those involved in planning roles and functions in the state agency.

Designing the Project: Inclusion of an Implementation Phase

The original proposal for Project SERVE outlined a three-year process including a full year of implementation activities in year three. Although

TABLE 16.3 Categories of Identified Unmet Needs

Health-related services
  Specialty care
    pediatric neurology
    pediatric cardiology
    ophthalmology
    unspecified specialty care
  Primary out-patient care
  Physical therapy—with pediatric
    specialization
  Primary dental care
  Occupational therapy
  Home health/nursing care
  Nutrition services
  Speech therapy
  Adaptive equipment and supplies
  Early diagnosis and assessment
  Medicaid provider availability
  Extensive specialty diagnostic
    evaluations (developmental, language,
    etc.)
  Home health/behavior management
    services
  Improved x-ray and laboratory services
  Pediatric nursing
  Multidisciplinary model for health care
  Emergency services
  Genetic counseling services

Counseling and support services
  Counseling and suport services to
    parents (hot line)
  Unspecified counseling or support
    services
  Psychological services including
    diagnosis and assessment for behavior
    problems
  Counseling or support services to
    disabled or chronically ill child
  Counseling or support services to
    siblings
  Psychiatric services

Case management, advocacy, and follow-up
  Case management and advocacy
  Service coordination and integration
    (interagency & within DFHS)
  Follow-up services (e.g., high-risk
    infants or adults over 22 years)
  Information and referral to community
    resources
  Education of community agencies
    regarding special needs

Respite care
  Unspecified respite care
  Specialized daycare
  Homemaker services
  After-school care
  Summer camp

Out-of-home living
  Specialized group residential (e.g.,head-
    injured, autistic, adolescent, etc.)
  Foster care
  Hospice services for terminally ill

Health education training
  Patient/client education regarding health
    needs (including sex education)
  Parent and family education regarding
    health needs
  Staff development/professional training
    regarding health needs
  M.D. training regarding team model
  M.D. training regarding special health
    needs

Financial services
  Family subsidy or other direct support
  Information on financial resources,
    benefits, etc.
  Improved benefits/health insurance
    coverage
  Decreased family liability—SHC
    eligibility guidelines

Environment
  Adaptive housing
  Environmental access

Other services
  Early intervention
  Legal services
  Translator services/bilingual
  Transportation
  Social/recreational services
  Summer education programs

Other system needs
  Computerized records
  Computerized resource systems
  Outreach/public relations regarding
    SHC programs
  Clinic hours and location—facilities

the specifics of those implementation activities could not be defined in advance, the agency was clearly committing itself to serious consideration of all recommendations that would emerge from the project and to implementing some changes in the final year. This open and public commitment to an implementation phase gave notice to personnel within and outside the agency that this was a serious effort. It had the additional effect of increasing people's motivation to cooperate and participate in project activities so that they could affect the eventual content of the recommendations.

Ensuring Project and Agency Goal Congruence: Using Overlapping Staff to Maintain Communication

When a planning project stretches over a protracted period of time, there is always the risk that immediate needs for policy decisions may result in changes that will be inconsistent with eventual recommendations for long-term policies. This project sought to avoid situations in which the state health agency moved in one direction while the project collected data and findings pointed in another.

The participation of two key decision makers from the agency as steering committee members and the use of periodic briefings, described below, assured effective and timely communication regarding current activities within the Division. In this way, staff resignations and replacements of medical consultants did not result in premature decisions regarding changing staff roles or clinic services, even though those very questions were the focus of project attention.

Developing the Recommendations: Using Periodic Review of Findings to Facilitate Acceptance

Early in the project, a decision was made to provide periodic briefings to key agency staff. Taking the time along the way to describe interim data or findings to the senior leadership within the agency facilitated the flow of valuable feedback to the project. Were the right questions being asked? Were any major areas of information neglected? Were interpretations of the preliminary data consistent with agency staff perceptions? Key personnel were asked to preview and validate project effectiveness in order to involve them in the development of the conclusions. This strategy helped to prevent any surprise recommendations and fostered acceptance of the recommendations once they were presented and endorsed.

Presenting the Recommendations:
Transferring the Planning to the Agency

In order to get formal feedback on the project's recommendations before they were finalized, a meeting was held involving key agency personnel, parent representatives, and other state and legislative staff. Drafts of the final report were circulated and feedback was solicited, which proved valuable both in correcting data on current program operations and offering suggestions for modifying the recommendations themselves. The result was a more accurate final draft.

The state health agency then held a statewide meeting for approximately 150 staff members in the Division of Family Health Services at which Project SERVE formally presented its report to the Division. The director of the Division sponsored the meeting and encouraged the attendance and participation of all staff, which gave the report high visibility in the agency and communicated a sense of legitimacy concerning the report and its recommendations. A key element was the statement that no one would lose his or her job as a result of these program changes because there were many new roles proposed that existing personnel could fill.

Following this main presentation conference, Project SERVE joined central administrative staff in conducting regional meetings with the medical consultants to elicit individual responses to the report's recommendations. These meetings allowed an exchange of ideas about the expected impact of the proposed changes on the role of the public agency vis-à-vis the private health care system in caring for children with special health needs.

The Advisory Council of the Division, which included consumer, professional, and provider membership, received periodic updates at all stages of the project's development and a full presentation of the recommendations.

Developing an Official Response:
The State Health Agency Assumes Leadership

A final process within the state health agency was designed by the Division of Family Health Services in order to build support for the recommendations and to develop preliminary work plans. Task forces were created to review and evaluate each recommendation and to develop initial strategies for the implementation of the recommendations that were accepted. Membership in these task forces was designed to assure representation from the regional office, central office (both the Maternal and Child Health and the Services for Handicapped Children units), medical consultants, parent groups, personnel from other state agencies, and the private medical sector. Each of these working groups included Project SERVE staff and steering committee members, who provided both substantive interpretation of the recommendations and administrative support. Project staff provided a record of committee proceedings, decisions, and discussions by reproducing minutes for the committee members.

Developing a Broader Constituency: Building Support for the Recommendations

Throughout the project, the strategy was to elicit as much interest and support for the recommendations as possible from persons outside of the state health agency in order to enhance eventual implementation. These supporters would serve to provide knowledgeable pressure to promote significant changes.

It was hoped that parent groups would help generate public awareness of the recommendations. Parent advocacy groups that had assisted in disseminating the parent questionnaire were mailed a copy of the final report and invited to send representatives to an open discussion with project staff. Subsequently, parent groups used their newsletters to help inform the public of a statewide conference sponsored by the project.

The full set of recommendations was widely disseminated in the state through mailings of the written report and oral presentations of the findings and recommendations. All interviewees were provided the report and invited to comment. Presentations were made throughout the state at academic and training institutions and to professional organizations such as the Massachusetts Chapter of the American Academy of Pediatrics, the Massachusetts Nurses Association, and the New England Chapter of the Association for Persons with Severe Handicaps.

Other agencies were instrumental in informing the public and health providers of the report and follow-up activities through their newsletters. These included the League of Neighborhood Health Centers, the Federation for Children with Special Needs, the State House Watch (a publication of the Massachusetts Human Services Coalition), the Association for the Care of Children's Health Network, the Boston Parents' Paper, and the newsletter from the Division of Family Health Services. Ultimately, copies of the report were sent to directors of Title V programs for children with special health care needs in all fifty states, all University Affiliated Centers for Developmental Disorders, and schools of public health.

Building a Network for Future Advocacy Efforts: Holding a Statewide Forum

In addition to those strategies that focused on internal dissemination and acceptance of the report, the project also sponsored a statewide forum on issues of access to and financing of health care for children with special health care needs. These issues had emerged as critical ones during the data analysis from the perspective of both parents and health care providers.

However, improving access and health care financing obviously required action that was beyond the scope of Project SERVE or the Department of Public Health. Appropriate remedies would necessitate reform of the private insurance system, including guaranteed access to comprehensive, affordable coverage for all children with special health needs through the establishment of a public insurance system and/or an expanded system of publicly funded services for these children and their families. The forum was held at the state capitol building, and the audience of more than 500 people included parents, providers, policy makers, and legislators. A Platform for Reform was developed by the project and distributed at the forum for discussion by panelists.

An effort was made to obtain media coverage and to use the occasion to highlight the needs of this special population. Another objective of the forum was to bring together people who represented a broad range of disability groups and to create an awareness on their part of the common issues and needs that cut across these different groups. The forum sought to build a broad-based coalition of many parents and providers who could act in concert in the future in advocating with the legislature and state agencies on behalf of children with special health care needs.

CONCLUSION

In order to define a rational public role that can complement and enhance the private health care system and utilize public resources in an equitable manner, other states may wish to consider changes in responsibilities to children with special health care needs. To maximize the effectiveness of such a planning effort, states need to involve local leaders from both the private and public health care sectors, ensure interdisciplinary participation, and reach out to families as partners in the planning process. Participation from a broad constituency in determining the statewide needs of children with special health care problems lends increased credibility to future recommendations and enhances the potential for implementation.

Each individual state or region that attempts such a project will have its own set of planning questions, identified priorities for data collection, and preferences for who should participate in and lead the process. The experience in Massachusetts suggests the efficacy of an externally based participatory needs assessment process, integrating public health department staff with private academic and service provider personnel. However, each state must consider its own constellation of public services, the availability of resources in the private health care sector, and the level of organizational support and readiness to participate in a planning activity that has as its goal the redefinition of existing public services.

Despite the absence of a preexisting, comprehensive, program-based data system and without the ability to count individual children with chronic illnesses or disabling conditions, a state can still approach difficult long-term planning questions with integrity and responsibility. The abundance of existing qualitative information and professional expertise within a state can be utilized.

When involved in statewide planning to improve the system of services to children with special health care needs, it is critical to give adequate attention to constituency-building efforts. Parents, health care providers, and their professional and academic organizations, as well as state agency personnel, can join forces to increase advocacy and visibility regarding the unmet needs of these children and their families. We hope that the lessons learned from the Project SERVE experience in Massachusetts will be of use to professionals and parents in similar planning efforts in other states and regions.

POSTSCRIPT

We are pleased that the Division of Family Health Services in the Massachusetts Department of Public Health, in June 1987, issued a report and recommendations from its own internal process and review of the Project SERVE recommendations. The DFHS endorsed all of the new directions and major recommendations of the Project Serve effort and is developing formal work plans to implement the recommendations in future years.

Acknowledgments: This project was supported by the U.S. Department of Health and Human Services through the Bureau of Health Care Delivery and Assistance, Division of Maternal and Children Health, as a special Project of Regional and National Significance (SPRANS), Project Number MCJ-253316, through a grant to the Massachusetts Health Research Institute. The principal investigators were Allen C. Crocker, M.D. (Children's Hospital), Deborah Klein Walker, Ed.D. (Harvard School of Public Health), and Gerald A. Tuttle, Ph.D. (DFHS, Massachusetts Department of Public Health).

V

Strategies for the Future

17

Preventing Mental Health Problems

Morton M. Silverman, M.D.,
Doreen Spilton Koretz, Ph.D.

This chapter describes a conceptual framework for understanding and developing interventions to prevent secondary mental health problems associated with chronic physical illness in children. Because we are working with a rapidly increasing population of chronically ill children, who, being the beneficiaries of modern medical technology, are living longer, we must begin to forecast the stresses and strains these children will experience as they mature and enter adolescence and young adulthood.

DEFINITIONS AND CONCEPTS

Probably the most commonly used definition of chronic physical illness in the literature is one used in Pless and Douglas (1971). From another perspective, these are conditions that "continually or repeatedly threaten to disrupt normal development in the physical, intellectual, emotional, or social sphere" (Ireys, 1981, p. 322).

These physical conditions thus include problems that vary widely in the amount of special medical care they require, their origin (i.e., genetic

The opinions expressed in this chapter are those of the authors and do not necessarily reflect the support or endorsement of the National Institute of Mental Health; the Alcohol, Drug Abuse, and Mental Health Administration; or the Public Health Service. Portions of this material are in the public domain.

or traumatic), the extent of dependence they impose, the age at which they appear, their stability, their duration (e.g., acute, gradual, chronic), and the predictability of their progression (Ireys, 1981). Nevertheless, once any physical handicap becomes chronic, conditions develop that can potentially result in attendant psychological dysfunctions. The term *chronically* connotes a long-term or permanent change, a need for reorientation of body image, the establishment of routines, certain real or potential limitations of growth and development, and, most damaging of all, a diminished sense of the future as holding promise and hope. With chronic illnesses, "confidence and hopes are undermined; the exprience is usually difficult to account for, no end is in sight, and self-perception—the sense of identity—is assaulted by changes in the body and its functional performance" (WHO, 1980, p. 24).

EPIDEMIOLOGY OF CHRONIC PHYSICAL ILLNESSES

On the average, approximately 6% to 20% of all children under the age of 18 have some type of chronic physical impairment (Stein, 1983; Pless & Roghmann, 1971). This figure corresponds roughly to the 12% average used in The Education for All Handicapped Children Act of 1975 (PL 94-142), although the population of children included in these two estimates does not entirely overlap. Various reviews of the literature show that most children with chronic disorders have mild to moderate disability, with 12% to 17% of those affected facing severe disability (Ireys, 1981; Pless & Roghmann, 1971; Werner, Bierman, & Frency, 1971). The most common physical conditions are asthma (2%), epilepsy (1%), cardiac conditions (0.5%), cerebral palsy (0.5%), orthopedic illness (0.5%), and diabetes mellitus (0.1%).

The World Health Organization (WHO), in discussing the consequences of disease, contrasted the characteristics of acute versus chronic illness (WHO, 1980). In offering a unifying framework from which to approach the study of chronic disease objectively, WHO made necessary distinctions between terms that are often interchanged.

An *impairment* is "any loss or abnormality of psychological, physiological, or anatomical structure or function." An impairment is more inclusive than a *disorder*, because it is not contigent on etiology and it also covers losses; for example, "the loss of a leg is an impairment, but not a disorder." A *disability* is "any restriction or lack (resulting from an impairment) of ability to perform an activity in the manner or within the range considered normal for a human being." Hence, the concept of disability can be objectified by performance measures. Finally, a *handicap* is a "disadvantage for a given individual, resulting from an impairment or a disa-

FIGURE 17.1 Consequences of disease onset.

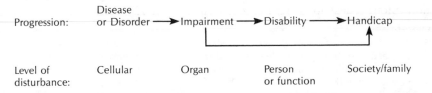

SOURCE: Adopted from WHO (1980).

bility, that limits or prevents the fulfillment of a role that is normal (depending on age, sex, and social and cultural factors) for that individual." The emphasis here is on the value (personal or societal) that is attached to a departure from a structural, functional, or performance norm. A handicap is characterized by "a discordance" between the individual's performance or status and the expectations of the society to which he or she relates. Figure 17.1 presents a modification of the WHO linear schema of the progression and consequences of disease onset to highlight the potential opportunities for preventive interventions at each level of disturbance. The disease process progresses sequentially through a number of steps before reaching the state where society determines that an individual is suffering from a handicap. A handicap is thus the end product of a causal chain of dysfunctional states beginning with a disease/disorder first measured at the cellular level, through an impairment stage often associated with a particular organ dysfunction, to a disability stage, which is defined at the level of the person. Interventions to prevent the development of a physical handicap can occur at the cellular, organic, or personal level of dysfunction. The sequence can be interrupted or modified at any step, using appropriate biological, psychological, educational, or environmental interventions specifically targeted to the level of disturbance associated with the state of dysfunction.

A MENTAL HEALTH PERSPECTIVE

Noncategorical Approach to Psychosocial Effects

Despite the wide range of medical conditions that fall under the umbrella of chronic disorder, there is some evidence to suggest that psychosocial outcomes are not specific to particular diseases but rather cross disease boundaries. Barry Pless and Ruth Stein are strong proponents of this noncategorical approach, which argues that the adjustment of chronically ill children and their families appears to be related to a number of cross-disease dimensions, such as time of onset, prognosis, the predictability

of the disease course, types of routines required for care, degree of intru-
siveness of care and treatment regimens, and the visibility of the condition (Stein & Jessop, 1982; Pless & Pinkerton, 1975). As noted by Stein
(1982):

> irrespective of the specific disease, children with diverse medical problems
> have great similarities in life experiences and in the preventive and rehabilita-
> tive aspects of their lives (Mattson, 1972; Pless and Pinkerton, 1975; Strauss,
> 1975). The limitation of the medical model has become increasingly recog-
> nized when the concern is with the *consequence* of the disease or disorder
> for the person afflicted, the family, and those involved in giving care (WHO,
> 1980). The chronicity of illness and the impact that it has on the child, his
> parents, and his siblings is more significant than the specific character of the
> disorder, be it diabetes, cerebral palsy, hemophilia, etc. In other words, there
> are certain problems common to all chronic illness over and above particular
> challenges posed by individual needs (Pless and Pinkerton, 1975)
> . . . The lives of children and families are affected by such things as whether
> the condition is visible or invisible; whether or not it is life-threatening, stable,
> or characterized by unpredictable crises; and whether or not it involves mental
> retardation, affects sensory or motor systems, or involves intrusive and
> demanding routines of care. Other issues that vary across diseases also appear
> to be important. For example, the effect on children of repeated hospitaliza-
> tions and days lost from school can be examined regardless of whether the
> hospitalizations were because of crises associated with asthma or sickle cell
> anemia. . . . Work done at Albert Einstein College of Medicine (Stein and
> Jessop, 1982) documents the lack of relevance of disease categories for the
> study of behavioral, psychological, and social consequences of chronic ill-
> ness. (p. 40)

In short, for purposes of studying secondary psychological effects, children with different chronic conditions can often be grouped together
because they face similar problems. The implication of the noncategorical
or generic approach is that there are cross-cutting psychological effects,
such as on perceived locus of control, body image, and self-esteem, that
can lead to increased risk for psychiatric symptomatology.

Chronic Physical Illness Seen from a Psychological Perspective

Steinhauer, Mushin, and Rae-Grant (1974) see the prolonged disruption
in life experience secondary to chronic illness as having lasting effects on
the cognitive and emotional development of children. Aside from the disruption of life experience, Mattson (1972) points out that uncertainty as
to why pain and suffering occur is a stress that needs to be addressed.
Preschool children have little ability to comprehend the causal nature of
an illness and tend to interpret pain and other symptoms as resulting from
mistreatment, punishment, or "being bad." From a child's perspective,
nothing happens by chance and reasons for an event such as an illness

are sought in the immediate past. Children up to the ages of 8 to 10 often attribute illness and injury to recent family interactions, such as disappointing one's parents. If the illness is of hereditary origin, other problems of adjustment may result. Such awareness of a likely genetic transmission, often resulting in anger, sadness, and anxiety, can result in a hostile child–parent relationship, blame, guilt, and the child's recognition of an added burden of responsibility when considering his or her plans to marry and have a family (Freeman, 1968; Tizard & Whitmore, 1968; M. R. Johnson, 1979).

The epidemiology of these emotional and mental problems has been summarized by Stein (1982):

> A considerable body of empirical work documents that severely ill infants, children, and adolescents and their families are at increased risk for mental disorders. Several features of illness contribute to this increased risk: the actual physical symptoms of illness, the therapeutic regimens the children experience, the unpredictable outcomes and poor prognosis, periodic crises, and the potential trauma of hospitalizations and new technologies. In general, these features can create stress for childen and families leading to emotional disorders of varying types, including depression, adjustment disorders, acute and chronic anxiety states, and family problems. In addition, the stress of a serious illness can alter normal growth and development.
>
> The epidemiological data are clear that children with physical health problems have higher rates of mental health problems. . . . Walker et al. (1981), in a population based sample of children in Genesee County (Michigan), demonstrate children with physical health problems have significantly more psychosocial problems including behavior, learning, social and school problems. In a survery of patients being seen in private practice settings in Monroe County (New York), Goldberg et al. (1979) show that children with chronic physical illness have rates of emotional, behavioral, and school problems twice that of children without ongoing physical illness.
>
> A few more recent studies have shown that serious illness may lead to less severe forms of psychopathology than early case studies indicated, but seriously ill children and their families still have more mental health problems than the general population of children and their families. For example, Drotar et al. (1981), studying the psychosocial functioning of children with several different types of chronic illness, found that the chronically ill children had more psychosocial problems than normal controls, though the frequency of severe psychopathology was rare. (p. 43)

One major problem in untangling the mental health effects of chronic illness is the paucity of data on subgroups who may be at particular risk for poor outcome. A few mediating variables have been identified—such as location of organ system affected, cosmetic effect, socioeconomic status, family functioning, family composition, the status of the child's physical functioning (severity of impairment), and the comprehensiveness and sensitivity of the service delivery system—but there has been little exploration of this topic using population-based studies. Fortunately, a recent population-based study (see Pless & Wadsworth, Chapter 12) has begun to examine the long-term effects of chronic illness on psychological functioning and to identify variables that may be important in mediating such effects.

The findings of this population-based study suggest significant and persistent patterns of psychological dysfunction related to chronic illness, with outcomes mediated by a variety of factors, including type of dysfunction, severity of the condition, duration of the disability, sex, and age of onset. This important study has therefore confirmed a number of mediators identified in smaller, cross-sectional studies on the effects of chronic illness on the child.

Psychological Reactions of the Family Unit, the Siblings, and the Mother

In addition to effects on the identified patient, we now know that a chronically ill child has profound effects on many aspects of society, including the family, the community, the schools, the health care institutions, and local, state, and federal legislative activities. Thus we may see the secondary mental health consequences of chronic physical illness throughout the child's entire ecological system.

Although there is disagreement in the literature about the long-term consequences to the family unit, siblings, and/or mother of chronic physical illness in a child (Drotar & Bush, 1985; Drotar & Crawford, 1985; Haggerty, Roghmann, & Pless, 1975; Jessop, Riessman, & Stein, 1988; Klein, 1975; Minde, Hackett, Killour, & Silver, 1972; Pratt, 1976; Schulman, 1979), a number of investigators have identified potential problems and dysfunctional patterns. Because it is unknown which dysfunctional reactions are transient and which may progress to more permanent, disruptive states, it is incumbent on the primary care provider system to be sensitive to the development and emergence of these patterns and reactions in family members. For this reason, we present a brief overview and selective summary of the literature highlighting disorders and dysfunctions in family members that may be amenable to preventive interventions.

Effects on the Family

Pless, Roghmann, and Haggerty (1972) have suggested that the rate of breakdown in families with severe chronic disease is high. The range of family emotional reactions often includes the following: denial, anxiety, depression, resentment and rejection, sibling reactions, shame, embarrassment, and feelings of guilt, responsibility, and self-blame (Steinhauer et al., 1974). Bruhn (1977) has suggested that chronic illness creates role changes for both the ill individual and other family members. These role changes have a "see-saw effect," creating new or reviving former symptoms in the identified family member or other family members. A number of factors that influence the family's response to chronic illness have been identified by researchers and practitioners (e.g., Mattson, 1972; Power & Dell Orto, 1980; Steinhauer et al.). These include (1) severity of the illness, likely prognosis, and availability of an effective treatment; (2) whether the disease is congenital or acquired; (3) age of onset of illness and diagnosis; (4) child's developmental level and coping skills; (5) how well the child understands the condition; (6) presence of preexisting emotional disturbance within the family; (7) nature and effect of the illness itself (visibility of the defect, degree of dysfunction); (8) effects of the home management program and restrictions on family life; (9) quality of the parent–child relationship and the parents' acceptance of the child; (10) presence or absence of other affected siblings; (11) repeated hospitalizations and surgical procedures; (12) cost of the illness (degree of financial burden); and (13) availability of community resources.

These various factors result in various constellations of family reactions to chronic physical illness in identified children. The family size, structure, and religious beliefs, as well as the stage of the family lifecycle, are often key variables in the stability equation (Power & Dell Orto, 1980). The key concept here is the interactional nature of the family system, in that the parents and siblings are in a constantly evolving relationship with the chronically ill child, and the child, in turn, may serve as both initiator and reactor in the unfolding family dynamics related to the illness.

Effects on Siblings

Steinhauer and colleagues (1974) have discussed sibling reactions to chronic physical illness. They have identified as important jealousy and resentment toward the child who siphons the attention and energies of the family unit. The parental preoccupation with the sick child and their own reactions to his or her illness may result in their experiencing a certain degree of emotional deprivation. Feelings and expressions of jealousy, resentment, and hostility that are not allowed to be adequately expressed often result in withdrawal, school problems, adolescent delinquency, and behavioral problems or other acting-out behavior among the physically intact siblings.

Effects on the Mother

Although there is debate about the exact nature and lasting effects of chronic physical illness on family members and siblings, it is generally accepted that the mother is the primary care provider for chronically ill children and often is the one member of the family who is in constant and regular contact with the child (Stein, 1982). The burden of the child's care is often more of an emotional than a practical one, and this results in increased tendencies to depression and stress. Again, however, the extent of problems experienced by mothers may be influenced by factors such as social support and the degree of acceptance of the chronic condition (Thomas, 1978).

In sum, we see that there are secondary mental consequences of chronic physical illness for both the child and the family. The child with a serious, chronic disease has to cope with threats of exacerbations, lasting physical impairments, and even a shortened life expectancy. Hence the degree to which a child develops adequate coping behavior and appropriate psychological defenses will determine the degree to which adaptation occurs. Adaptation and coping for the child with chronic physical illness cannot take place in a vacuum. The interplay among the affected child and siblings, parents, and extended family members, and between the family and the health care system, is critical. The opportunities for preventive interventions, then, take many forms, can occur at many developmental points, and can be targeted at the affected child as well as siblings, parents, and the family as a whole.

A PREVENTION PERSPECTIVE

Definitions

In order to orient the reader toward a prevention perspective, we first present some definitions in order to highlight the goals of preventive interventions as seen within the framework of the epidemiological concepts of incidence, prevalence, and duration. As Table 17.1 illustrates, primary intervention can be achieved by reducing the incidence of the measurable problem in the population and by reducing the number of children

TABLE 17.1 Prevention Approaches

Primary prevention: reduce prevalence by reducing *incidence*

Secondary prevention: reduce prevalence by reducing *duration*

$$\text{Incidence} = \frac{\text{prevalence}}{\text{duration}}$$

Prevalence = incidence × duration

FIGURE 17.2 A psychosocial definition of incidence.

$$\text{Incidence} = \frac{\text{organic factor + stress}}{\text{coping skills + self-esteem + support groups}}$$

SOURCE: Albee (1982).

who develop mental disorders or behavioral dysfunctions. In an attempt to translate these epidemiological terms into understandable psychosocial concepts, Albee (1982) developed an equation to define the roles of community, professional, and individual efforts in accomplishing the goal of reduced incidence of mental disorders or behavioral dysfunctions (see Figure 17.2.). Albee argues that the reduction in the incidence of mental disorders and behavioral dysfunctions can come about by either reducing the numerator or by increasing the denominator, or by doing both. For purposes of this chapter, decreasing stress and increasing the triad of coping skills, self-esteem, and social support would all lead to a decrease in the incidence of mental dysfunctions among the chronically physically ill.

Research Framework

Consistent with this approach, the U.S. Public Health Service's definition of prevention research highlights the importance of recognizing the role of biological, environmental, and behavioral factors in the development and implementation of preventive interventions (see Table 17.2). In moving from research definitions to developing prevention research, many disciplines and basic research findings must be coordinated and integrated. Figure 17.3 illustrates the essential building blocks of preventive intervention research and suggests an interplay and interdependence of various disciplines and research paradigms. Such research, if well designed, well executed, and well evaluated, has the potential to help answer a number of related questions about:

1. the etiology and pathogenesis of disorder,
2. the who, when, where, what, and how of interventions,
3. the essential ingredients of an intervention, the relative roles of components of an intervention, and the significance of timing, frequency, duration, and intensity,
4. the role and function of mediating variables in the development of a disorder, the maintenance of a disorder, or the interruption in the development and expression of a disorder, and
5. the interplay among subject variables, intervention/mediating variables, and outcome variables.

TABLE 17.2 U.S. Public Health Service Definition of Prevention Research

Prevention research: Prevention research includes only that research designed to yield results directly applicable to interventions to prevent occurrences of disease or disability, or the progression of detectable but asymptomatic disease.

Pre-intervention

- Identification of risk factors for disease or disability
- Development of methods for identification of disease controllable in the asymptomatic state
- Refinement of methodological and statistical procedures for quantitatively assessing risk and measuring the effects of preventive interventions

Intervention

- Development of biologic interventions to prevent occurrence of disease or disability, or progression of asymptomatic disease
- Development of environmental interventions to prevent occurrence of disease or disability, or progression of asymptomatic disease
- Development of behavioral interventions to prevent occurrence of disease or disability, or progression of asymptomatic disease
- Conduct of clinical and community trials and demonstrations to assess preventive interventions and to encourage their adoption

Prevention-relevant research: More broadly defined, prevention research also includes that research which has a high probability of yielding results which will likely be applicable to disease prevention. Included are studies aimed at elucidating the chain of causation—the etiology and mechanisms—of acute and chronic diseases. Such basic research efforts generate the fundamental knowledge which contributes to the development of future preventive interventions.

In order to answer these questions, the essential ingredients for developing preventive intervention research are as follows:

1. well-defined populations at risk for a disorder,
2. well-defined disorders and/or dysfunctions that one is trying to prevent,
3. well-defined theory/hypothesis of the etiology and pathogenesis (pathophysiology, psychopathological process) of the disorder, and
4. well-reasoned intervention that conceptually takes into account the above three points.

Such an orientation allows for a range of preventive interventions to be tested in various settings, with various at-risk populations, and aimed at various targeted disorders.

FIGURE 17.3 Preventive intervention research: essential building blocks.

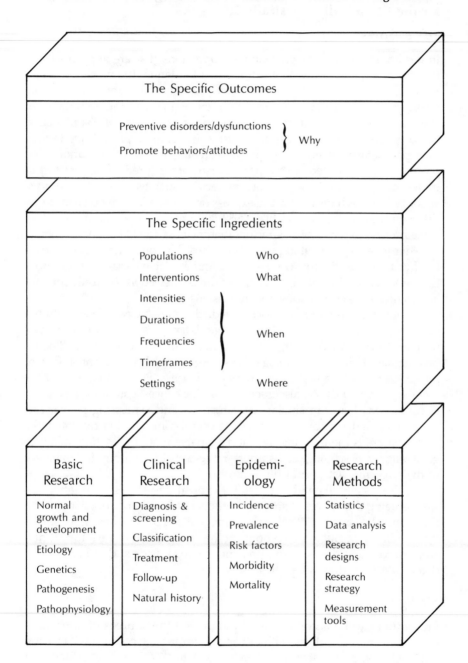

Applying Prevention Concepts to the Design of Interventions for the Chronically Physically Ill

Role of Stress

In designing and testing preventive interventions that are appropriate for the chronically physically ill, it is important to identify the process through which the physical conditions may precipitate the development of mental disorders or dysfunctions. Bloom (1979) has highlighted the importance of stress as a causal agent in the development of psychological disorders and called for a shift of interest from *predisposing* factors to *precipitating* factors. This paradigmatic shift moves from searching for a specific underlying precondition associated with a particular disorder (predisposing factor) to understanding the role of precipitating factors, such as stressful life events, as triggering mechanisms for the expression of maladaptive behavior in at-risk populations. Similarly, Caplan (1980, 1981) has conceptualized the pathogenic process in terms of risk factors that increase the likelihood of mental disorder given stresses that precipitate crises. The outcome of these crises is a function of individual competencies and available social support. From this perspective, chronic physical illness can be viewed as a chronic stressful life event with exacerbations and remissions.

Hence perceived stress becomes a mediating variable associated with the development of any number of psychological disorders or negative outcomes (Eichler, Silverman & Pratt, 1986). In some important respects, Bloom's paradigmatic shift for psychological disorders parallels the recent shift from categorical to noncategorical views of physical illness (Pless & Pinkerton, 1975; Stein & Jessop, 1982). As discussed earlier, these investigators see physically ill children as being in similar risk situations and expressing similar risk behaviors as a direct consequence of their compromised physical status. For Bloom, stress is the unifying mediating variable that, if present, could trigger a range of psychological disorders in these at-risk children, independent of their specific, categorical physical disorder.

The chronically ill child is at risk for exposure to stressful situations as well as being the source of stress for others in his or her support network. Stress then becomes a critical variable in the life of the child as either stimulus, mediator, or outcome/response. How the child and the support network perceive and assess the presence of chronic or sudden stress will determine how they adapt to it.

Strategies

Prevention can be accomplished by reducing the sources of stress that accompany chronic physical illness and by improving coping, self-esteem, and social support. More specifically, Hollister (1977) has suggested four preventive intervention strategies to deal with the presence of, or potential for, stress:

- stressor management
- stressor avoidance
- stress resistance building
- stress reaction management

This approach implies the need to examine environmental interventions to minimize stress on family members and to develop age-appropriate and situation-specific skills to prevent the exacerbation of psychological problems related to the underlying physical condition.

Prevention implies prediction. Predicting the unique psychological, cognitive, behavioral, emotional, and developmental tasks that this "aging" population of chronically physically ill children will need to identify and master is a challenge. In order to stay ahead of the potential difficulties and stumbling blocks, we will need to continue adapting some of the existing preventive intervention approaches that seem to have promise for other populations and situations to a uniquely at-risk population (see Table 17.3).

These strategies can involve the use of cognitive functions (perception, memory, speech, judgment, reality testing), motor activity, emotional expression, and psychological defenses. Successful coping behavior results in adaptation, which implies that the individual is functioning effectively. Denial is the most common psychological defense used in addition to isolation in coping with emotional distress caused by pain, malaise, and interrupted plans. Identification with others who have a similar chronic handicap is another defense often used by children. Learning about and associating with others who are successful in dealing with similar problems can effectively support the development of a positive self-image. Such mastery of their condition leads to pride, confidence, and the ability to face an uncertain future in a positive manner.

Emerging psychological problems are a function of the interaction among the stresses of the illness, the environment's response to it, and the child's developmental level. Thus preventive interventions should be designed to decrease risk factors, decrease stress, and increase competencies and social support. All these interventions must be geared to the developmental levels of and specific issues faced by the ill child.

CONCLUSION

Childhood physical illnesses of any type or duration are stressful to all concerned and may have the potential to chronically alter normal functioning

TABLE 17.3 Preventive Intervention Approaches

The consequences of disease (WHO model)		Examples of types of preventive interventions
Level of disturbance	Progression	

Cellular	Disease/ disorder	Nutrition and diet
		Exercise
		Education
		    primary care providers
		    parents and siblings
		    individuals at risk
		Communication skills

Organ	Impairment	Stressor management Stressor avoidance Social support networks

Person	Disability	Cognitive/behavioral training
		    self-control/self-help
		    problem solving
		    personal responsibility training
		    coping skills
		    interpersonal skills
		Stress resistance building
		Stress reaction management

Society/ family	Handicap	Parent training in interpersonal skills
		Family management skills training for
		    parents
		Sibling cognitive skills training
		Family/parent social support
		    environmental alternatives

and age-appropriate development growth in the patient, the siblings, and the family unit. The ability to predict and prevent such psychological sequelae in any family member rests in part on our ability to:

1. Determine the nature and extent of psychological sequelae to chronic physical disorders in affected children and their families (i.e., definitions, classifications, measurement, etc.).
2. Assess the coping strategies used by chronically ill children and their families to resist the psychological impacts of the stress associated with chronic illness.
3. Identify and assess effective preventive interventions for reducing the risk of childhood disorders.

Despite the impressive amount of thinking, writing, and research that has already addressed this issue, much more work needs to be done. It has only been within the last decade that serious, consistent, and rigorous attention has been directed at the prevention of psychological sequelae to chronic physical illness in children. Other chapters in this book highlight the missing data points, the complexity of the issues, and the interplay between risk factors, risk behaviors, risk situations, and risk settings.

Although chronically ill children are at increased risk for mental health problems, it is important to remember that a large proportion of this group show little or no disturbance. This raises an important issue for the design and implementation of cost-effective preventive interventions for mental health—the need to identify particularly vulnerable subgroups of children and to target the interventions to those most in need of them or most able to benefit from them (Crawford, & Gonofsky, 1984). Future work will also need to pay careful attention to the effects of other risk factors and concurrent stressors, to the intervention service delivery modes and locations, and to the long-term effects of preventive interventions.

Society must have readily available specific interventions for specific individuals at specific times to prevent specific disorders or dysfunctions. Such preventive interventions—which can take the form of education, social support, environmental engineering, health protection, and health enhancement—can provide guidance and assistance in promoting healthy coping and adaptation to an ever-changing and increasingly uncertain future.

REFERENCES

Albee, G. W. (1982). Preventing psychopathology and promoting human potential. *American Psychologist, 37*(9), 1043–1050.

Bloom, B. L. (1979). Prevention of mental disorders: Recent advances in theory and practice. *Community Mental Health Journal, 15*(3), 179–191.

Bruhn, J. G. (1977). Effects of chronic illness on the family. *The Journal of Family Practice, 4*(6), 1057–1060.

Caplan, G. (1980). An approach to preventive intervention in child psychiatry. *Canadian Journal of Psychiatry, 25,* 671–686.

Caplan, G. (1981). Partnerships for prevention in the human services. *The Journal of Primary Prevention, 2,* 3–5.

Drotar, D. (1981) Psychological perspectives in chronic childhood illness. *Journal of Pediatric Psychology, 6*(3), 211–228.

Drotar, D., & Bush, M. (1985). Mental health issues and services. In N. Hobbs & J. M. Perrin (Eds.), *Issues in the care of children with chronic illness* (pp. 517–527). San Francisco: Jossey Bass.

Drotar D., & Crawford, P. (1985). Psychological adaptation of siblings of chronically ill children: Reasearch and practice implications. *Developmental and Behavioral Pediatrics, 6*(6), 355–362.

Drotar, D., Crawford, P., & Gonofsky, M. (1984). Prevention with chronically ill children. In M. C. Roberts & L. Peterson (Eds.), *Prevention of problems in childhood: Psychological research and applications* (pp. 234–256), New York: Wiley.

Drotar, D., Doershuk, C. F., Stern, R. C., Boat, T. F., Boyer, W., & Matthews, L. (1981). Psychosocial functioning of children with cystic fibrosis. *Pediatrics, 67,* 338.

Eichler, A., Silverman, M. M., & Pratt, D. M. (1986). *A scientific debate: How to define and research stress.* Washington, DC: American Psychiatric Press.

Freeman, R. D. (1968). Emotional reactions of handicapped children. In S. Chess & A. Thomas (Eds.), *Annual progress in child psychiatry and child development* (pp. 379–395). New York: Brunner-Mazel.

Goldberg, I. D., Regier, D. A., McInerny, T. K., Pless, I. B., & Roghmann, K. J., (1979). The role of the pediatrician in the delivery of mental health services to children. *Pediatrics, 63,* 898–909.

Haggerty, R. J., Roghmann, K. J., & Pless, I. B. (1975). *Child health and the community.* New York: Wiley (Interscience).

Hollister, W. G. (1977). Basic strategies in designing primary prevention programs. In D. C. Klein & S. E. Goldston (Eds.), *Primary prevention: An idea whose time has come. Proceedings on the pilot conference on primary prevention, April 2–4, 1976* (pp. 41–47). (DHEW Publication No. ADM 77-447). Washington, DC: U.S. Government Printing Office.

Ireys, H. T. (1981). Health care for chronically disabled children and their families. In *The Report of the Select Panel on the Promotion of Child Health for Our Children: A National Strategy,* Vol. IV. (pp. 321–353). Washington, DC: U.S. Government Printing Office.

Jessop, D. J., Riessman, C. K., & Stein, R. E. K. (1988). Chronic childhood illness and maternal mental health. *Journal of Developmental and Behavioral Pediatrics, 9,* 147–156.

Johnson, M. R. (1979). Mental health interventions with medically ill children: A review of the literature, 1970–1977. *Journal of Pediatric Psychology, 24,* 147–163.

Johnson, S. (1980). Psychosocial factors in juvenile diabetes: A review. *Journal of Behavioral Medicine, 3,* 95–116.

Klein, S. D. (1975). Chronic kidney disease: Impact on the child and family and strategies for coping. Unpublished doctoral dissertation, University of Minnesota, Minneapolis.

Mattson, A. (1972). Long-term physical illness in childhood: A challenge to psychosocial adaptation. *Pediatrics, 50*(5), 801–811.

Minde, K. K., Hackett, J. D., Killou, D., & Silver, S. (1972). How they grow up: 41 physically handicapped children and their families. *American Journal of Psychiatry, 128*(12), 1154–1160.

Pless, I. B., & Douglas, J. W. B. (1971). Chronic illness in childhood. I. Epidemiological and clinical characteristics. *Pediatrics, 47,* 405–414.

Pless, I. B. & Pinkerton, P. (1975). *Chronic childhood disorders promoting patterns of adjustment*. London: Henry Kimpton.

Pless, I. B., Roghmann, K. J., & Haggerty, R. J. (1972). Chronic illness, family functioning, and psychological adjustment: A model for the allocation of preventive mental health services. *International Journal of Epidemiology, 1,* 271–277.

Power, P. W., & Dell Orto, A. E. (1980). General impact of child disability/illness on the family. In P. W. Power & A. E. Dell Orto (Eds.), *Role of the family in the rehabilitation of the physically disabled* (pp. 173–179). Baltimore: University Park Press.

Pratt, L. (1976). *Family structure and effective health behavior*. Boston: Houghton-Mifflin.

Rutter, M., Tizard, J., & Whitmore, K. (1968). *Handicapped children: A total population prevalence study of education, physical and behavioral disorders*. London: Longmans.

Schulman, J. (1979). *Coping with tragedy: Successfully facing the problems of a seriously ill child*. Chicago: Follett.

Stein, R. E. K. (1982). *Preventive intervention research center for child health*. Preventive Intervention Research Center Grant Application, NIMH Grant #P50 MH38280. Public Health Service, DHHS, 40–43.

Stein, R. E. K. (1983). Growing up with a physical difference. *CHC 12* (2), 53–61.

Stein, R. E. K., & Jessop, D. (1982). A noncategorical approach to chronic childhood illness. *Public Health Reports, 97*(4), 354–362.

Steinhauer, P. D., Mushin, D. N., & Rae-Grant, O. (1974). Psychological aspects of chronic illness. In *The Pediatric Clinics of North America, 21,* 825–840. Philadelphia: Saunders.

Strauss, A. L. (1975). *Chronic illness and the quality of life*. New York: Mosby.

Thomas, D. (1978). *The social psychology of disability*. London: Methuen.

Walker, D. K., Gortmaker, S., & Weitzman, M. (1981). *Chronic illness and psychosocial problems among children in Genesee County*. Boston: Harvard School of Public Health, Community Child Health Studies.

World Health Organization (1980). *International classification of impairments, disabilities, and handicaps* (p. 24). Geneva.

18

An Interdisciplinary Approach to Research, Services, and Treatment

Ronnie Halper, M.S.W., M.P.H., Henry T. Ireys, Ph.D.

The needs of children with chronic illnesses and their families are multifaceted. In addition, there is a complex interplay of physical and mental health factors and social circumstances. Therefore, in most instances, no single disciplinary perspective is adequate for conducting the research needed to develop and evaluate effective programs. Progress in understanding chronic illness demands an effective blend of disciplinary perspectives, including the knowledge, training, and methods of pediatrics, biomedical sciences, epidemiology, psychiatry, sociology, clinical and community psychology, social work, public health, and prevention, which must be well integrated into such a sustained research program. This chapter describes a center that focuses on one set of issues: the prevention of mental health problems in the children themselves and their families. It is an example of an interdisciplinary research center where individuals from multiple backgrounds work together and where the intellectual, theoretical, and programmatic home for such an effort is provided. It establishes an environment for nurturing and sustaining a variety of projects and activities that would lack the resources to thrive on their own.

Since its inception in 1983, the Preventive Intervention Research Center (PIRC) for Child Health at the Albert Einstein College of Medicine/ Montefiore Medical Center has had the opportunity to develop and expand a research program dedicated to preventing mental health problems in children with serious physical health conditions and in their families. The PIRC builds on research in health care delivery that has yielded and continues to yield contributions to the science and methods of preventive intervention in the field of childhood chronic illness (Escalona, 1982; Stein & Jessop, 1984). Rather than reviewing the research, this chapter is devoted to a discussion of the structure and nature of the environment that encourages effective research about children with serious physical health conditions and about their families.

THE CENTERS

The Preventive Intervention Research Center for Child Health was established in late 1983 at the Albert Einstein College of Medicine/Montefiore Medical Center as one of five original centers funded by the National Institute of Mental Health in the country. It is the only one devoted to the prevention of mental health problems in children and their families with ongoing physical illnesses/disabilities and to the interface between physical and mental health. The Center provides an opportunity to study the relationship between a child's physical and mental health over the course of development as well as the complex interaction of physical and mental health factors in family members. As Long notes, "The powerful interplay between mind and body, together with the biological, social, and environmental influences on the individual, make up the complex base on which prevention programs can be built" (1986, p. 826).

The main purpose of the Center is to create an environment where interdisciplinary research and training in the area of preventive intervention will flourish. The Center's research examines how different types of interventions may benefit the children and their families and focuses on an age spectrum from birth through adolescence. In addition, the Center seeks to become a regional and national resource for information and ideas in the field of prevention in child health by (1) supporting a group of professionals knowledgeable about emerging problems, research, policy, and legislative solutions for this group of children and their families, and (2) developing resources at the Center that investigators within the field may consult or draw upon.

Need for the Center

As summarized by Silverman and Koretz (see Chapter 17), children of all ages with serious or chronic physical health problems and their families often experience significant emotional, social, and economic difficulties as a result of the illness. These secondary consequences can be as severely disabling as the biological conditions themselves. Research has shown that these children have higher rates of mental health problems than healthy children (Goldberg, Regier, McAnerney, Pless, & Roghmann, 1978; Pless & Roghmann, 1971; Walker, Gortmaker, & Weitzman, 1981). The mental health and social consequences of physical health problems are especially severe for children and families who are poor (Egbuono & Starfield, 1982).

The opportunity to develop the PIRC around the theme of childhood physical illness was timely. As described throughout the book, health problems among infants, children, and adolescents now pose formidable challenges, not only to their families but also to the nation as a whole, and this group of children consumes a vastly disproportionate share of the nation's health care dollars (Butler, Budetti, McManus, Stenmark, & Newacheck, 1985; Zook & Moore, 1980). Because individuals who would have died during childhood in former times now live into adolescence and adulthood, the cumulative costs of their medical and mental health problems have increased and are likely to continue to rise. Indeed, the problems posed by childhood illness clamor for lasting national attention because the affected population is large, the difficulties it faces are complex, and its needs are urgent.

Regardless of their socioeconomic environment, children with chronic illness are at risk for mental health problems. Furthermore, poverty can add to this risk enormously (Egbuono & Starfield, 1982; Stein & Jessop, 1985). In addition to the child with the illness, all of the people with whom the child lives are also more vulnerable to increased stress and mental health problems.

As this book shows in detail, although each particular condition requires specific medical treatment, chronically ill children have many similarities. The psychological, social, and economic difficulties encountered by these children and their families are not unique to any one diagnosis. Therefore, research, program planning, and public policy decisions should consider the broad group of children with chronic illness as a whole rather than as individual disease entities competing for limited resources. This philosophy forms a major conceptual building block for the Center's work.

As stated in the original proposal, a basic premise of the Center is that the mental health consequences of physical health problems should be addressed during childhood, when relatively simple and low-cost interventions may prevent greater problems in later life, when costs to the individual, the family, and society are much greater. Because the pediatrician is frequently the first professional to see the child and family in distress and is, by tradition, oriented to the health of the whole child and family, the pediatric health care practitioner is in an ideal position to identify such high-risk children during regular contacts, even before mental health problems become manifest. As a result, pediatricians represent community-based services available to a wide segment of the population who may be at risk for developing mental health problems. The pediatrician who identifies a given child as "at risk" is in a unique and trusted position to provide a preventive intervention directly or to refer the child to appropriate sources of help in the community (Academy of Pediatrics, 1982; Hamburg, Elliott, & Parron, 1982). The Center seeks to influence the training of pediatric and mental health professionals who will enter clinical practice to integrate the prevention perspective into their work in the community. This is an approach that has potentially powerful and far-reaching effects.

Goals and Objectives of the Center

The objectives of the Center are to:

1. Foster an interdisciplinary research environment targeting the identification and prevention of mental health sequelae of physical illness in childhood.
2. Implement interventions to prevent significant mental health problems arising from these health problems, determine how the mental health consequences of physical health problems in childhood are mediated by factors in the immediate life experience or the medical services of the ill child and family, and use this information to guide prevention strategies.
3. Increase understanding of the relationship of physical and mental health among physically ill children and their families.
4. Incorporate a developmental perspective into prevention programs as a means of assuring that an intervention rests on emotional, cognitive, and psychological factors appropriate to the child's age and the family's development.
5. Bring diverse research and intervention activities located within our academic medical center into closer working relationships.
6. Serve as a local, regional, and national resource in focusing on preventive intervention for children and their families.
7. Disseminate research findings and knowledge about the implementation of effective interventions.

These objectives are realized through a series of research projects, training programs, and related activities in the Center. At any time, the Center is involved with a dozen research projects, ranging broadly across the age span, based on diverse methodological approaches, and investigating a variety of specific issues. Collectively, the projects serve to evaluate different aspects of an overall conceptual model of the relationship between physical and mental health variables and their individual and combined effects on the behavioral and psychological well-being of the child and family.

AN OVERVIEW OF THE RESEARCH PROGRAM

Under its auspices, the Center has a range of faculty and graduate student research projects that regularly produce publications in the pediatric and mental health literature. Current examples included a controlled trial of the effects of family advocates on parents with a chronically ill child in respect to enhancing support and problem-solving skills; the effect on ego development and mental health status of a peer counseling training program for chronically ill adolescents; a school-based survey of adolescents to ascertain their knowledge about AIDS and to develop an appropriate educational program in the school system to enhance understanding of AIDS and promote appropriate prevention measures; and a randomized clinical trial of an educational approach to the management of asthma through an interactive computer game.

Some of these projects have been part of the Center since its inception, others are small pilot projects sponsored by the Center, and some have associated themselves with the Center to participate in its activities and to share resources. The projects' investigators come from different disciplines and backgrounds and include pediatricians, sociologists, pediatric and psychiatric fellows, clinical and school psychologists, and graduate students in health, developmental, and clinical psychology programs. In its pilot project program, the Center, one or twice each year, announces a request for applications of up to $10,000 to support projects related to the Center's theme.

THE STRUCTURE OF THE CENTER

It is useful to think of the PIRC as a Center without walls. All of the Center's administrative activities are concentrated in one area, whereas the numerous research projects and training activities occur in different locations in a variety of settings. The core staff is an interdisciplinary unit with backgrounds in pediatrics, public health, sociology, and psychology. This group oversees the Center's activities and provides an important model of interdisciplinary work. Virtually all of the major research, training, fund-raising, and administrative decisions are made within the context of the scheduled weekly meetings of this core group and numerous other ad hoc discussions. Often the solutions to difficult issues are reached only after extensive discussion, in which the issues are debated from different disciplinary points of view.

The Senior Advisory Committee includes prominent members of the scientific community from the Albert Einstein College of Medicine and Yeshiva University. The committee advises on major research issues and serves as the review panel for the pilot project program mentioned above. Individual members also often provide informal consultation on research projects.

Virtually all research centers, at some point, must develop a long-range plan for building a financial base that extends beyond a single source. To this end, the Center has assembled an Advisory Board composed of corporations, businesses, foundations, and individuals interested in helping children with chronic illness. This board also includes several representatives and civic leaders from the local community. This affords a link to groups in the community who otherwise might not be aware of the Center's activities and what it offers.

The Co-Director for Research and Evaluation and the Center's statistical analyst are jointly responsible for the day-to-day operation of the Center's computer facility, which is a major resource for all of the Center's investigators and trainees and has become an important source of consultation for researchers throughout the university.

In addition to its research program and computer facilities, the Center has begun to establish a resource center for families with children who have a serious condition and for local professionals and clinicians concerned with this population. We anticipate that this resource center will have a full-time staff person with access to computerized data on referral sources, including information on health services, housing, education, welfare, and ancillary programs. In order for it to be successful, this system will need to be publicized and made readily accessible to the community. The system will also require a carefully considered evaluation component in order to assess utilization, identify unmet needs and services, and develop methods for improved functioning.

TRAINING AND EDUCATION ACTIVITIES

From its inception, the PIRC has been committed to the training of professionals in preventive interventions and preventive intervention research. Pediatric house staff, fellows, faculty, graduate students in psychology, medical students, and psychiatry trainees have all been involved in the Center's educational forums, which include formal course work, periodic seminars and workshops, symposia, and informal consultation, technical assistance, and supervision.

One of the Center's new educational programs arises from a research and development training grant from NIMH to support the development, evaluation, and dissemination of a model curriculum in the prevention of mental health problems in child health care. The project is an interdisciplinary training program designed to enhance the knowledge and skills of mental health clinicians in the area of preventive interventions and their application to children, youth, and families at risk for mental illness. It uses the relationship between physical and mental health risk in children to illustrate basic prevention concepts and to teach specific preventive interventions. The project's overall goals are to help students conceptualize child mental health issues within a framework of prevention and to prepare them to utilize preventive intervention research data in clinical settings.

In addition, the preceptee program has been a key element in the Center's functioning since its inception. As part of its original mission, the Center included support for graduate students in a wide range of disciplines to learn about and participate in preventive intervention research. The preceptees have been unanimous in identifying the center as an important resource in their education and have noted several specific areas where their skills have been enhanced. Overall, the core staff of the Center have served as mentors and role models for individuals who are likely to integrate prevention concepts and research into their professional careers.

Another key element of training and education has been the Center's monthly seminars, topics for which have ranged from specific research projects within the Center to more general research and intervention issues. The Center has also sponsored several national conferences and symposia that have attracted professionals from many states, as well as from the university community and metropolitan area. Less tangible, perhaps, but of equal importance has been the ongoing information exchange and consultation among the Center's core staff and members of the university community from every level. In the context of working on existing research projects, discussing new research possibilities, or planning a presentation of research findings, the core staff communicates the concepts and ideas central to the field of preventive intervention research. We believe strongly that working together on common projects is an especially effective method for achieving two primary goals: (1) disseminating throughout the university a common set of ideas, assumptions, and methods about preventive intervention research in order to strengthen a broad foundation on which new preventive intervention projects can grow, and (2) developing diverse models for effective interdisciplinary cooperation, illustrating how physicians can work with social scientists and how clinicians and researchers can productively draw from each other's body of knowledge. The development of such models is an essential ingredient for the growth of true interdisciplinary research.

The Center has had a profound impact on the Department of Pediatrics and the university as a whole by bringing to the forefront issues concerning the psychological and social effects of illness in children and pioneering methods for preventing negative consequences secondary to serious health problems. This is accomplished through the integration of teaching and research activities conducted in multiple clinical sites. Alerting faculty, fellows, house officers, and other professionals about prevention of mental health problems in children with chronic illness has been a gradual yet steady process. As more students and trainees within other departments request information and assistance from the Center's staff, this influence is likely to spread.

THE CONTEXT AND SETTING

The PIRC has its headquarters on the Albert Einstein College of Medicine/Bronx Municipal Hospital Center (AECOM/BMHC) campus but, because of its transinstitutional affiliation, is able to conduct its activities at several sites in the Bronx and within the AECOM/Montefiore complexes. The Center also has affiliations with many extramural programs and institutions within the university with an interest in the mental health of children and their families. In 1985, in the Department of Pediatrics alone, there were approximately 290,000 ambulatory and emergency room visits (Department of Pediatrics, 1985). The population served, primarily working class and poor, is predominantly Hispanic and black, but also includes other minorities as well as whites.

In any research project the socioeconomic, cultural, and ethnic composition of the population must be considered carefully. Research that fails to do this runs a high risk for major problems in design and implementation. A careful and critical analysis of the environment in which people live, and the daily stresses that they encounter, is essential for effective prevention (Price & Smith, 1985). A large percentage of children and families receiving care from hospitals in the Bronx live in poverty, with unemployment, lack of financial resources for food and clothing, housing problems, lack of heat or hot water, electricity shutdowns, and an absence of phones a part of day-to-day life. The structure of the health care delivery system itself is fragmented, complicated, and difficult to understand. A child's health status may be only one of a number of stressors affecting both child and family. These stressors affect and often prohibit intervention to prevent adverse mental health consequences of chronic illness.

Careful scrutiny must also be given to understanding the role of a research center within an academic medical complex. On the positive side, the PIRC's location in a medical school makes available a wealth of resources. There are innumerable possibilities for establishing relationships with many affiliated programs and institutions that permit access to an enormous array of areas for exploration and research. On the negative side, highly charged political issues are ever present in an academic medical center. Problems related to turf, allocation of scarce resources, and complex bureaucracies often impede innovative prevention approaches. It is incumbent on the Center to integrate and maximize the positive aspects and to anticipate and minimize the drawbacks. Becoming a part of the environment as a whole is crucial. Sensitivity both to the needs of the population and to the needs of the institution is an important factor in the Center's operation.

OBSERVATIONS OF LIFE IN A RESEARCH CENTER

As part of the core staff of the Center, we have encountered numerous administrative and organizational issues, many of which have a direct influence on the conduct of research. These issues include communication problems between professionals with different backgrounds, questions of resource allocation, and resolution of competing demands. We discuss these issues here partly because they are especially relevant to interdisciplinary research centers. Furthermore, the *way* in which these issues are addressed sets an important tone for the Center and can contribute to the emergence of a productive ambiance.

Integrating the Clinical and Scientific Approaches to Research

Our Center includes (1) individuals trained primarily as clinical pediatricians who understand the value of research in the social sciences, but who have had relatively little experience in actually designing and implementing such research, and (2) individuals trained primarily as social scientists with considerable background in research but with relatively little hands-on clinical experience. Because our Center is based in a Department of Pediatrics, much of the research derives from clinical experience, from hunches and observations about what works in a particular situation. Furthermore, there exists a desire to test these hypotheses. The nature of clinical life often leads to a special focus on the unusual case, the idiosyncratic response, or the nonnormative pattern. The impetus for experimental research derives from a desire to investigate clinical observations in a methodologically sound and systematic way. In contrast, much research within the social sciences derives from a theoretical model about a particular phenomenon. Experimental designs thus serve to test aspects of a model. This vantage point leads to a focus on theory, on normative patterns, and on typical cases. These two perspectives can at times be difficult to integrate.

Of course, the distinction between the clinical and research perspectives is rarely as sharply drawn in practice as this dichotomy might suggest. In fact, the best "applied" research draws on both vantage points. In the Center, we have tried to integrate the two by assuring that clinical questions are set in the context of pertinent theoretical models and that questions deriving from theory are framed to address pertinent clinical issues. No single discipline has a monopoly on the issues and questions. For example, a neonatologist might observe that mothers who seem to have good social support are able to visit their babies more often; an intervention involving social support suggests itself from this observation. Yet the design of the intervention and its evaluation must be connected to a theory of how social support works, how it might be measured, and how it interacts with other important factors. While this marriage of clinical observation and theory building appears obvious, an enormous amount of work is required for maintaining a successful union. Rarely does a single person have sufficient knowledge about all the relevant issues in neonatology, social support, and research design. As others have observed (Ellison & Kopp, 1985), the study of such a complex phenomenon as child development in the context of health problems requires an interdisciplinary effort.

The Nature of Interdisciplinary Research

Embedded in the concept of interdisciplinary collaboration is a recognition that individuals from different disciplines have important contributions to make to one another, contributions that will in turn enhance the development of knowledge in this field. The interdisciplinary approach works effectively when individuals trained in one way of understanding the world are sufficiently flexible to incorporate the viewpoints of another perspective.

Such collaborative work can be challenging, stimulating, and rewarding. Yet problems arise. Ellison and Kopp (1985) note some of these difficulties:

> The maintenance of a solid physician and psychologist research collaboration requires thoughtfulness, understanding, tact, and nurturance. Consider the status and responsibilities of the physician. He or she often outranks the psychologist, has access to the subject population, daily confronts ethical issues surrounding patient diagnoses, and controls communication of information to child and family. A sense of being in charge develops. Con-

sequently, the psychologist may be perceived as being an adjunct to the research, responsible for day-to-day operations and committing ideas to paper. This is not a good formula for research. (p. 885)

A good formula requires mutual respect and support as well as dedication to the democratic decision-making process. Concepts that are taken for granted by one discipline are often major points of contention in another. The languages of two disciplines can also be surprising sources of misunderstandings, which take time and effort to resolve. However obvious it appears, interdisciplinary collaboration is a process that must evolve over time and be built on trust.

Professional Development in the Context of Center Building

One of the most enduring and problematic concerns for an interdisciplinary research center involves the reward system for professional activities. In most academic environments, professional advancement rests on relatively tangible products: the number of papers in peer-refereed journals, the number of classes or students taught, the number of presentations at national conferences, the number and size of grants received, and so forth. Activities related to developing a Center—that is, to the effort needed for creating a supportive research environment—generally receive less recognition in promotion committees. In our Center, for example, we schedule "research retreats" at least twice a year to discuss the progress of current research, develop new ideas, and identify new techniques. We believe that one of the most important functions of a center is to bring together persons with common interests who would not otherwise be in contact with each other, in the hope of stimulating new ideas and identifying new research opportunities. The pressures of prior commitments, however, coupled with the inherent tensions of interdisciplinary work, can result in major obstacles to collaborative work. We have come to appreciate the powerful disincentives within the academic environment toward activities needed for institution building or center development. In response to these disincentives, we must acknowledge that certain intellectual and educational benefits are afforded only by the presence of a vigorous interdisciplinary center.

From the inception of the Center, some of the investigators have been able to devote the time necessary to developing preventive intervention strategies. Others found it more difficult to incorporate mental health prevention strategies into their medical background. Early on, many resources were devoted to educating the professional community about prevention research. It is now apparent that the investment of time and effort has benefited and strengthened individual investigators and projects as well as the Center as a whole. Long-term investment without immediate rewards is based on the belief not only that preventive intervention research is a viable and fruitful domain for an interdisciplinary research center, but also that the field cannot proceed without it.

Value Added: The Benefits of a Center

Biased though we may be, we believe strongly that the existence of an interdisciplinary research center brings special benefits both for the individual investigators within the Center and for the field as a whole. From an investigator's point of view, the presence of a Center can lead to increased efficiency in the development and conduct of a research project. For example, in our Center we have collected information on a wide variety of measures related to the Center's theme, and the Center's core staff has considerable experience in the use of these measures. The presence of this resource can save investigators new to this field a great deal of time and effort in identifying appropriate tools. Furthermore, because we have available individuals trained in the methods and techniques of implementation frequently used in mental health research with children, the application of appropriate approaches and the analysis of data can be accomplished with relative efficiency. The existence of a core staff knowledgeable in a particular area leads to continuing chances for informal consultation and networking that otherwise would rarely occur.

The presence of the Center also stimulates the growth of new research opportunities that would otherwise be impossible. For instance, it has aided in the creation of a data base on subjects across all research projects. This information allows for long-term follow-up and interproject analysis. This type of longitudinal data base is essential (1) to generate innovative projects in the area of long-term development of children with serious illness and (2) to provide investigators with an opportunity for using comparative information available within the data base. The development and use of this resource requires a substantial initial investment of time and energy and is feasible only within the context of a center.

The analysis and discussion of different but related projects also affords the opportunity to validate findings more rapidly. For example, parallel findings in two studies, each of which alone would appear inconsequential, may together suggest an important direction for further study. This type of discovery, which has occurred repeatedly within the short life of the Center, represents one of the most fruitful consequences of a center to an investigator.

In addition to benefiting individual investigators, an interdisciplinary research center benefits the field as well. The PIRC has become a national clearinghouse for a wide array of issues related to the field of prevention and child health.

SUMMARY

Establishing an interdisciplinary research center devoted to the prevention of mental health problems in children with chronic physical health problems requires fortitude, perseverance, and vision. Like other prevention efforts, the PIRC must break new ground and build new structures for interdisciplinary applied mental health research. As Long (1985) notes:

> The prevention of mental–emotional disabilities as a focused area in the mental health field is a new dimension compared to treatment and rehabilitation. Developing the knowledge base for prevention requires planning, systematic interdisciplinary communication, coordination of research efforts, persistence, and time. The knowledge base for prevention comes from insights of clinicians, from prevention research, from epidemiological and biomedical research, and from the behavioral sciences. To prevent mental–emotional disabilities, attention must be given to organic and biological factors, the development of competence and coping skills, social support, the relationship of stressors to the development of disorders, and the context and interrelationships of these factors. (p. 826)

The efforts to accomplish these goals are often extraordinarily complicated, both methodologically and administratively. For the benefit of these children and their families, professionals in this field must not let these complications deter development of the innovative strategies and creative responses needed for the prevention of mental health problems in children.

Acknowledgments: The authors acknowledge the many ideas contained in this chapter that emerged from discussions with Laurie Bauman, Dorothy Jessop, and Ruth Stein. Their contributions to the interdisciplinary process made possible the Preventive Intervention Research Center for Child Health and helped to establish the intellectual and professional foundation of our interdisciplinary teamwork. The work for this chapter was supported in part by the National Institute of Mental Health (Grant MH38280).

REFERENCES

Academy of Pediatrics Committee on Psychosocial Aspects of Child and Family Health. (1982). Pediatrics and the psychosocial aspects of child and family care. *Pediatrics, 79* (1), 126–127.

Butler, J., Budetti, P., McManus, M., Stenmark S. & Newacheck, P. (1985). Issues in cost and financing. In N. Hobbs, J. Perrin, & H. Ireys (Eds.), *State of knowledge papers: Vol. 1: Public policies affecting chronically ill children and their families.* San Francisco: Jossey-Bass.

Davis, F. (1963). *Passage through crisis: Polio victims and their families.* Indianapolis: Bobbs-Merrill.

Department of Pediatrics, Albert Einstein College of Medicine/Montefiore Medical Center, (1985). *Annual report*, Bronx, NY.

Egbuono, L., & Starfield, B. (1982). Child health and social status. *Pediatrics, 69*, 550–557.

Ellison, P., & Kopp, C. (1985). A note on interdisciplinary research in developmental/behavioral pediatrics/psychology. *Pediatrics, 75*, 883–886.

Escalona, S. (1982). Babies at double hazard: Early development of infants at biologic and social risk. *Pediatrics, 70*, 670–676.

Featherstone, H. (1980). *A difference in the family*. New York: Basis Books.

Fowler, M., Johnson, M., & Atkinson, S. (1985). School achievement and absence in children with chronic health conditions. *Journal of Pediatrics, 106*, 683–687.

Goldberg, I. D., Regier, D. A., McAnerney, T. K., Pless, I. B., & Roghmann, K. J. (1978). The role of the pediatrician in the delivery of mental health services to children. *Pediatrics, 63*, 898–909.

Haggerty, R. J. (1981). Challenges to maternal and child health research in the 1980s. In L. V. Kerman (Ed.), *Research priorities in maternal and child health* (pp. 245–251). Washington, DC: U.S. Government Printing Office.

Hamburg, D. A., Elliott, G. R., & Parron, D. L. (1982). *Health and behavior: Frontiers of research in the biobehavioral sciences*. Washington, DC: National Academy Press.

Klerman, L. V. (Ed.). (1981). Research priorities in maternal and child health. Washington, DC: U.S. Government Printing Office.

Long, B. (1986). The prevention of mental-emotional disabilities: A report from a National Mental Health Association Commission. *American Psychologist, 41*, 825–829.

Pless, I. B., & Perrin, J. (1985). Issues common to a variety of illnesses. In N. Hobbs, & J. M. Perrin (Eds.), *Issues in the care of children with chronic illness*, (pp. 41–60). San Francisco: Jossey-Bass.

Pless, I. B., & Roghmann, K. J. (1971). Chronic illness and its consequences: Some observations based on three epidemiological surverys. *Journal of Pediatrics, 79*, 351–359.

President's Commission on Mental Health. (1978). *Report on the Task Panel on Community Support Systems*, (Vol. 2), Washington, DC: U.S. Government Printing Office.

Price, R. H., & Smith, S. S. (1985). *A guide to evaluating prevention programs in mental health*, [DHHS Publication No. (ADM) 85-1365]. Washington, DC: U.S. Government Printing Office.

Sabbeth, B., & Leventhal, J. (1984). Marital adjustment to chronic childhood illness: A critique of the literature. *Pediatrics, 73*, 763–768.

Select Panel on the Promotion of Child Health. (1978). *Better health for our children. A National Strategy* (Vols. 1–4). Washington, DC: U.S. Government Printing Office.

Stein, R. E. K., & Jessop, D. J.. (1982a). A noncategorical approach to chronic childhood illness. *Public Health Records, 97*, 354–362.

Stein, R. E. K., & Jessop, D. J. (1982b, May). *What the diagnosis does not tell: The* case for a noncategorical approach to chronic physical illness. Paper presented at the annual meeting of the Society for Pediatric Research, Washington, DC.

Stein, R. E. K., & Jessop, D. J. (1984). *Evaluation of a home care unit as an ambulatory ICU, Final Report* (Division of Maternal and Child Health, Grant No. MC-R360402).

Stein, R. E. K., & Jessop, D. J. (1985) Delivery of care to inner-city children with chronic conditions. In N. Hobbs & J. M. Perrin (Eds.), *Issues in the care of children with chronic illness* (pp. 382–401). San Francisco: Jossey-Bass.

Walker, D. K., Gortmaker, S. L., & Weitzman, M. (1981). *Chronic illness and psychological problems among children in Genesee County*. Boston: Harvard School of Public Health, Community Child Health Studies.

Weisman, M. (1982). *Intensive care*. New York: Random House.

Zook, C. J., & Moore, F. D. (1980). High-cost users of medical care. *New England Journal of Medicine, 302,* 966–1002.

19

Applying New Technology to Improve the Treatment of Adolescents

Karen Hein, M.D.

The expansion of new technologies offers an opportunity to widen treatments for and improve understanding of the management of chronic illness. The focus of this chapter is how improved understanding of the hormonal regulation of puberty and of pharmacology can be put to use in dealing with chronic illness in adolescence. After a brief review of the ways in which chronic illness and hormonal function affect one another, a model study assessing the mechanism by which puberty affects the disposition of medications will be examined. It is but one example of how advances in traditional subspecialties, such as endocrinology and pharmacology, now permit investigators to apply basic concepts to clinical problems presented by chronically ill adolescents. Because of the increased prevalence of chronic illness in this age group—stemming from increased survival rates engendered by research efforts over the past four decades—and because this population (along with chronically ill children) consumes a disproportionate amount of health dollars, it is essential that we research advances on the interaction of chronic illness and puberty.

INTERACTION OF CHRONIC ILLNESS
AND THE HORMONAL REGULATION OF PUBERTY

Adolescence is characterized by the marked changes in body size and function caused by the hormonal influences occurring during puberty. Chronic illness affects puberty, and puberty affects chronic illness. The majority of chronic illnesses require some medical intervention, such as medication, on a continuous or episodic basis. Therefore research on the nature, extent, and effects of such treatments is an integral part of this topic.

Research on the effects of chronic illness on physical growth has become possible only as the basic chronobiologic mechanisms of puberty have been elucidated. Over the past two decades, the sequence of normal events in the evolution of function of the hypothalamic–pituitary–adrenal–ovarian/testicular axis has been described. It is now possible to study the impact of various illnesses on this normal sequence. We know that chronic illness can affect linear growth rate, the appearance of secondary sexual characteristics, and sexual organ functioning. Now that there is a fuller understanding of the development of the hypothalamic–pituitary–gonadal axis in normal adolescents, comparisons with chronically ill youngsters are possible. Until recently, most studies were limited reports on the timing of a specific pubertal event, such as menarche, in patients with specific disease entities. Puberty can also serve as a mediating factor in the appearance of chronic illness. We can unravel pathophysiology of disease from long-term consequences by studying youngsters at the time the condition is developing rather than studying adult patients who have had the illness for many years.

People with chronic illnesses face different problems or issues, depending on their stage of physical and emotional development. In adolescence, three factors are of particular importance: (1) the dramatic physical changes occurring during puberty, (2) the shift in dependency (economic, emotional, and physical) away from the family and toward peers and society, and (3) the change in physiological functioning resulting from changes in cognition, ego functioning, and reasoning ability.

Although it appears that the increased prevalence of chronic illness is a result of improved survival rather than increased incidence (Newacheck, Budetti, & McManus, 1984), it must be emphasized that many chronic illnesses presenting before adulthood have a bimodal distribution. That is, there are two peak periods when the disease is likely to present: early childhood and adolescence. Examples include epilepsy (Woodbury, 1978; Epilepsy Foundation of America, 1975) and tumors (Connecticut State Department of Health, 1966; Maurer, 1978; Young & Miller, 1975). Morbidity and motality rates are also influenced by puberty (Hein, Cohen, Litt, et al., 1978; Wegman,

1985). The prognosis for many forms of leukemia has improved dramatically since the 1950s (Maurer, Simone, and Pratt, 1977). However, one of the prognostic indicators for poorer outcome is age at presentation. Patients presenting in adolescence with acute lymphoblastic leukemia have a poorer prognosis than younger children.

Even for common conditions such as asthma, a change in severity of illness accompanies puberty. Some studies report an improvement during puberty (Balfour, 1985), while others report a marked increase in mortality rate. For example, in one study from the United Kingdom in the 1960s, an "epidemic" of deaths among young people with asthma was noted. Among those aged 10 to 14, the mortality rate increased sevenfold, and asthma became the fourth leading case of death at that time (Benatar, 1986). The mechanisms proposed for the increase in morbidity and even mortality in adolescence include differences in severity of illness, effectiveness of treatment, compliance, and organization of care.

Many examples exist of the central role that puberty plays in initiating or exacerbating chronic illnesses. Puberty plays a role in the incidence of many other chronic conditions, including migraine headaches, epilepsy (Newmark & Penny, 1980), von Willebrand's disease, and late-onset congenital adrenal hyperplasia (Emans & Grace, 1984).

Studies of long-term sequelae of hypertension have highlighted the importance of adolescence as the time when borderline or mildly elevated levels of blood pressure present (Kannel, 1976; Joint National Committee on Detection, Evaluation, and Treatment of High Blood Pressure, 1984; Kilcoyne, Richter, & Alsup, 1974; Blumenthal, Epps, Heavenrich, et al., 1977; Katz, Heidiger, Schall, et al., 1980; Loggie, 1970). The role of the rise of sex steroids on lipoprotein levels is now being investigated. This line of research is particularly important because heart disease, cerebrovascular accidents, and associated mortality in adulthood may be ameliorated or prevented by interventions in adolescence (Voors, Webber, Frerichs, et al., 1977; Gruskin, Perlman, Balvarte, et al., 1984; Berenson, Voors, Webber, et al., 1983).

The treatments used to ameliorate, cure, or prevent chronic illnesses can affect pubertal development; the ultimate impact of such treatments—even life-saving ones—on the timing or completion of puberty has recently become a focus of research. Long-term survivors of childhood cancer, for example, are now being evaluated for long-term effects of radiation chemotherapy given prior to puberty (Scott, 1981); some studies demonstrate differential effects on gonadal structure and function following treatment. And differing effects of pre- and post-pubescent bone marrow transplants on gonadal function and relationship of outcome can now be determined (Sklar, Kim, & Ramsay, 1984).

The role of adjunct therapies on promoting pubertal development has also been assessed. For example, the addition of vitamin D3 to the hemodialysis regimen improved bone maturation in patients on hemodialysis (Johannsen, Nielsen, & Hansen, 1979). Although renal transplantation is a more effective means of restoring growth, the addition of anabolic steroids to the hemodialysis regimen may have merit (Jones, Bishti, Bloom, et al., 1980). The use of anabolic steroids in other conditions, such as cystic fibrosis, has recently been studied (Landon & Rosenfeld, 1984).

The effect on pubertal development and function of treatments for chronic illnesses that are not life-threatening are similarly being studied. For example, in male epileptics, anticonvulsant medications are being studied by themselves and in relation to other medications, including methylphenidate, used in the treatment of youngsters with attention-deficit disorders, and theophylline, used for the treatment of asthma.

As new treatments evolve, these too should be studied for their potential influence on puberty. For example, heart transplants have been successfully completed in older children and adolescents. In addition to improved mechanical and technical modes of therapy, the addition of cyclosporine to the medical treatment of transplant patients has been a major breakthrough in improving long-term viability of transplanted organs. The influence of this medication and the impact of the transplant itself on pubertal growth maturation and function are unknown at this time.

Lately, criteria are being developed to predict when it is safe to discontinue medical treatment for chronic illnesses. Criteria now exist to permit some patients with epilepsy to discontinue anticonvulsant therapy (Holowach, Thurston, & O'Leary, 1972; Shinnar, Vining, Mellits, et al., 1985).

USE OF HORMONES AND OTHER TREATMENTS TO REGULATE PUBERTAL EVENTS IN ADOLESCENTS WITH CHRONIC ILLNESS

In recognition of the negative impact of specific chronic illnesses and their treatments on pubertal development, there has been an attempt to ameliorate the consequences by introducing treatment to induce or maintain puberty. "Hormonal regulation of puberty" refers to those systems that initiate, maintain, and regulate the physical changes in body composition and organ response and function that comprise the pubertal states differentiating adults from children. As our ability to diagnose chronic conditions earlier in the life cycle improves, the advantages and disadvantages of therapeutic interventions can be evaluated. Replacement of missing, defective, or deficient sex hormones has been possible for several decades.

A MODEL STUDY OF THE INTERFACE BETWEEN CHRONIC ILLNESS AND HORMONAL REGULATION OF PUBERTY: EFFECT OF PUBERTY ON DRUG DISPOSITION

Many conditions, acute or chronic, require medication during the teenage years. Physiologic changes occur during puberty that result in changes in body composition and organ function necessitating special adjustments of medications. The basis of selecting a proper medication dose for a rapidly growing youth has only recently become the focus of systematic investigations. Prescribing practices vary enormously depending on the type of provider and whether he or she views the teenager as a small adult or a big child. By studying teenagers themselves, using asthma as a model illness and theophylline as a model compound, we have begun to identify which factors are related to changes in drug requirements during adolescence.

The purpose of presenting this model is to emphasize the following:

1. The way in which research on treatments for chronic illness in adolescence can be designed to adequately characterize the diversity of study subjects.
2. The way in which basic research can now be applied to clinical problems presented by adolescents with chronic illnesses. In this example, we have demonstrated the application of basic concepts of pubertal development to improving treatment by using concepts of pharmacokinetics in conjunction with knowledge of body composition and organ function to improve disease control during adolescence. In this way, research of various traditional disciplines (endrocrinology, pulmonary medicine, adolescent medicine, biomathematics, and developmental pharmacology) can work together to apply what information has been learned over the past few decades to more targeted, appropriate treatment of adolescents.

A new method was developed by our group for determining the appropriate medication dose in a rapidly growing adolescent. During the past five years, in collaboration with other investigators (principally Ralph Dell, M.D.), I have developed a method for characterizing the effect of puberty on drug disposition in pharmacological terms. This process involved three stages: (1) defining certain aspects of adolescent physical growth that were most likely to affect drug distribution and metabolism, (2) defining pharmacologic parameters that would best reflect or be affected by pubertal changes, and (3) choosing two model compounds to test the method. The two model compounds chosen were imipramine (Hein, Dell, Puig-Antich, et al., 1983) and theophylline (Hein, Dell, Pesce, et al., 1985).

Since most asthmatics are diagnosed in childhood, a dose of theo-phylline is chosen before puberty. The dose (mg/kg) and dosing interval (number of times taken per day) do not usually change during the years between early childhood and puberty. However, by adulthood, the dose is decreased by half (mg/kg/day), and the dose interval lengthens. The need to know when and how to adjust the dose of theophylline between childhood and adulthood is particularly pressing for moderate and severe asthmatics. For the mild asthmatic this titration, even if performed inac-curately, rarely has serious consequences. However, for the moderate or severe asthmatic, failure to adjust accurately during years of rapid growth may well contribute to poor disease control, patient discomfort, and excess use of emergency room and hospital facilities, because disease destabili-zation is exacerbated by the improper amount of medicine taken.

The hypothesis being tested is that an iatrogenic factor—namely, the physician's failure to adjust medication dose properly during a time when the dose is likely to change—is a major reason for destabilization in dis-ease control during adolescence. The result of improper dosing is an inade-quate amount of drug to control or prevent symptoms, a situation often wrongly assumed to be noncompliance on the patient's part. Conversely, if the dose is too high, toxic side effects, such as nervousness, tachycardia, and gastrointestinal upset, will discourage the patient from continuing medications as prescribed and result in true noncompliance. Until the medication dose is adjusted for state of development, the cycle of poor control or toxicity contributing to noncompliance will continue. This occur-rence is documented by the high percentage of patients presenting to the emergency room for treatment with low levels of theophylline.

If a simple predictive method were devised to tailor the dose indiv-idually, physicians could then prescribe medication in such a way as to avoid, rather than react to, disease destabilization or drug toxicity. Patients would then suffer less from symptoms of their disease resulting from improper medication doses. Those patients who use emergency room facilities because of poor disease control would decrease their use of these health care resources. In addition, rates of hospitalization would decrease if disease exacerbation was caused by undermedication producing ineffec-tive control or overmedication leading to drug toxicity.

It is now possible for many physicians in this country to obtain esti-mates of the plasma concentration of many drugs, including theophyl-line. However, this technological advance is usually employed only when disease symptoms or signs of toxicity appear. Although this is a useful rule for making decisions for adult asthmatics whose metabolism and body composition are relatively stable, it is not useful for adolescents. We have determined a specifically timed schedule for plasma theophylline concentration measurements so that $t_{1/2}$ can be computed. Half-life is being used for two purposes: (1) $t_{1/2}$ is being related to stage of pubertal development in a 3-year longitudinal study; and (2) $t_{1/2}$ is being used to adjust dosage (mg/kg/day) and dose interval (number of doses per day) in a randomized clinical trial to determine if a better dosage schedule will result in better disease control, decreased loss of school time because of asthma, and decreased use of medical resources (specifically, decreased visits to the emergency room and decreased episodes of hospitalization).

We believe that puberty affects theophylline disposition via changes in body composition and organ function. The model for this hypothesis is shown graphically in Figure 19.1. Theophylline enters the body and is then distributed into body water and is relatively fat insoluble. The amounts of fat and water differ between males and females and among youngsters of various body habitus. Theophylline is eliminated by being metabolized in the liver and then conjugated and excreted by the kidneys.

In pharmacological terms, the "tank" into which the theophylline is distributed is estimated by the volume of dilution (V_d). The main site of elimination is the liver. The rate of the metabolite production is known to change with age. The rate of metabolism is described by the elimination rate constant, from which the half-life $t_{1/2}$ is derived.

FIGURE 19.1 Schematic representation of the effect of pubertal development on drug disposition.

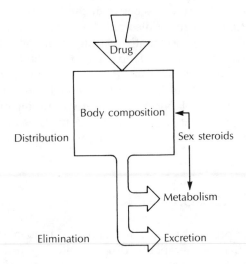

SOURCE: Hein, K. (1987). The use of therapeutics in adolescents. *Journal of Adolescent Health Care, 8*, 8–35.

The demographic and anthropometric variables were selected that, in combination, accurately define an individual adolescent developmentally. The ten variables are: age, sex, sexual maturity rating scale (Tanner, 1962), growth velocity (height or weight gain per unit time), body compositional variables (lean body mass, percentage of fat, or total body water), surface area, and a newly developed composite score (based on Tanner stage, growth velocity, sex, and body composition combined). Data from 70 patients aged 8 to 18 requiring theophylline for the treatment of asthma have been analyzed (Hein, Dell, Reuben, & Ulrich, 1987). Half-life is related to sex (it is significantly longer in females than males), age, height, and lean body mass. From these preliminary studies, we have gained sufficient expertise in measurements and classification to be able to select from the list of variables and to develop our own composite score for assessing teenagers at various stages of development.

The next step was to select certain pharmacologic variables that show a change between childhood and adulthood and that might bear some relationship to the changes in body composition and liver function that occur during puberty. The variable drug half-life ($t_{1/2}$ elimination) was chosen because $t_{1/2}$ changes quite dramatically between childhood and adulthood for most classes of drugs. In the case of theophylline, for instance, our own measurements show a range of $t_{1/2}$ of 2–12 hours in youngsters aged 8–18. Other studies have demonstrated a similar range between children and adults (mean $t_{1/2}$ child "x" hrs vs adult "y" hrs). Other pharmacological parameters, such as volume of distribution (V_d) and clearance, show differences between children and adults, which we have now documented for adolescents.

A series of outpatient and inpatient studies were designed and carried out that investigated the relationship between pubertal development and drug distribution and metabolism. Pharmacokinetic models have been developed and fitted to the data for two model compounds. Sampling strategies had to be developed to assure proper timing of blood samples to enable accurate calculations of drug $t_{1/2}$. A more detailed set of studies was done in inpatients to enable calculation of clearance and volume of distribution.

SUMMARY AND CONCLUSION

The goal of this project has been to apply two innovations—measuring drug levels as part of therapeutic drug monitoring and applying pharmacokinetic principles—to achieve and maintain proper medication dosing for youngsters and adolescents during periods of rapid growth.

Teenagers account for 18% of the population in the United States, and 10% to 20% of these young people have chronic conditions. The total amount of medication consumed by this group (prescribed, over-the-counter, illicit) plus the number of youngsters with chronic illnesses extending into the teenage years beyond childhood is staggering. Frequently, precise dosing recommendations are not available from the drug manufacturer because they fall under the "orphan drug" category, that is, a drug used in treatment of patients under the age of majority or for a condition that does not justify large expenditures by the pharmaceutical manufacturers to define adequately the exact requirements for a specific age group. With the basic capabilities of measuring blood or other body tissue levels of a drug (therapeutic drug monitoring), when a range of levels can be defined as safe and effective (therapeutic range), studies such as the ones described will enable clinicians to define the correct dose for individuals to maximize the length of time they remain within the therapeutic range.

We are at a unique point in the history of medicine vis-à-vis adolescents with chronic illness. We now have the technical capability to prolong life and to begin to measure the impact of chronic illness on puberty and, conversely, the impact of puberty on chronic illness. By providing a new conceptual framework for research in these areas in the coming years, we have an opportunity to minimize, ameliorate, or even reverse some of the adverse biological consequences of chronic illness in adolescence.

REFERENCES

Balfour, L. L. (1985). Childhood asthma and puberty. *Archives of Disease in Childhood, 60*, 231–235.

Benatar, S. R. (1986). Fatal asthma. *New England Journal of Medicine, 314*, 423–428.

Berenson, G. S., Voors, A. W., Webber, L. S., et al. (1983). A model of intervention for prevention of early essential hypertension in the 1980s. *Hypertension, 5*, 41–53.

Blumenthal, S., Epps, R. P., Heavenrich, R., et al. (1977). Report of the task force on blood pressure control in children. *Pediatrics, 59*, (Suppl.) PI–II, 797–820.

Connecticut State Department of Health. (1966). *Cancer in Connecticut. Incidence and rates 1935–1962.*

Emans, S. J., & Grace, E. (1984). Management of late onset 21-hydroxylase deficiency congenital adrenal hyperplasia complicated by obesity and polycystic ovary syndrome. *Pediatric and Adolescent Gynecology, 2*, 173–184.

Epilepsy Foundation of America. (1975). *Basic statistics on the epilepsies.* Philadelphia, PA: Davis.

Gruskin, A. B., Perlman, S. A., Baluarte, H. J., et al. (1984). Primary hypertension in the adolescent: facts and unresoved issues. In J. M. H. Loggie, M. J. Horan, A. B. Gruskin, A. R. Hohn, J. B. Dunbar, R. J. Havlik (Eds.), *NHLBI workshop on juvenile hypertension* (pp. 305–333). New York: Biomedical Information Corp.

Hein, K., Cohen, M. I., Litt, I. F., et al. (1978). Neo-plastic disease during adolescence. *Clinical Pediatrics, 17,* 178–180.

Hein, K., Dell, R., Pesce, M. et al. (1985). Effects of adolescent development on theophylline half-life. *Pediatric Research, 19,* 173.

Hein, K. Dell, R., Puig-Antich, K. et al. (1983). Effect of adolescent development on imipramine disposition. *Pediatric Research, 17,* 89.

Hein, K., Dell, R., Reuben, N., Ulrich, S. (1987). Influence of pubertal development on theophylline kinetics. *Pediatric Research, 21,* 175.

Holowach, J., Thurston, D. L., & O'Leary, J. (1972). Prognosis in childhood epilepsy: Follow up study of 148 cases in which therapy had been suspended after prolonged anticonvulsant control. *New England Journal of Medicine, 286,* 169–174.

Johannsen, A., Nielsen, H. E., & Hansen, H. E. (1979). Bone maturation in children with chronic renal failure. Effect of 1 alpha-hydroxy vitamin D3 and renal transplantation. *Acta Radiologica: Diagnosis (Stockholm), 20,* 193–199.

The Joint Committee on Detection, Evaluation, and Treatment of High Blood Pressure. (1984). The 1984 report of the Joint National Committee on Detection, Evaluation, and Treatment of Hypertension. *Archives of Internal Medicine, 144,* 1045–1057.

Jones, R. W., El Bishti, M. M., Bloom, S. R., et al. (1980). The effects of anabolic steroids on growth, body composition, and metabolism in boys with chronic renal failure on regular hemodialysis. *Journal of Pediatrics, 97,* 559–566.

Kannel, W. B. (1976). Some lessons in cardiovascular epidemiology from Framingham. *American Journal of Cardiology, 37,* 269–282.

Katz, S. H., Heidiger, M. L., Schall, J. L., et al. (1980). Blood pressure, growth and maturation from childhood through adolescence. Mixed longitudinal analysis of the Philadelphia blood pressure project. *Hypertension, 2* (Suppl. 1), 55–69.

Kilcoyne, M. M., Richter, R. W., & Alsup, P. (1974). Adolescent hypertension 1. Detection and prevalence. *Circulation, 50,* 758–764.

Landon, C., & Rosenfeld, R. G. (1984). Short stature and pubertal delay in male adolescents with cystic fibrosis. Androgen treatment. *American Journal of Diseases of Children, 138,* 388–391.

Loggie, J. M. H. (1979). Prevalence of hypertension and distribution of causes. In M. I. New, L. S. Levine (Eds.), *Juvenile hypertension.* (pp. 1–12). New York: Raven Press.

Mauer, A. M., Simone, J. V., & Pratt, C. B. (1977). Current progress in the treatment of the child with cancer. *Journal of Pediatrics, 91,* 523–539.

Mauer, H. M. (1978). Current concepts in cancer. *New England Journal of Medicine, 299,* 1345.

Newacheck, P. W., Budetti, P. P., & McManus, P. (1984). Trends in childhood disability. *American Journal of Public Health, 74,* 232-236.

Newmark, M. E., & Penny, J. K. (1980). Catamenial epilepsy: A review. *Epilepsia, 21,* 281–300.

Scott, J. E. (1981) Pubertal development in children treated for nephroblastoma. *Journal of Pediatric Surgery, 16*(2), 122–125.

Shinnar, S., Vining, E. P. G., Mellits, E. D., et al. (1985). Discontinuing antiepileptic medication in children with epilepsy after two years without seizures: A prospective study. *New England Journal of Medicine, 313,* 976–970.

Sklar, C. A., Kim, T. H., & Ramsay, N. K. (1984). Testicular function following bone marrow transplantation performed during or after puberty. *Cancer, 53*(7), 1498–1501.

Tanner, J. M. (1962). *Growth at adolescence* (2nd Ed.) (pp. 162–165). London: Blackwell Scientific Publications.

Voors, A. W., Webber, L. G., Frerichs, R. R., et al. (1977). Body weight and body mass as determinants of basal blood pressure in children: The Bogalusa heart study. *American Journal of Epidemiology, 106,* 101–108.

Wegman, M. E. (1985). Annual summary of vital statistics—1984. *Pediatrics, 76,* 861–871.

Woodbury, L. A. (1978). Incidence and prevalence of seizure disorders including epilepsies in the United States of America: A review and analysis of the literature. In *Plan for nationwide action on epilepsy* (Vol. 4). Washington, DC: U.S. Department of Health, Education and Welfare.

Young, J. L., & Miller, R. W. (1975). Incidence of malignant tumors in US children. *Journal of Pediatrics, 86:* 254–258.

20

Computer-Assisted Care

David H. Rubin, M.D.

Programs for children with chronic illnesses have recently begun to include computer-assisted technology. These programs have contributed to a more standardized approach to patient and family education, to educational and assistive interventions designed to reduce deficits, and to monitoring illness status. They hold great promise for affecting child health in the future. However, the controlled evaluation of these programs prior to their release to the public is still in a very primitive stage and requires as much attention as their technical development. For most chronic illnesses, there are specific educational needs for both patient and family. These illness-specific needs are primarily related to the day-to-day medical and/or psychological demands posed by the illness (e.g., medication, physical therapy, etc.). In addition, some illnesses cause specific educational handicaps or have associated disabilities that potentially could be reduced through computer technologies. Computers are also beginning to be used to assist in outpatient monitoring of illness and its management.

This chapter includes (1) a review of some of the theoretical concepts underlying special educational uses of computers for children with chronic illness, (2) a discussion of the emergence of the computer as an educational instrument, and (3) a presentation of illness-specific examples of computer-assisted programs now in use.

THEORETICAL BACKGROUND FOR EDUCATIONAL USES OF THE COMPUTER

Educational services are available to children with chronic illnesses through public programs (Lesser, 1985), self-help and mutual aid groups (Borman, 1985), and disease-specific national organizations. For example, the American Lung Association sponsors educational meetings for children with asthma and their families to discuss common problems in the management of asthma.

One of the most common goals of these educational programs is to provide information that will help patients and their families better understand and better manage daily issues and problems. Such improved control could result in improved child behaviors related to the specific illness. Examples of improved child behavior in childhood asthma include avoidance of specific allergens and appropriate use of medication. The hoped-for final result of any educational program is a reduction in disease-related morbidity. A proposed model of this interaction is shown in Figure 20.1.

Hobbs, Perrin, and Ireys (1985) have divided children with chronic illnesses into three groups when defining school-related educational needs. These divisions could also apply to educational programs aimed at improving disease management. The first group includes children who have severe cognitive or perceptual deficits in addition to, or as a result of, illness. Examples of this group are children with spina bifida and muscular dystrophy. The second group includes children with temporary or permanent physical impairments without any associated deficits in cognitive or intellectual functioning. Examples of this group are children

FIGURE 20.1 Proposed interaction of education and behavior in children with chronic illness.

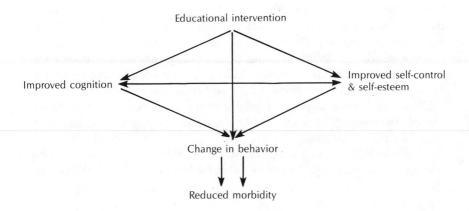

with arthritis and hemophilia. The third group includes children who have no intellectual or physical impairment directly attributable to their illness. Examples of the group are children with asthma, diabetes, and malignancies. Based on the limitations imposed by the specific chronic illness, each of these three groups has specific requirements to be met when designing an educational program.

The success of any educational program requires that the program be fine-tuned to the cognitive and developmental level of the target group. For example, educational programs even for children in group three could not be expected to be used successfully in children less than approximately 7 years of age. This is the age that Piaget described as the stage of concrete operations, or the age at which the child can start to apply the principle of inductive reasoning (Lewis, 1982). Physical impairment is also an important consideration, especially for children in group two. One possible solution to the problem of physical impairment has been the recent development of voice-activated text. If successfully implemented, this would eliminate the need to push buttons on a keypad.

Door (1981) has suggested that health education programs must address four issues. The first three include (1) the presentation of messages in such a way that they will be understood, (2) the presentation of material in ways that are appealing, and (3) the focusing of material on the specific experiences of the target age group. The fourth criterion is the creation of an educational experience that will influence behavior related to the management of the condition. Two additional behaviors have been emphasized by Bandura (1977), who suggests that learning the specific behaviors in a "safe" environment is the best method of affecting behavior.

Computer games and educational materials have changed the way children spend their free time. The popularity of these games, which can intensely attract children's attention, stems from their challenge and the chance they give children to control action on the screen (Butterfield, 1983). Computer-assisted instruction has been shown to (1) improve inductive reasoning and the ability to handle multiple variables interacting simultaneously and (2) improve skills related to study habits and self-concept (Gadzella, 1984). Thomas (1979) found that computer-assisted instruction in secondary schools resulted in achievement levels equal to or higher than those attained with traditional instruction.

There has been a dramatic increase in the presence of computers in school. Between 1981 and 1983 the number of school districts with microcomputers increased from 6,473 to 12,517, or to approximately 78% of all school districts in the United States. The number of schools using microcomputers increased from 14,132 in 1981 to 55,175 in 1983 (Deninger, 1985).

The recent emergence of computer-assisted educational instruction programs has profoundly affected the relationship between the chronically ill child and his or her environment. These programs are the result of research and development that attempt to produce a standardized teaching medium. This medium does not require the active participation of health care professionals in didactic teaching sessions, which characterized prior instructional formats. Deardorff (1986) has compared a computerized format for patient education with written and verbal methods of instruction, finding that the computerized health education format was the best method of patient education. Not only did computerized health education produce good recall of medical information, but it was also more popular than the written instructional method.

Computer-assisted educational programs have been produced using the formats of (1) educational text, (2) interactive computer games, and (3) interactive video. An educational text is the simplest approach to patient education using computer technology. This approach concentrates on a series of questions and answers without extensive attention to graphic design. For example, a computer educational text on hemophilia would include basic information on the treatment of common childhood injuries sustained by children with this disorder. Following the instructional screen, there might be a multiple-choice question based on the information presented. If the patient chooses the correct response, he or she would advance to the next screen for another lesson in the management of hemophilia.

Interactive games add an exciting dimension to computer-based education. The interactive capacity of these programs creates a unique environment for children. There is instantaneous feedback on any decision made by a player. The feedback indicates whether the player has made a correct response in offering a solution to a particular problem.

Interactive video combines the technology of video and computer-assisted instructional methods. A video segment is displayed, and the computer selects a specific program related to the video segment. Interactive video has two advantages: the videotape advantages of visual images and sound, combined with the instantaneous interactive capability of computer-assisted instruction (Pollard, 1985).

A recent review of the medical literature revealed the availability of a variety of computer-assisted educational programs for children with several chronic illnesses. One problem with reviewing this particular topic is that the literature does not reflect the true availability of all programs. There is no national clearinghouse for computer-assisted educational programs for children with chronic illness, and many software packages are not marketed nationally. Furthermore, research evaluating the efficacy of computer-assisted programs has been less than satisfactory. Even though specific educational programs may exist for particular illnesses, the programs are rarely tested in a controlled manner. Most prior studies have been solely descriptive, with very few controlled evaluations.

ILLNESS-SPECIFIC COMPUTER PROGRAMS

There are two models of program development: (1) health education, focusing on help in the management of a condition, and (2) increased communication and deficit reduction, focusing on methods of bypassing problems and increasing communication. Computer-assisted educational programs now exist for children with asthma (Rubin, Leventhal, Sadack, & Letovsky et al., 1986), cerebral palsy (Bruno & Stoughton, 1984), diabetes (Lefebvre, Houziaux, Godart, & Scheen-Lavigne, 1981; McAdoo, 1987), hearing impairment (Grant & Semmes, 1983), learning impairment (Fulton, Larson, & Worthy, 1983), autism (Colby & Kramer, 1975), mental retardation (Lally, 1981), and motor and speech impairment (Fried-Oken, 1985).

Health Education Programs

Asthma

Asthma Command is an interactive computer game for children with asthma (Rubin et al., 1986). The game was written to emphasize four basic principles in the management of childhood asthma: (1) the recognition of symptoms and allergens, (2) the appropriate use of medications, (3) the appropriate use of the emergency room and physician's office, and (4) the encouragement of school attendance. The object of *Asthma Command* is to simulate a daily routine of asthma management and score as many points as possible. *Asthma Command* is not a question-and-answer computerized text of the principles of the management of asthma; rather, it attempts to force players to develop strategies for scoring points. Players must use their knowledge of asthma management to maneuver through the many obstacles presented in the game. For example, if a player is allergic to cats, a pictorial representation of a cat is presented during the game. Using a joystick, the player must maneuver himself around the cat or risk a loss of points. Players must also remember to choose the option of taking their regularly prescribed medications. They must learn the correct frequency and dosage to protect them if they find themselves close to an allergen or if they run (as opposed to walking). A high score is achieved by avoiding allergens and appropriately using medications, the emergency room, and the physician's office. Subjects use their own specific medications and allergens, entering both into the game's memory during the first playing session. At the end of a 45-minute session, the player is presented with a computer printout detailing strengths and weaknesses in the management of asthma based on his or her performance in the game.

The efficacy of *Asthma Command* was evaluated in a randomized clinical trial. Control subjects played routine computer games, children assigned to the experimental group played *Asthma Command*. Compared with children in the control group, experimental subjects showed improvement in knowledge about asthma ($p < .001$), behavior related to the management of asthma ($p < .008$), and a trend toward the reduction of acute visits related to asthma ($p < .13$). Children in the experimental group also scored higher on the assessments of behaviors related to the management of asthma that were specifically addressed by the intervention provided by *Asthma Command* ($p < .01$). This randomized clinical trial was performed using a graphically immature version of the game. Recently the game was substantially upgraded with improved graphics and is being tested once again using a controlled trial design.

Diabetes

Lefebvre and colleagues (1981) designed a computer-assisted instructional text and tested its efficacy in improving knowledge related to diabetes care. Evaluation of the program was by pre- and postexposure testing. The diabetes text focused on (1) carbohydrate metabolism, (2) pathophysiology of insulin-dependent diabetes, (3) insulin—different types of preparations and usage, (4) correct adapting of doses to daily situations, (5) hypoglycemia, (6) dietary principles, and (7) urine testing for glucose and ketone bodies. Results of the evaluation showed a significant improvement in diabetes-related knowledge after exposure to the text ($p < .001$).

McAdoo developed an interactive computer game for children with diabetes called *Diabetes Adventure* (distributed by Picodyne Corporation, Portola Valley, CA). The purpose of the game is to teach children with diabetes to assume greater control over their illness. This includes knowledge of correct insulin dosage as well as the correct role of exercise and diet in the management of diabetes. The program takes the form of an adventure game that simulates real-life problems for diabetic children. The testing of the efficacy of this game is now in progress (McAdoo, 1987).

Programs in Increased Communication and Deficit Reduction

Cerebral Palsy

Bruno and Stoughton developed a computer-based communication device for children with cerebral palsy and tested it on one child, who improved his communicative abilities as a result of the program. The program was developed on a battery-operated portable computer that contained a built-in printer and a microcassette tape recorder for saving computer programs and patient vocabularies. Voice output capability was included in the program through a speech synthesizer. Messages typed (via a head pointer for children with cerebral palsy) on the computer keyboard are displayed on the monitor and may be optionally printed or spoken. The vocabulary portion of the software allows commonly used words and/or sentences to be stored in memory for easy access by the user (Bruno & Stoughton, 1984).

Hearing Impairment

Computer-assisted education has been used extensively for hearing-impaired children who are subject to potential problems in language acquisition and verbal expression. In one program, the computer language LOGO was used with a hearing-impaired 5-year-old twin (whose sibling was a control) to enhance spatial visualization and introduce an organized symbol system in addition to spoken language (Grant & Semmes, 1983).

LOGO has several advantages for use in language development, including vocabulary and syntax that are parallel to human language and serve as an introduction to the use of metaphor in everyday language (Cazden, 1982). In this particular program, LOGO was used with a single keystroking program involving a simple graphics program. The twins participated in the instructional program for eight sessions over a 2-week period. Although no formal evaluation was performed, it was felt that the program objectives were achieved for both the hearing-impaired and normal twin. Spatial visualization was enhanced, as demonstrated by familiarity with direction. The introduction of a new language through the use of keystroking was felt to be successful based on the observation that both children had grasped the concept that a single keystroke could command an activity.

Learning Impairment

Fulton and colleagues (1983) developed a computer-assisted audiovisual program for investigating auditory–visual discrimination among learning-impaired children. The program presents computer-generated symbols (text or graphic), video images (still or motion), and auditory stimuli (video–audio track, audiocassette, and speech digitizer) independently or simultaneously. Young children can respond by pointing instead of interacting with a keyboard, which older children have the option of using. Subject responses are printed out immediately for analysis.

Handicapped Children

Thorkildsen (1985) developed the interactive video social skills (IVSS) training program to develop the social skills of handicapped children. The IVSS program teaches children how to use appropriate verbal communication in social interactions. The videodisc presents examples of appropriate and inappropriate social behaviors along with models to imitate in subsequent role-playing. The components of this program include a printer, videodisc player, and color monitor. A microcomputer is part of the videodisc player.

A randomized clinical trial was performed to test the efficacy of the IVSS program. Children assigned to the experimental group were exposed to the IVSS program over a 4-month period. Those assigned to the control group did not receive the IVSS program. Evaluation included data on social behavior, acceptance by nonhandicapped peers, and self-esteem. Children in the experimental group scored significantly higher on a measure of peer acceptance and social skills. There was no significant difference in self-esteem or social behavior between the two groups.

Nonspeaking Children

Colby and Kramer (1975) developed a computer-assisted audiovisual program to stimulate language behavior in nonspeaking children. When a key is pressed on the keyboard, a symbol, letter, word, expression, or drawing appears on the display screen. This image is accompanied by the appropriate human or animal sound. It is hoped that nonspeaking children will be able to use the program to improve language by attempting to imitate and respond to the sounds accompanying the various images. The efficacy of this program is not known. However, from recorded data in the program, a nonspeaking child's capability for producing language can be followed over time by comparing his or her responses to those of a normal child.

Mildly Retarded Children

Lally (1981) used a computer-assisted training program to teach sight vocabulary to mildly retarded children. An interesting part of the program was the elimination of the child's need to use a keyboard. Verbal instructions were included as part of the text displayed on the screen.

A list of 105 words was used in the program. During the training sessions, a plastic overlay of 16 words was placed over a matrix of 16 large buttons; each button covered a different word. Twelve overlays were used to include all 105 words. The object of the program is to match the word displayed on the display screen with the word contained in the overlays. Sixteen children 9–16 years of age participated in a randomized clinical trial testing the efficacy of the program. The mean IQ was 60 (range 40 to 74, SD = 10). The control and experimental groups were matched for age, IQ, and initial sight vocabulary and tested on the list of 105 words. Children in the experimental group correctly recognized more words than did those in the control group after a 4-week training course ($p < .001$). This recognition remained constant for more than 23 weeks after the completion of the course.

Speech Impairment

A voice recognition device used as an interface between motor- and speech-impaired individuals and computers was developed by Fried-Oken (1985). The device enables the subject to bypass a computer keyboard and control the computer through voice activation. This device could enable persons with disabilities to increase their independent functioning by activating currently available environmental control systems. Various interfaces have been in use by disabled persons, including a mechanical joystick and touch-sensitive buttons. However, the use of a voice recognition device appears to be a step forward in the rehabilitation of these individuals. (Fried-Oken tested this device on a 10-year-old quadriplegic boy who was able to create a vocabulary for computer storage to run educational software packages. The resulting accuracy rate for speech recognition was between 45 and 60%.) Refinement of this device is currently being performed.

MONITORING OF ILLNESS

The other major new application of computers is their use in monitoring care. This technology is being used extensively in inpatient services and is beginning to be seen in ambulatory treatment.

Diabetes

Mazze, Pasmantier, Murphy, & Shamoon (1985) have used a computer-based storage system of blood glucose measurements designed to improve patient self-monitoring. Reflectometers were designed with memory chips capable of storing blood glucose readings with time and date. Data from the reflectometer were off-loaded into an Apple IIe microcomputer and displayed to subjects. Using historical controls, patients who used the modified reflectometer showed improvement in self-monitoring. During the study, the common practice of fabricated test results was almost nonexistent. However, even though there was improvement in self-monitoring behavior, there was no significant change in metabolic control during the short 6-week study.

CONCLUSION

The overall development and evaluation of computer-assisted educational teaching programs for chronically ill children is in a primitive stage. The preceding description of a few of the currently available programs indicates the potential range of research and development. There is a need for a central clearinghouse responsible for cataloguing and critically evaluating these programs. Such a critical review prior to their release to the public would protect families from the dissemination of misinformation. Second, it would reduce expectations for the attainment of unrealistic goals in some programs. Third, it would allow for evaluation of appropriate monitoring of specific programs. Finally, evaluation of the effect of these programs could increase our understanding of the relationship between education programs and the cognitive, behavioral, and mental health status of children with chronic illnesses.

Several of the currently available programs have shown promising results. It is clear that the use of this type of educational medium has tremendous potential for positively affecting children's health. Further work in this field might well produce a series of programs for each chronic illness, each tested in a controlled manner. Because of the constant improvement in computer software packages, such as improved user friendliness and improved graphics, this task should become easier in the next few years.

Acknowledgments: Support for this work was provided in part by The Robert Wood Johnson Foundation Functional Status Grant #10836. The author appreciates the review of this chapter by Henry T. Ireys and its typing by Fran Erenberg.

REFERENCES

Bandura, A. (1977). *Social learning theory.* Englewood Cliffs, NJ: Prentice-Hall.
Borman, L. D. (1985). Self-help and mutual aid groups. In N. Hobbs & J. M. Perrin

(Eds.), *Issues in the care of children with chronic illness: A sourcebook on problems, services and policies* (pp. 771–789). San Francisco: Jossey-Bass.

Bruno, J., & Stoughton, A. M. (1984). Computer-aided communication device for a child with cerebral palsy. *Archives of Physical Medicine and Rehabilitation, 65,* 603–605.

Butterfield, F. (1983, May 24). Video games specialists meet at Harvard to praise Pac-Man, not to bury him. *New York Times,* pp. A22–A23.

Cadzen, C. B. (1972). *Child language and education.* New York: Holt, Rinehart & Winston.

Colby, K. M., & Kramer, H. C. (1975). An objective measurement of nonspeaking children's performance with a computer-controlled program for the stimulation of language behavior. *Journal of Autism and Childhood Schizophrenia, 2,* 139–146.

Deardorff, W. W. (1986). Computerized health education: A comparison with traditional formats. *Health Education Quarterly, 13,* 61–72.

Deninger, M. L. (1985, November). Is it still an apple for the teacher? *American Annals of the Deaf,* 332–339.

Dorr, A. (1981). How children related to educational materials. In *Self-Management Educational Programs for Childhood Asthma* (Vol. 2) (pp. 305–326). Bethesda, MD: National Institute of Allergy and Infectious Diseases.

Fried-Oken, M. (1985). Voice recognition device as a computer interface for motor and speech impaired people. *Archives of Physical Medicine and Rehabilitation, 65,* 678–681.

Fulton, R. T., Larson, A. D., & Worthy, R. C. (1983, September). The use of microcomputer technology in assessing and training communication skills of young hearing-impaired children. *American Annals of the Deaf,* 570–576.

Gadzella, B. M. (1984, January). *Study skills, self-concept and academic achievement for high school students.* Abstract presented at the Southwest Educational Association research meeting.

Grant, J., & Semmes, P. (1983, September). A rationale for LOGO for hearing-impaired preschoolers. *American Annals of the Deaf,* 564–569.

Hobbs, N., Perrin, J. M., & Ireys, H. J. (1985). *Chronically ill children and their families.* San Francisco: Jossey-Bass.

Lally, M. (1981). Computer-assisted teaching of sight-word recognition for mentally retarded school children. *American Journal of Mental Deficiency, 4,* 389–395.

Lefebvre, P. J., Houziaux, M. O., Godart, C., Scheen-Lavigne, M., Bartholome, M., & Luyckx, A. S. (1981). Computer-assisted instruction for diabetics: An original project developed at the University of Liege, Belgium. *Diabete et Metabolisme, 7,* 127–134.

Lesser, A. J. (1985). Public programs for crippled children. In N. Hobbs & J. M. Perrin (Eds.), *Issues in the care of children with chronic illness: A sourcebook on problems, services and policies* (pp. 733–757). San Francisco: Jossey-Bass.

Lewis, M. A. (1982). *Clinical aspects of child development.* Philadelphia: Lea and Febiger.

Mazze, R. S., Pasmantier, R., Murphy, J. A., & Shamoon, H. (1985). Self-monitoring of capillary blood glucose: Changing the performance of individuals with diabetes. *Diabetes Care, 8,* 207–213.

McAdoo, T. (1987). Diabetes power. Unpublished communication.

Pollard, G. (1985, November). The nuts and bolts of interactive video: How it works and how to get started. *American Annals of the Deaf,* 385–387.

Rubin, D. H., Leventhal, J. M., Sadock, R. T., Letovsky, E., Schottland, P., Clemente, I., & McCarthy, P. (1986). Educational intervention by computer in childhood asthma: A randomized clinical trial testing the use of a new teaching intervention in childhood asthma. *Pediatrics, 77,* 1–10.

Thomas, D. B. (1979). The effectiveness of computer-assisted instruction in secondary school. *AEDS Journal, 12,* 103–116.

Thorkildsen, R. (1985, November). Using an interactive videodisc program to teach social skills to handicapped children. *American Annals of the Deaf,* 383–385.

21

Facing the Financing of Care

Arthur F. Kohrman, M.D.

The discussion of the needs of chronically ill and disabled children usually turns quickly to the financial problems they create and of which they are victims. While there are many self-evident reasons for that focus of discussion, it might be useful for a moment to look into some of the less obvious reasons for our concerns. The most common association with the term *cost* is the concept of *value* (see Fleischman, Chapter 7). In a society that has traditionally not valued the less competent, the less mobile, or the less attractive, it is appropriate to ask if the concern about the cost of care and support of the ill and disabled (who have many of those characteristics) is not, in fact, a constant debate over their value to that society—can we afford them? Or, put differently, is their value sufficient to justify the costs of keeping them alive and attending to their admittedly disproportionate needs for support? Society, through its policy processes and mechanisms, supports without question the vast majority of services and establishments that are seen to be essential to its function and safety—defense, sanitation, education—yet continues to wrestle with the financial needs of those of its members who are temporarily or permanently dependent as a consequence of age (both the very young and the very old), illness, or congenital or acquired disability, as if their claim on the society's resources is very tenuous—always uncertain or in question. In other spheres, the issues are not *whether* to support but rather *how* to do so most efficiently and effectively. For the chronically ill, disabled, and dependent, it seems that we are always asking the question of whether to support them, as if this endlessly revisited territory will someday yield an answer that will get us off the hook in a way that is morally and ethically acceptable.

We also focus on cost because public policies are practically expressed in terms of dollars and because the abstraction of a child who will be dependent on others for an incalculable period of time is too difficult to comprehend and measure. The relatively high direct costs of care of the individual child are well described in this book (see especially Rowland, Chapter 2) and elsewhere (Butler, McManus, & Newacheck, 1986; McManus & Norton, 1984). We know that families of chronically ill children are less likely to have any or adequate insurance and that alternate sources of financial support are uncertain and difficult to obtain and coordinate (Butler et al., 1986; Kutza, Richman, & Kohrman, 1987). In addition to these obvious problems are the less calculable and more frightening uncertainties of figuring out how to pay for (or plan to pay for) the costs of illnesses or disabilities in children who may remain totally or partially dependent for years or decades, for a long but unknown period of time. The high costs of the child's care in the present are only the beginning of a lifetime of concerns about money to support a burden of unknown duration or magnitude.

The issue of cost of care for chronically ill children forces us to acknowledge their extreme political vulnerability. A group making up only a small part of the population of sick children and of children in general, they nonetheless consume a disproportionate part of the resources devoted to child health (McManus & Norton, 1984). Because of the very high costs of the care of some of them, they are extremely evident to the policy maker looking for targets for cost-cutting. That these children are also likely to be dependent on society for a variety of supports for a long time conflicts with the American concern for physical, emotional, and financial independence. In combination with the present ambivalence toward children in general in contemporary policy initiatives, these forces conspire to make the situation of the chronically ill child in public policy shaky; the guarantees of continuing concern and support (both fiscal and political) seem uncertain to both their caretakers and their caregivers. These circumstances beg for long-range planning that transcends year-to-year budget making and ensures stability on the unpredictable seas of the political process.

As we become clearer on the real long-term needs of chronically ill children and their families, it becomes evident that the existing and traditional sources of payment are not necessarily directed toward those needs; thus, even for families who have some sort of insurance, out-of-pocket expenses may be great. Ambulatory visits, the services of professionals other than physicians, home care, respite services, various forms of transitional care, special educational services—all important needs of some or all chronically ill children or their families—have not been covered by traditional forms of insurance, public or private (Fox & Yoshpe, 1986).

This misfit between needs and existing payment mechanisms becomes yet another factor that focuses attention on financing problems as central issues in the lives of chronically ill and disabled children.

The family of the chronically ill or disabled child must nearly always deal with the problem of money—to pay for care, to purchase appliances and medicines, to buy the services of others for the treatment, education, or transportation of their child. Wage earners must also consider the salary lost in meeting their child's needs; the price of forgoing vacations and other opportunities to renew their psychic energy; the toll that the constant presence of their child's illness or disability takes on other human relationships and on personal freedom, whether the freedom just to play or the freedom to change jobs and homes as others are able to do. Many of these costs can easily be calculated in specific terms; some can only be approximated. Because the intangible costs are in domains that are difficult to measure, the tangible and countable costs take on an even greater importance, both in their own right and as symbols for the unspoken opportunity costs and losses.

The secondary and unmeasureable costs of having a child with a chronic illness or disability may, in fact, take an even higher emotional toll on parents than the monies required for the direct care of the child. The denial or limitation of insurance or the complex scheduling that the child requires have high emotional as well as monetary costs. Primary wage earners sometimes have to make the difficult choice between leaving a job or going uninsured because the cost of their children's care has led to an intolerable rise in the insurance premiums of their co-workers. How do we calculate the cost of such a dilemma to families or to the children themselves, if they are aware of the problem?

One of the most worrisome current trends clouding the long-term futures of these children is the growth and threatened dominance in American health care of so-called managed-care organizations such as health maintenance organizations (HMOs) and preferred provider organizations (PPOs), in all their various and changing combinations and permutations. These and other present and contemplated forms of collective risk sharing across closed patient panels must see the long-term patient with many and expensive needs as "bad risks." How chronically ill and disabled children will find care in settings where individual patient cost control is the driving force and dominant motive is both unclear and unsettling. Yet the present climate is one that is encouraging the growth of managed-care systems, and, as they grow, the concern about their adequacy to meet the needs of chronically ill and disabled children also grows. The population of chronically ill children consumes the largest portion of all pediatric hospital days, requires a large number of specialty and subspecialty consultations, uses many more ambulatory services and visits than well children, and will continue to need such extensive services for an unknown length of time. Thus they are quintessentially those patients whom successful managed-care programs should avoid or to whom they should limit services in the name of cost containment.

The problems of financial support for chronically ill children are complicated and unavoidably colored by the inextricable connections between chronic disease and poverty. The burden of chronic illness is greater among the poor, both in incidence and in morbidity. The poor are less likely to have insurance, to have access to needed care, to receive needed special education services, or to have the family stability so essential to good outcomes for their disabled children. The high likelihood of financial dependence of these children and their families may have several important consequences for the attitudes of the professional and lay communities with which they come into contact. The first financial resource sought by those who would help them is usually one or another of the welfare-type programs (because that may be all that is available), and the perception of chronically ill children as welfare recipients (with all the connotations of that status) is thus reinforced. Both explicitly and implicitly, welfare recipients are judged by means tests, or by a calculus that postulates that some children are "more deserving" than others in the battle for the limited resources our society provides for its less well-off members.

FINANCING IN THE PRIVATE SECTOR

The most common means of payment for health services for the nonelderly in the United States is by private health insurance. However, the availability and effectiveness of private insurance for children with chronic illness is limited and appears to be diminishing in recent years (Fox & Yoshpe, 1986). Between one-fifth and one-quarter of all American children are without any health insurance protection for all or part of the year. Children with special problems seem to have some insurance coverage at the same general rate as all children. However, as a group they appear to have greater burdens because of the larger proportion who live in poverty; this group is more likely to be assisted by public funds (primarily Medicaid) and thus more likely not to be covered by insurance for a part of any given year.

Even those families with chronically ill children who have private insurance coverage may have large, possibly crushing, out-of-pocket expenses because of the limitations in their policies. Many insurance plans restrict coverage for "prior existing conditions"; thus the parent who switches jobs may be deprived of coverage for the child with a long-standing illness or disability. Traditional insurance plans also more or less restrict payment for outpatient services, including special therapies, psychological or mental health services, appliances or equipment, and home care services—all of the special needs for which chronically ill children are most likely to require payment. In addition, most private insurance plans have ceilings on total lifetime payments for a family or for any of its individual members. These ceilings can rapidly be reached by children with a serious chronic illness or disability requiring extended hospitalization, high technology, or complex home care arrangements.

Recent trends in the private insurance sector show both encouraging and worrisome elements. There appears to be a growing awareness by insurers of the advantages, both human and fiscal, of well-covered home care programs for the chronically ill; careful case-management programs are being initiated and evaluated by some insurers, with generally favorable early results. The number of employers who provide for an unlimited or very high ceiling on lifetime benefits is growing; a significant number are now incorporating out-of-pocket spending limitations.

Other trends, however, are less positive. The growth of self-insurance by small- to medium-sized employers places a great burden on the parent of the high-cost child whose expenses may be single-handedly responsible for raising the premiums or co-payments of the entire insured group— they may be singled out for extraordinary premium payments or even dropped from the group, either by job termination or by the employer's change of insurers. With a clear trend toward increased cost sharing by employees, parents may be required to make larger out-of-pocket co-payments and accept larger deductibles; parents of chronically ill children face a particular problem when the deductible is a fixed percentage of all costs (or even of hospital costs) and their child requires a long period of intensive therapy and/or hospitalization in a given policy period. Another trend is the development of so-called cafeteria benefit plans—in these, the employee may choose from a list of available benefits up to a ceiling employer cost. These plans have resulted in an increase of the proportion of all children who are uninsured or under-insured because of the willingness of the parent to "bet" on the relatively low risk of problems occurring to a previously well child. If, however, that child then sustains an illness or injury that results in a long-term disability and high costs for care, the child is essentially uninsured, even though the parent is technically covered.

There is much recent interest in the development of risk pools in the private insurance industry, with encouragement and oversight from individual state insurance agencies. In these, there are either pooled funds for all high-cost clients, with mandatory contributions from all the private insurers doing business in the particular state, or so-called assigned risks, with each insurer (or a designated group) responsible for clients with one or another diagnostic entity. As these programs are conceptualized, they might or might not receive contributions from state or federally derived funds to underwrite the anticipated high payouts and thus limit the exposure of the private insurers.

Similarly, "catastrophic insurance" plans have emerged in several state initiatives and in proposed federal legislation; these are primarily directed toward relieving the problems of the impoverished aged, whose limited resources can easily be devastated by out-of-pocket payments. The state plans generally are intended to provide at least some coverage for the un- or under-insured or uninsurable; but they nonetheless require that the client have sufficient money to purchase the insurance available under the new scheme. They do not seem to address the problems of poor parents with a disabled child who have no additional funds available. Individuals particularly left out of these plans are those who are poor but do not meet eligibility requirements for Medicaid or other forms of public support.

Risk pools and catastrophic insurance plans may evolve into programs that are favorable to families of chronically ill and disabled children. If they ultimately lead to an acceptance of the permanent (or at least long-term) nature of the dependency of these children, and become funds essentially held in escrow for the children's future care, then they will be realistic and predictable sources of support into the now-too-uncertain future. However, if access to these pools and plans for the poor and near-poor is brokered through present welfare systems (e.g., Medicaid), then the status of chronically ill children as welfare recipients will not have changed: access to insurance will just have become another means-tested "benefit," subject to all the shortcomings of present systems—spend-downs, state-to-state variation, time-to-time eligibility changes, and determinations of relative worthiness.

As discussed earlier, the most rapidly growing forms of medical care organization and payment are the various managed-care alternatives, all of which have cost containment as one of their major incentives and organizing principles. In different ways, each of these is required to meet a "bottom line"; some are clearly intended to make money for their organizers and professional participants. These financial imperatives require, in turn, that the organizations control utilization of expensive services, especially hospitalization, and screen out or limit services to high utilizers.

In these organizations families with chronically ill or disabled children may find themselves at particular jeopardy; "prior existing condition" clauses may exclude their children from coverage at the times of job or insurer change, or needed services may simply not be provided or covered under the constraints of cost containment. There is particular sensitivity to high-cost clients in small or newly started managed-care organizations which do not have large enough reserves to absorb, nor client bases over which to distribute, the fiscal burden of such persons.

Whether fiscal incentives to managed-care organizations to take on such high-cost clients (such as the federal experiments subsidizing Medicare recipients in HMOs) will emerge remains to be seen. These might arise from either federal or state initiatives, or they might be made part of high-risk insurance pools by including managed-care organizations in those mandated to participate in those pools. One can also imagine private–public joint initiatives (e.g., among insurance companies, managed-care payers, and state Title V—Crippled Children Services—agencies) that would both spread the costs over a larger payer base and assure that the children receive the necessary services and have them paid for, regardless of the type of insurer/payer involved. Until these alternatives are explored and developed, however, the chronically ill child's status in managed-care systems will be uncertain at best, potentially seriously compromised at worst.

Another source for support in the private sector for the chronically ill child lies in the many disease-oriented voluntary associations (DOVAs). Although these organizations command relatively little of the total monies spent on children with chronic illness or disability, they can make an important difference for the child whose needs fall into their general categorical (specific diagnosis- or disease-related) interests. However, there is great variability in the support offered, both between programs and within the same agency from place to place. Depending heavily, as most of them do, on volunteer staff for fund raising and for service delivery, it is not surprising that there are wide variations in the level and quality of services offered. Many of the DOVAs see their primary mission in research support; in these, the availability of funds for direct service is further constricted. Nonetheless, in many communities and for many children and families, various DOVAs are important sources of direct support, especially for ancillary therapies, equipment, and home care services; they can be especially important and useful as information sources for families with children with complex needs and as political advocates for the children whose interests they represent. In the latter function, they occupy a unique and important role, in that their advocacy is free of conflict of interest with the various governmental programs or private insurance initiatives that provide the greatest amount of monetary support for children with special needs; they can thus be vigorous advocates or adversaries of change as they see their interests helped or threatened. In that sense, they ultimately become important voices in influencing the financial climate and possibilities in both the public and private sectors.

FINANCING IN THE PUBLIC SECTOR

While this section will not describe the many public sector programs available for financing the care of chronically ill or disabled children (see Rowland, Chapter 2), it will discuss some salient features of the present systems (or nonsystems) of governmental payment. The most evident characteristic of the public sector financial supports is the notable lack of coordination between the various federal and state agencies that bear responsibility for the support of these children and their families (see Rowland, Chapter 2). The maze of overlapping agency responsibilities, varying eligibility rules, and apparent deficiencies of interagency communication around a given child can be perplexing or impenetrable even to the most aggressive and sophisticated parent or advocate (Kutza et al., 1987). Although there is great promise in the mandates of PL 94-142 (the Education for All Handicapped Children Act), the funds available for chronically ill and disabled children are clearly inadequate in many instances; those monies that are available are administered with great inconsistency, both within and among school districts. There are similarly wide variations in the other publicly funded services and in eligibility criteria from place to place (Butler et al., 1986), particularly between states. While the greater portion of available funds (in most states) is derived from federal sources, the mechanisms for gaining access to those funds are not at all uniform.

Medicaid (Title XIX) is the major governmental payer for services for chronically ill children, usually after certification and with oversight by the State Title V agency; however, it is virtually impossible to obtain from Medicaid offices the total amounts spent on the population of chronically ill children. Without these data it will be difficult, if not impossible, to estimate the total financial burden to government of their care. Thus, planning for more rational systems is impeded because of an inadequate data base on which to make reasonable estimates of the anticipated public-sector burden for the adequate care of these children in the future.

With the exception of Title V, SSI (Supplemental Security Income), and variously funded programs for handicapped children in education agencies, the majority of public funds available to children with chronic illness are administered through Medicaid, which is fundamentally a welfare program. Thus these funds are provided as charity rather than as an entitlement, such as are the guarantees to the elderly under Title XVIII (Medicare). While there have been effective manipulations of the Medicaid program in recent years which have helped many chronically ill children (such as the various waivers for home-based care), the basic requirement to establish eligibility and need, whether for an individual child or for the entire class of children at risk, remains. This situation symbolizes the societal discomfort with recognizing the permanence of these children's dependency and the (unspoken) hope that somehow their individual and collective problems will disappear. Public education should lead to recognition of the innappropriateness of this sort of thinking, then to a more permanent and logical kind of financial support, federal trust funds that project into the child's future, can emerge as the alternative. Until that time, chronically ill children and their families will live under the shadow of welfare or a welfare-like program, with the continuous need to demonstrate worthiness and an inherent uncertainty about their financial future in a political process notable for its fickleness about welfare recipients.

RECOMMENDATIONS

The financing of care for chronically ill children is complex, and changes or improvements must occur in many different areas, each interrelated with the others. Changing social values and political realities affect an environment in which technological change, with all its implications for good and bad, will not stop; new diseases with unimagined consequences and new treatments, some only partially effective, will bring new demands and hopes. Payment systems will have to be not only flexible from child to child and from time to time but also from place to place; the great diversity of the United States will require regional and local systems that respond to geography, ethnicity, social class, and differing disease and disability profiles.

How much we pay and how we pay for the care of chronically ill children in the future will be strongly influenced by the shape of three separate but closely related systems: the institutions (both social and physical) in which care takes place, the ways in which we manage and coordinate care on a day-to-day basis, and the form of the evolving governmental and private cost-sharing schemes as they change to reflect changing public attitudes about young chronically ill and disabled people and their futures.

Institutional Organization

With the current general recognition of the excess capacity of the American health care system and its attendant costs, it is unreasonable and unnecessary to imagine the development of new institutions for the care of the relatively small population of chronically ill and disabled children. Rather, we must design regionally tailored, comprehensive, and integrated institutional care systems that utilize existing physical and human resources. Community hospitals and clinics, private physicians, transitional facilities, schools, and voluntary and public-sector assessment and treatment programs and agencies should be linked in local consortia with the tertiary care institutions from which most of the present care of chronically ill and disabled children is now directed. The goals of these consortia should be to ensure that the child is in or has available a care setting and resources that provide for the least restrictive, most supportive, and lowest-cost continuing care. This goal will require new comprehensive and easily communicated forms of record keeping, and easy mobility for the child between caretakers and settings, in the physical as well as operational sense. Especially important are the linkages with educational institutions: the child spends (or should spend) the greatest proportion of time in school when not at home, and it is there that the child's most important "job" is performed. In addition, and of great present and potential importance, it is within school systems that mandates for and expenditures of funds for disabled and disabled children already exist.

New referral patterns, based on the child's needs rather than on traditional professional imperatives and convenience, will emerge. As an additional benefit, the consortia should be able to identify and provide needed but not presently available services in concert, with greater effectiveness and lower cost than if done by any of the institutions alone, for example, respite services or group care settings that can serve as resources for the entire community.

Professional roles and traditional guild boundaries should be scrutinized. The needs of many different categories of chronically ill and disabled children are similar; better community organization should be able both to reduce the numbers of professionals doing the same tasks for different subgroups of children and to provide opportunities to look anew at professional career definitions and the educational programs that prepare professionals. There may be categories of caregivers not now in existence because of traditional territorial divisions among professionals (and the certification and licensure mechanisms that support and reinforce those divisions) who could more effectively and more efficiently deliver and coordinate services.

The consequences of these attempts at integration, reorganization, and redefinition will not only have immense benefits for the children but should also result in significant redistributions and efficiencies in the utilization of funds now applied to their care.

Individual Case Management

Individual children with chronic illnesses and their families may use many services, be in contact with many agencies, and need many forms of support, from information about opportunities to financial counseling. Great inefficiencies, lost opportunities, and unnecessary costs ensue when the needs of the individual child lack integration. On the other hand, there may be costs *not* incurred that *should* be, if they are costs for services that will make the child more functional or the family less stressed; in these cases, the increased short-term tangible costs resulting from better integration must be measured against the long-term tangible and intangible costs to the child, family, and society. In either case, there is a great need for systems of case management for the chronically ill child; this would involve not only financial planning, which is only one (albeit important) part of the total plan for care and follow-up, but also a comprehensive, responsive, creative management plan. What distinguishes true case management from traditional care plans is the incorporation of continuous monitoring, quality assessment of services delivered, investigation of reasons for services not delivered, and constant revision of the plan in response to the child's changing needs and developmental status as well as the family's resources, both financial and emotional.

What is described is really only what all competent parents do for their children; in unstressed families with adequate resources and well children, we usually do not even question that this sort of "case management" is logically the parents' assumed responsibility, and society only intervenes when some catastrophic resource depletion or family disintegration exposes the child to serious risks that become evident to outsiders. The family of the chronically ill child, however, is likely to be subject to constant material and emotional stress, with variations in that stress as circumstances change, acute illness intervenes, the child enters a new developmental stage, or some external event unbalances an already tenuous family system. The breakdown of a care plan has tremendous costs—to the family, to society, and especially to the child. Thus there is a need to establish a case management plan for each child and each family and to identify the coordinator or overseer of that plan carefully and deliberately. The case manager may be, in many instances, the well-trained and competent parent(s), but the assumption cannot automatically be made that parents can or will assume that role initially, or without relief, or without intermittent or constant help.

The financial impact of good case management is significant for many parties. Family resources can be stretched and applied where most effective, agency resources are better used and thus available for more children, and insurance payers and other fiscal guarantors can realize great savings (and thus provide longer periods of financial support to families to whom they have a fixed obligation). Private insurance payers and managed-care organizations should be prepared to pay for case management services, since the overall savings will be great. Public agencies should also either provide or pay for well-conceived and well-run case-management services, since their limited funds will thereby be significantly extended.

There are great opportunities for public–private sector collaborations in applying case management services to the careful allocation and expenditure of funds for chronically ill children; one can imagine several possible configurations for cooperative ventures in which the goal is the best utilization of the combined public and private funds available for each child. These would require anticipatory planning of the projected long-term needs of the child and conjoint commitment of each of the funding partners from the outset, rather than the situation that now occurs in so many instances—using public funds only as the last resort to "rescue" the child and family from the catastrophes threatened or precipitated by the exhaustion of private insurance. These often harmful disruptions need not occur; anticipatory planning and good case management can help to avoid them, with obvious and important benefits, both financial and programmatic, to chronically ill children, their families, and the responsible payers.

Trust Funds for Chronically Ill and Disabled Children

Present payment mechanisms in both the public and private sectors are based on assumptions and social constructions that are neither correct nor appropriate and that reflect a basic and pervasive ambivalence about the nature of the social obligation to chronically ill children and their families. Public monies, with the exception of the relatively small amounts available through Title V and related programs, are lodged in and administered by welfare bureaucracies. The purpose of private health insurance is to offer relief and cost sharing for unexpected occurrences to the individual. The problems of the chronically ill child that create long-term or permanent dependency on outside financial resources are neither reflective of a welfare status nor unexpected in the usual sense of insurance risk. We have, as a society, accepted and responded to the anticipated dependency of the elderly and, with Medicare, have placed monies in trust against the anticipated costs of caring for that dependency. The projected costs and necessary deposits to meet those costs in a future-discounted manner are calculated from actuarial estimates based on national demographics. The elderly thus have a form of social insurance, not against the unexpected but rather in anticipation of their needs. While we are learning that the present Medicare program does not meet all the long-term care needs of the elderly and are responding with new national policy initiatives (e.g., catastrophic insurance plans), the assumption remains that the needs of a population with anticipated dependency should be met with planned entitlements rather than with ad hoc resort to a welfare system only after the inevitable exhaustion of personal resources finally occurs.

The needs and attendant exhaustion of personal resources are as inevitable for families of chronically ill children as they are for the elderly. Because the aggregate time of dependency of the population (and thus the total burden) is less certain than in the case of the elderly, the actuarial assumptions to establish trust funds for these children will, at least at first, necessarily be less precise; these can be refined with accumulating experience from further research. However, because the population at risk is small, the funds necessary to establish such trusts will be relatively small (compared to those for Medicare or for prudent reserves for private health insurers), and the degree of uncertainty surrounding actuarial assumptions should be tolerable in the early years. The advantages of establishing trust-like funds for chronically ill children are not limited to the public sector. Private insurers will benefit from investing funds against already obligated payouts in order to capture the savings realizable from the time value of such investments. If the period of payout can additionally be extended by effective case management and utilization of facilities and services in the most cost-effective manner, the resulting savings will be large; some portion of them can be plowed back into the trust funds to reduce the amount of new capital needed to assure adequacy of future coverage from subsequent new recipients.

There are in these recommendations many opportunities for new collaborations between the public and private sectors as well as indications for well-thought-out and evaluated demonstration projects, which might be sponsored by insurance companies, state and local agencies, philanthropies, or the Health Care Financing Administration, in various combinations. It is unlikely that a single program will meet the needs of the diverse population of children and families in need, nor will a single model be appropriate for the entire United States. However, if the principles of regional institutional integration, comprehensive case management, and establishment of funding mechanisms based on social insurance rather than welfare assumptions are used, we should be able to devise realistic programs for financing the care of chronically ill children that are reassuring, dignified, and effective.

REFERENCES

Butler, J. A., McManus, M. A., & Newacheck, P. W. (1986). Issues in the financing of care for chronically ill children and their families. *Topics in Early Childhood Education, 5*(4), 58–69.

Fox, H. B. (1984). *A preliminary analysis of options to improve health insurance coverage for chronically ill and disabled children.* Paper prepared for the Office of Habilitation and Rehabilitation Services, Division of Maternal and Child Health, U.S. Department of Health and Human Services, Washington, DC.

Fox, H. B., & Yoshpe, R. (1986). *Private health insurance coverage of chronically ill children.* Paper prepared for the Georgetown University Child Development Center, Washington, DC.

Kutza, E., Richman, H. A., & Kohrman, A. F. (1987). *Chronically ill children in Illinois.* Report prepared for the Colman Fund of the Chicago Community Trust, Chicago.

McManus, M. A., & Norton, C. H. (1984). *Health care utilization and expenditures for chronically ill children by condition: A preliminary review of selected data sets.* Paper prepared for the Office of Habilitation and Rehabilitation Services, Division of Maternal and Child Health, U.S. Department of Health and Human Services, Washington, DC.

Epilogue

Bruce C. Vladeck, Ph.D.

Hard cases, according to the old aphorism, make bad law. In other words, when the facts are particularly complicated, or in dispute, or when the decision between competing parties involves a particularly close call, then it is difficult to formulate or apply clear, general policy principles.

In a different sense, the problems of many chronically ill children also constitute hard cases, in that the provision of optimal care over time for these children and their families is hard, and even harder to do well. If the tasks were less formidable, or the policy questions they raise less complex, there would be no need for a volume like this one at all; yet the scope and difficulty of the issues leads even those of us who are very proud of this book to acknowledge that it raises more questions than it resolves—which is, of course, as it should be. Making good "laws" from these hard cases is not an easy task.

The instincts of program administrators and of academic physicians—and certainly the needs of policymakers—all insist on at least a level of abstraction and generalization, yet one cannot think for very long about the needs of chronically ill children without being constantly brought back to the concrete, the specific, the variety of particular human needs, frailties, and strengths. In thinking about the hard cases of individual ill children, it is critical not to lose a sensitivity to that diversity and that specificity, even while engaged in necessary summary and speculation.

The hard cases of chronically ill children also make for bad law in the sense that most of our systems for providing and paying for health services, not to mention our systems of elementary and secondary education, do not do a very good job of taking care of them. Often, those systems can barely cope with meeting the minimal needs of those whose needs are most simple; we should hardly be surprised when they have great difficulty in dealing with more complex problems. We must do better by the millions of individual children with very serious needs, yet we must also begin from a recognition that doing better will not be easy, that hard problems generally do not have simple or uniform or quickly attained solutions, and that blaming the providers of care or funding for not coping adequately with problems they were never equipped to address is an error comparable to, if less morally objectionable than, blaming the victims themselves.

These general observations provide a kind of preamble to the discussion of a number of themes that emerge from the earlier chapters in this volume. In a book with so much material covering so broad a range of topics so extensively, an epilogue neither can nor should provide either a comprehensive summary or a grand synthesis; at best, it can restate or put a slightly different interpretation on some of the points made earlier. That is what I hope to do in what follows, addressing specifically the topics of support for families; integration of medical and social services; the relationship of chronically ill children and high technology; the dilemmas of managed care; and the particular problems that arise from the intersection of poverty and chronic illness in children.

SUPPORT FOR FAMILIES

To begin with, if one conclusion emerges clearly from the literature—including this book—on children with chronic illness, it is that effective services support not only the ill child but the child's entire family. As Julianne Beckett writes at the beginning of her remarkable chapter, "if the child is to survive, the family must also survive." One is tempted to add that for the child to thrive, the family must also thrive, or at least muddle through. Yet while support of the family and of "family values," whatever they are, are basic stock-in-trade of every politician's vocabulary, we have in fact, in the United States, hardly any precedent or capacity for dealing with families as the objects of public policy. Our public statistics count "households" or "taxpaying units"; our income maintenance programs support "dependents." Families are supported when they are single-parent families or, in a minority of states, when the principal wage-earner is unemployed. Our "family service" agencies revolve organizationally around the process of making decisions as to when children should be removed from their biological families and on administration of adoption and foster care programs. Even in programs to care for the dependent elderly, we give extensive lip service to the importance of "informal caregivers"—mostly family members—but have yet to figure out how to avoid impinging on their roles when public support is made available, let alone how to assist them.

The parents, extended family, and, often, siblings of children with chronic illness are, in most instances, the primary givers and managers of care, just as they are for other children. In most instances, however, they need considerable help in coping both with their caregiving tasks and with the financial, psychological, and social burdens that the child's illness presents. Providing such help, however, is not the kind of thing we tend to do well in public policy in this society. It is also not, it should again be emphasized, something that is easy to do well, without creating excessive dependency and passivity on the family's part, on the one hand, or incomplete and inadequate supports, on the other. But instead of finding creative ways of helping such people, we tend, in too many instances, to punish them in a variety of subtle, and sometimes not so subtle, ways. We refuse to require accommodations in the workplace to permit working parents to care adequately for chronically ill children, limit or take away health insurance benefits, and reduce public payments if the child remains at home. If we cannot find more effective and creative ways to assist the families of chronically ill children, the least we should be able to do, it seems to me, is to remove some of the obstructions that so often make it impossible for them to assist themselves.

INTEGRATION OF MEDICAL AND SOCIAL SERVICES

Rigid, artificial, and often quite arbitrary boundaries between medical and social services abound in all parts of the human service system, affecting clients of all ages suffering from a wide variety of problems. But as is made clear at many points in this book, the distinction between "medical" and "social" is often almost entirely meaningless in defining the care needs of a chronically ill child, so that generic difficulties in integrating those two systems can have particularly harmful effects when chronically ill children are involved.

One of the reasons the problem arises so frequently is that we have set up our services in ways that make them particularly hard to integrate. Not only are the professionals who work within them trained in different disciplines, but they tend to work for different kinds of organizations with different sorts of cultures and values, paid for from different sources and often with wildly different methods. Just for starters, professionals of similar backgrounds may be paid considerably different amounts if they are working for agencies from two different subsystems. So while those managing care for chronically ill children tend to be very much aware of the need for integration of medical and social services, it should not be surprising that they often face considerable difficulties in carrying that out.

CHRONICALLY ILL CHILDREN AND HIGH TECHNOLOGY

The principle that hard cases make bad law applies in a somewhat different way to another troubling aspect of the situation of chronically ill children—their relationship to high technology. In a sense the problems of the growing number of chronically ill children might be seen as one of the kinds of "failures of success" with which our medical care system is increasingly confronted. The fruits of modern medical technology permit many children with chronic illnesses to survive when even within recent decades they might not have, but with that survival comes the whole array of problems that dominate the discussions in this book, many of them problems tied to the technologies themselves.

Another way of looking at this same phenomenon, however, might be to conclude that we are substantially better with some kinds of technologies than with others. The mechanical or biomedical devices to assist with ventilation, control blood sugar levels, or perform delicate reconstructive surgery are better developed than the technologies of remote monitoring, educational assessment, information provision and retrieval, or even scheduling of services. The latter kinds of technologies are far more dependent on "human factors" such as ignorance or simple forgetfulness, and thus are much more difficult to make work reliably and effectively. In a sense, it is not that we have too much technology that creates the problem, but rather that the technologies we have for solving or coping with the problems of giving care are not adequately developed, simply because they are harder to develop. We are more skillful at diagnosis and treatment than we are at caring, or at organizing systems of care.

DILEMMAS OF MANAGED CARE

One place where our relatively primitive skills at organizing systems of care becomes acutely evident is the idea of "managed care," especially when such care management involves both organizational arrangements and some sort of financing package. The authors in this volume are ambiguous about "managed care"; to take one example, Arthur Kohrman, in the book's final chapter, both argues strenuously for good case management, on economic as well as clinical grounds, and rails against health maintenance organizations (HMOs) and preferred provider organizations (PPOs). Yet to the extent that HMOs or PPOs are more than mere financial gimmicks—and in all too many instances, financial gimmicks are all they are—then something that looks very much like what Kohrman calls good case management must be the very core of the way in which they operate.

The problem, again, is that "good" case management, like good support of family caregivers, is something that everyone believes in theory should be done, but that is in practice very hard to do. In the instance of case management tied to financing, Kohrman seems to be saying, doing it badly is worse than not doing it at all, and he may very well be right. But the question that must be dealt with, at both the public policy and the operational level, is not whether "case management" per se is good or bad—it is obviously good when it is done well, and bad when it is done poorly—but how to ensure that it will be done well. Financing incentives, in that sense, are probably not so much inimical to good case management as at least partially irrelevant.

THE INTERSECTION OF POVERTY AND CHRONIC ILLNESS IN CHILDREN

The final theme which emerges with this volume is less suffused with ambivalence but is no less a case of hard problems and bad policy: that is the particular difficulty and poignance of the problems arising from the intersection of chronic illness in children with poverty. Poor children, to begin with, like poor people of all age groups, are much more likely to be afflicted with chronic illness than the nonpoor. In some instances, this occurs because illness creates poverty, typically through earnings loss experienced by a caretaker or high medical expenses or both, but more significantly, poverty in and of itself is a major risk factor for poor health, including chronic childhood illness.

Family poverty means, by definition, the availability of fewer resources for the families to cope with the problems chronic illness presents. The most obviously inadequate resource is health insurance, but good housing, good social services, and good schools are important too, and tend to be much harder to find in the communities in which poor people live. Nor should the simple scarcity of cash be underestimated as a barrier to managing effectively any of life's exigencies, especially those of the sort encountered by families with a chronically ill child.

The fundamental problem, of course, is not so much what happens to poor children with chronic illness, but that in a society as affluent and proud of itself as this one, we have so many poor children. Indeed, a higher proportion of children—almost one in five—are poor than are members of any other age group. Poor children with chronic illnesses face particularly formidable problems, but the generic problem is that of childhood poverty. Massive interventions will be necessary, and must be undertaken, to ensure that the next generation of Americans have some reasonable chance of succeeding with their lives. Such interventions will, at the same time, provide additional benefits to chronically ill children precisely to the extent that their problems are exacerbated by poverty.

CONCLUSIONS

Chronically ill children pose very hard questions for service systems and for a society which in a variety of fundamental ways are not very well-equipped to meet their needs. There are, however, many people—if not enough—including many of the authors of this book's chapters, who are facing these challenges, often with considerable success. They are representatives of another, more positive aspect of contemporary American society: the commitment, skill, toughness, and resourcefulness of the thousands of people who do the most difficult jobs, generally without adequate recognition or reward. The examples they provide comprise, in some ways, the best things in this book, and in the communities in which they work.

Perhaps ironically, perhaps predictably, the very people whose own work provides such encouraging examples recurrently report their frustration and impatience with the systems in which they must operate, and with the absence of coherent, effective, and humane policies that would permit more effective care for their clients. Masters of the particular, they seek more general solutions. But more general solutions are, at the macrocosmic level, at least as hard to come by as optimal care is of the microcosmic.

On the evidence of this volume, in order to get all chronically ill children and their families the kinds of services they need, when they need them, we must discover and train professionals in better ways to support families and develop public policies more responsive to family needs; teach caregiving professionals from different disciplines to work together in teams and provide them with the right incentives to carry out those teachings; radically improve the technologies of service provision and care organization; square the conceptual circle of cost-effectiveness in case management; and make a major dent in childhood poverty. No one could argue with any of these objectives, but neither should even the most committed advocate hold his or her breath. What is most remarkable about this book's success stories is that they are true, even though none of those objectives is remotely close to being achieved.

In other words, the care of chronically ill children is going to constitute a hard case, enmeshed in inadequate public policy, for some time to come. The challenge is how to continue to achieve successes even in this context. We need to return, in conclusion, from the general to the specific. It is probably a mistake to fall into the trap of romanticizing children as being somehow better people than adults, but the matter-of-factness, openness, sense of perspective, and even good humor with which children face their problems can indeed provide a salutary model for the rest of us. They command, and deserve, all the help we can give them.

Author Index

Adler, B., 218
Aegrete, V. F., 69
Albee, G. W., 129,220,221
Alsup, P., 247
Altenstetter, C., 33
American Academy of Pediatrics, 167, 168,233
Apt, H. E., 32
Arras, J. D., 97
Ashcroft, S. C., 50

Bachman, G., 35
Baird, S. M., 50
Bajo, K., 80
Balfour, L. L., 247
Baluarte, H. J., 247
Bandura, A., 258
Bartholome, M., 261
Baskiewicz, A., 65
Benatar, S. R., 247
Bender, E. I., 130
Berenson, G. S., 247
Berkman, L. F., 129
Bierman, M., 37,38,214
Birch, H. G., 137
Bjorkman, J., 33
Blomfield, J. M., 148
Bloom, B. L., 224
Bloom, S. R., 248
Blumenthal, S., 247

Boat, T. F., 69,70,217
Borck, L. E., 13,133
Borman, L. D., 257
Boyer, W., 69,70,217
Bremner, R. H., 32
Bronfenbrenner, U., 145
Bruch, H., 69
Bruhn, J. G., 219
Bruno, J., 260,262
Budetti, P., 17,18,19,20,21,22,232,246
Bush, M., 69,218
Butler, J. A., 17,18,19,20,21,22,45,52, 232,269,280
Butterfield, F., 258

Caplan, G., 224
Capron, A., 93
Cazden, C. B., 262
Cerreto, M. C., 64,79
Charter for the 80s, 146
Children's Bureau, 37
Clemente, I., 260
Cohen, S., 36,46
Colby, K. M., 260,263
Comptroller General, 48
Connecticut State Department of Health, 246
Cooper, D., 63
Cooper, J. E., 152
Coury, D. L., 77,80,81

Subject Index